College Success
Strategies

About the Authors

Sherrie L. Nist is currently the Director of the Division of Academic Enhancement at the University of Georgia, where she also holds the rank of Professor. Before becoming the Director, she taught reading and studying courses to college students in the same division. Sherrie received both her master's and doctoral degrees from the University of Florida. It was as a graduate student that she first became interested in how students learn, particularly in the factors that seem to influence a smooth transition from high school to college, and the academic struggles that first-year students seem to face. She has published more than 80 articles, textbooks, textbook chapters, and other professional pieces all related to how college students learn and study. She has presented the results of her research at more than 100 national and international professional meetings. And she has received honors and awards for her contributions to both teaching and research. When not working, Sherrie loves traveling, cooking, and, of course, reading and learning new things.

Jodi Patrick Holschuh is currently an Assistant Professor in the Division of Academic Enhancement at the University of Georgia. She completed her doctoral degree in 1998 at the University of Georgia. (Sherrie Nist was her major professor.) An award-winning teacher, Jodi teaches courses to help students learn effective and efficient study habits. She has presented many conference papers and has written several articles, book chapters, and books on the topic of helping students learn in college. She became interested in learning more about strategies for academic success while working as a Tutorial Coordinator at the Philadelphia College of Textiles and Science. It was there that she realized students could be "studying hard" yet still struggling to pass their courses. Her research interests include students' beliefs about learning, making the transition from high school to college learning, strategies for academic success, and motivation. When she is not writing, teaching, or researching, Jodi loves rediscovering the world as her daughter learns new things. She also loves to read good books and travel to new places.

College
Success
Strategies

Sherrie L. Nist
University of Georgia

Jodi Patrick Holschuh
University of Georgia

PENGUIN ACADEMICS

New York   San Francisco   Boston
London   Toronto   Sydney   Tokyo   Singapore   Madrid
Mexico City   Munich   Paris   Cape Town   Hong Kong   Montreal

Vice President and Editor-in-Chief: Joseph Terry
Senior Acquisitions Editor: Steven Rigolosi
Senior Marketing Manager: Melanie Craig
Senior Supplements Editor: Donna Campion
Media Supplements Editor: Nancy Garcia
Production Manager: Donna DeBenedictis
Project Coordination, Text Design, and Electronic Page Makeup: Elm Street
    Publishing Services, Inc.
Senior Cover Designer/Manager: Nancy Danahy
Cover/Photo: © Getty Images/PhotoDisc, Inc.
Manufacturing Manager: Dennis J. Para
Printer and Binder: R.R. Donnelley & Sons Company/Harrisonburg
Cover Printer: Phoenix Color Corporation

Library of Congress Cataloging-in-Publication Data

Nist, Sherrie L. (Sherrie Lee), 1946–
College success strategies / Sherrie L. Nist, Jodi Patrick Holschuh.
        p. cm. — (Penguin academics)
Includes index.
  ISBN 0-321-10805-1
  1. Study skills. 2. Learning, Psychology of. 3. Academic achievement. 4. College
student orientation. I. Holschuh, Jodi Patrick. II. Title. III. Penguin academics.
  LB2395 .N545 2003
  371.3'028'1—dc21

                                                                2002016140

Please visit our website at http://www.ablongman.com/studyskills

For more information about the Penguin Academics series, please contact us by
mail at Longman Publishers, attn. Marketing Department, 1185 Avenue of the
Americas, 25th Floor, New York, NY 10036, or by email at **www.ablongman.com**

ISBN 0-321-10805-1

    5 6 7 8 9 10—DOH—05 04

Contents

Preface

The major premise behind *College Success Strategies* is rooted in the importance of academics. Although other success books have a chapter or two specifically dedicated to the academic side of college, *College Success Strategies* is entirely devoted to this focus. It takes you on an academic journey to help you understand yourself as a learner and to teach you the strategies you will need to be successful. The majority of this text focuses on four key academic factors, all of which must interact if learning is to be maximized: (1) your own characteristics as a learner; (2) the tasks you must complete in each of your classes; (3) the strategies that will help you read, understand, and remember what your professor expects you to learn; and finally (4) the texts with which you interact.

The key to academic success is being actively involved in your own learning. Students who gain the most from college are those who participate. Just as you participate in campus clubs and organizations, you must also recognize the importance of participating fully in each course you take and every academic experience you have. This translates to using active reading strategies, rehearsing as you prepare for exams, taking organized lecture notes and reviewing them, giving daily attention to your work, monitoring your learning, and a variety of other strategic approaches for studying. Studying actively means using your senses to learn—you write, you hear, you listen, you talk. You have a variety of strategies that you can use and you know the appropriate time to use them. Involvement means all of this and more. The strategies you learn in *College Success Strategies* will assist you in not only becoming an active learner, but also a life-long learner.

We have based *College Success Strategies* on many years of experience interacting with college students and professors, as well as our own research focusing on how college students study. We have learned from our students that they often enter college unprepared to meet the studying demands placed on them, even if they had been successful in high school. We have also learned that college students are sometimes overwhelmed with the reading and studying demands that college can bring, and sometimes they become frustrated when they believe they are "working hard" but not seeing their efforts pay off. We have learned that it takes more than knowledge of a few strategies for students to achieve academically. But perhaps the most important thing we have learned from our students is that they can be taught how to study actively, and in most cases, they are eager to learn new skills that will help them be successful in college.

We have also learned much from college professors with whom we have interacted over the years, especially those who teach large numbers of first-year students. We learned that professors believe it is the students' responsibility to be an active learner and they expect students to have the skills to do whatever it takes to be successful in their particular class and discipline. We learned that professors and students always don't see eye-to-eye on what a discipline entails or even on what a professor expects from them. The most important thing we learned from professors, however, may have been that they view the overall purpose of college to be much more than the memorization of facts, regardless of the particular discipline in which they teach. Rather, the purpose of a college education is to provide students with the skills to learn on their own in the future.

Finally, we learned from our own research efforts as well as those of others in our field. When we initially outlined this text and thought about the approach we would take when writing it, we both agreed on the importance of building the book on a strong research-based foundation. That is, many first-year and study skills books tout study methods that are based only on conventional wisdom, but are not necessarily grounded in research. *College Success Strategies*, however, is based on what current research on college learning has found to be important for success. Therefore, in preparation for writing this book, we reread some of the studies that influenced our own work and influenced the field of college studying in general. It became very clear to us that being an active learner included many factors that all had to interact and click together in order for learning to be maximized.

Using *College Success Strategies*

College Success Strategies was designed not only to get students reading about what it takes to learn actively but also to start them thinking and talking about it. Thus, the activities at the end of each chapter ask you to discuss important questions with classmates, to think critically, and to reflect on academic issues. We believe that active learners use numerous senses as they go about learning in college. They read, they write, they discuss, and they visualize. Interacting with information in a variety of ways encourages active processing, and active processing leads to academic success.

We have divided this text into six parts. Part One introduces you to active learning in college; Part Two helps you determine your own learning characteristics; Part Three discusses how to determine your tasks in college learning; Part Four introduces strategies for effective learning; Part Five discusses characteristics of college texts; and Part Six helps you prepare for college-level exams. In addition we have included brief text excerpts from a variety of disciplines: history, psychology, and biology. These excerpts are located at the beginning of Part Four. *College Success Strategies* is designed so that as you learn the strategies you can apply each one to these text excerpts.

College Success Strategies has several important features to note. First, you will find **"Real College"** scenarios located near the end of each chapter. Each scenario features a college student who has a problem related in some way to what you have learned in that chapter. By helping these college students solve their problems, you will be able to further apply the ideas and strategies discussed in the chapters. We believe that you may see part of yourself in many of the scenarios. These scenarios, by the way, are based on real issues that our students consistently face as they work toward becoming active learners.

You will also find **"Thinking Critically"** and **"Follow-Up Activities"** at the end of each chapter. These activities will help you apply the concepts learned in each chapter to your other college courses. They also will ask you to reflect and evaluate your experiences using the strategies.

In addition, *College Success Strategies* features informative boxes:

- **Quick Takes**—Focus on how you can use the strategies outside of class or in the workplace after you have graduated. The point is to help you understand that many of these strategies have practical application beyond the classroom.

- **College Campus Today**—Focus on the kinds of issues that college students currently face and provide suggestions for maximizing learning.

- **Networking**—Focus on using technology for learning actively.

- **Success at a Glance**—Depict key information in a visual way to help you remember it better.

VISIT OUR WEB SITE

College Success Strategies is supported by the Longman Study Skills Web site. For additional resources, exercises, activities, and Web links to help make your college experience a successful and rewarding one, be sure to visit the Web site at **http://www.ablongman.com/studyskills.**

For additional instructor and student support materials—such as the Longman Student Planner, the Longman Instructor's Planner, and our various reading and writing software—please contact your Longman sales representative or visit us on the Web at **http://www.ablongman.com/basicskills.** You can also send your questions to us at **BasicSkills@ablongman.com.**

ACKNOWLEDGMENTS

There are many individuals who contributed directly or indirectly to the contents of *College Success Strategies.* Certainly it is important for us to acknowledge the students whom we have had the privilege to teach and the professors from a variety of disciplines who have shared their views on what it takes to be successful in their respective areas. As is always the case, our students help to ground our writing in reality—the reality of the many pressures currently faced by today's college students and the reality of just how important life-long learning has become. We were especially struck as we wrote *College Success Strategies* of the major importance of understanding technology to being successful.

Today's students are truly the first generation of college students who are expected to know and keep abreast of new technological advances that can enhance learning.

In addition to our students, our thanks go out to the numerous professors and graduate students on the University of Georgia campus and beyond who have willingly shared their concerns and their expertise about learning in their particular disciplines. This text would have not been nearly as effective without their valuable insights. A special thanks to Denise Pinette Domizi for her insightful suggestions and her willingness to share her note-taking strategies in *College Success Strategies*.

Certainly, we acknowledge our respective families—our spouses, parents, siblings, and children—who always offered their continuous support, and sometimes even additional insights, as we worked to turn this book from a concept into reality. We appreciate their understanding, support, and advice as this text seemed to take over our lives at times.

We acknowledge the major support we have received from Steve Rigolosi, our editor at Longman. Steve's enthusiasm about offering *College Success Strategies* as part of the Penguin Academic Series was both challenging and contagious. We greatly appreciated all his wonderful suggestions, and his encouragement contributed to this book being completed in almost record time. We had worked with Steve at the conclusion of another project and continue to be impressed by his unstinting energy and terrific ideas.

Finally, we would be remiss if we failed to acknowledge all of the assistance we received from those we have worked with at Longman: Meegan Thompson, Melanie Craig, Donna DeBenedictis, and Nancy Danahy, and at Elm Street Publishing Services: Brandi Nelson, Zak Semens, Sue Langguth, Merisa Boveri, Angel Chavez, Emily Friel, and Anastasia Healy. Everyone's patience, attention to detail, and helpful suggestions made working on this book a pleasant experience.

Sherrie L. Nist

Jodi Patrick Holschuh

PART ONE

WELCOME TO COLLEGE SUCCESS STRATEGIES

College learning is very different from high school learning. If this is your first term in college, you may already have noticed many of those differences. In Chapter 1, we discuss the differences between college and high school as well as several special situations you will eventually encounter in college.

Chapter 2 introduces the concept of active learning. You learn about what active learning is and why becoming an active learner can help you succeed in college. You also learn about the four factors that influence learning: (1) characteristics of the learner, (2) the tasks, (3) the texts, and (4) the strategies. We talk about how the factors work together to influence student learning. These four factors guide the organization of the remainder of this book.

Chapter 3 presents several theories on how people learn. You will also learn about the role of learning styles and some strategies to help you stretch your memory.

CHAPTER 1

NOW THAT YOU'RE HERE

Read this chapter to answer the following questions:

- How does studying in college differ from studying in high school?
- What special situations can you expect to encounter in college, sooner or later?

SELF-ASSESSMENT

DIRECTIONS: On a scale of 1 to 5, with 1 being "strongly disagree," 3 being "somewhat agree," and 5 being "strongly agree," respond to each of the statements below. This should give you a good idea about how much your college experience differs from what you experienced in high school.

1. My college professors seem to expect much more of me.   1   2   3   4   5

2. My college classes move at a faster pace.   1   2   3   4   5

3. My college classes require more than just memorization.   1   2   3   4   5

4. My college classes give me few chances to earn extra credit.   1   2   3   4   5

5. My college classes require me to spend more time studying.   1   2   3   4   5

6. My college professors give less frequent exams.   1   2   3   4   5

7. I have more freedom in college.   1   2   3   4   5

8. I often feel anonymous in college.   1   2   3   4   5

9. I have experienced motivation problems in   1   2   3   4   5
college.

10. Managing my time effectively is more   1   2   3   4   5
challenging in college.

Now add up your score. The higher your score, the more differences you are experiencing in making the transition from high school to college. The more differences you experience, the more time it may take you to make the adjustment.

Starting college! You may feel as if you have been preparing for this day forever. You've taken a college preparatory curriculum in high school, you've talked with friends or siblings who are already in college, and you may have even visited several campuses before deciding which school to attend. Or you may be returning to college after several years working. Regardless of your situation, you are probably excited about what the next few years have in store for you. And some of you may even be a little wary and unsure of yourself as you begin down the college path.

In this chapter, we will discuss some of the ways in which college differs from high school. In addition, we will present eight situations that you are sure to encounter in college sooner or later and will offer suggestions about how you might deal with them. Keep in mind as you read this chapter that campuses differ in size and in the expectations they have of students. For these reasons, some of the generalizations and solutions offered here might not apply exactly to your particular situation.

How Does College Differ from High School?

How many times since high school graduation have you heard one of your relatives say something like this: "Oh _____ (insert your name)! Enjoy these college years. They will be the best of your life." Although this statement is probably true—college is enjoyable and memorable—it is also demanding and, in many instances, just plain different from high school. It's a time in your life when you will go through many changes as you prepare for the world of work that follows. In this section we will discuss some of the reasons why high school and college differ.

- **Reason 1: College Requires Greater Independent Learning.** Your high school teachers may have been willing to give you lots of test preparation help. They may have provided prepared study guides or even the exact questions they would ask. Although college instructors also want you to be successful—we have never met a professor who wants students to fail—they don't give students as much study help. Sure, most professors will answer questions about course content and things you don't understand, but they will not provide you with a variety of supplementary learning materials and they certainly will not give you test questions. They expect that you know effective and efficient study strategies and if you don't know how to study for their courses, they expect you to learn how.

QUICK TAKES

Learning How to Learn

Did you know that learning how to learn on your own may be one of the most important benefits of going to college? As you move into the world of work, most employers will expect you to do a considerable amount of learning on your own. Employees who need lots of guidance in learning new things aren't nearly as valuable as those who are self-starters. So one of the most important skills you want to foster early in your college career is the ability to learn on your own.

- **Reason 2: College Courses Move at a Faster Pace.** If you ask first-year college students about the differences between high school and college, one of their most common responses would be that college courses move much faster than high school classes. What might have taken a year to cover in high school will probably be covered in a semester in college. It's not uncommon for college professors to move through three, four, or more chapters in a week, expecting you to keep up. In addition, topics are generally covered in greater detail. However, college professors may also expect you to fill in many of the details on your own.

- **Reason 3: College Courses Require You to Think Critically.** In your high school classes, perhaps you were required to memorize lots of facts for exams. Perhaps you were discouraged from questioning either your high school textbooks or your high school teacher. But as you proceed through college, you will find yourself in more and more classes where your professor wants you to do more than memorize. You might have to critique an essay on gun control, read and respond to a historian's view of the Vietnamese Conflict, or compare and contrast conflicting scientific theories. All of these tasks require you to think critically.

- **Reason 4: College Classes Have Few Safety Nets.** Usually on the first day of a college class your professor will give you a syllabus. The syllabus outlines the course requirements and also generally tells you how your grade will be determined. Something that will become clear as you read your syllabus is that many of the safety nets that you had in high school, such as extra credit assignments or other bonuses to improve your grade, have all but disappeared. This means your course grade will be determined by the grade you earn on a limited number of tests or papers.

- **Reason 5: College Requires You to Study Longer and More Effectively.** You will probably find out pretty quickly that both the amount of time you put into studying and the way you study in college will have to change if you want to continue to earn high grades. Many of our students tell us that they really didn't have to study in high school. "Studying" was reading over a study guide or going over class notes for about a half-hour. Few students have ever had to read their texts and many begin college never having taken essay exams. It is important to realize that studying in college requires not only more time, but also a variety of study strategies to have at your disposal.

- **Reason 6: College Provides Fewer Chances for Evaluation.** In high school, it may have seemed as though you were always taking tests or writing papers. You were probably tested over small amounts of material (only one or two chapters) and you had numerous chances for evaluation. If you did poorly on one test, you could usually make it up on the next one. In college, on the other hand, you will probably have fewer chances to be evaluated. At first, the idea of taking fewer tests per course in a term may seem appealing. But think about the big picture. If you have only three exams, you are going to be held responsible for much more information at one time than you were in high school. What at first seems to be an advantage—fewer tests, homework that goes unchecked, a longer period of time between exams—may actually work against you, unless you know how to stay on top of things.

- **Reason 7: College Gives You Greater Freedom and Greater Responsibility.** Legally, you become an adult at age 18, which just happens to be at about the same time you graduate from high school. In college, no one makes you stay on top of your schoolwork or keeps track of your comings and goings or checks to see that you have done all of your reading and studying before heading out for a night on the town. This freedom comes with a tremendous amount of responsibility. It is your responsibility to prioritize the tasks you *have* to do against the things you *want* to do.

- **Reason 8: College Provides Greater Anonymity.** If you attend a moderate to large college or university, you will be faced with being somewhat anonymous, and in some cases, very anonymous. By anonymous we mean that you *can* become another face in the crowd. Most of you probably attended high schools where you got to know your teachers and your classmates fairly well. Your teachers not only knew your name, but were also concerned about whether or not you were learning and understanding the information presented in their classes. For the most part, in college, your professor has few opportunities to get to know you well. All is not lost, however. Most of the time, students are anonymous only if they want to be, regardless of how large or small their campus may be. You can become a "face" to your professors by making appointments to talk with them. You can join clubs that have faculty sponsors. You can take part in a variety of campus activities with other students who share your interests.

- **Reason 9: College Requires You to Be Proactive.** Being proactive means that it's your responsibility to take the initiative in a variety of situations. In high school, either your teachers or your parents may have "insisted" that you get help if you were having problems with a particular course. And you may have followed their advice reluctantly. In college, however, it becomes your responsibility to know the resources that are available on your campus, so that if you do run into difficulties, or need the services of some office, you'll know how to find the information you need or where to go to get assistance. If you are proactive and find out a little about them before you need their services, it will save you time in the long run. However, you don't want to wait until you are in dire need of these resources before seeking them out. Some of these services may include:

- **The Library.** In addition to providing resources, the library is a great place to study, to do research online, or to meet your study group. Most campuses have library orientations that help students learn to navigate large and complex systems.

- **The Learning Center.** The campus learning center can be an excellent source of assistance because most offer a variety of services, from academic counseling to assistance with writing, studying, and mathematics.

- **Tutorial Services.** Like learning centers, most campuses offer tutorial services for a broad range of courses. Generally, tutoring is provided by undergraduate students who earn top grades in the areas that they tutor. This tutoring is usually free, but appointments are often necessary.

- **Health Services.** Because getting sick enough to need the services of a doctor is inevitable, know where your campus health facility is and what the rules are to be able to see a medical professional. Don't wait until you feel as if you're on your deathbed. Find out where to go and what to do early on.

- **Student Center or Student Union.** On most campuses, the student center is the hub of campus where you can meet friends, but most also offer a wealth of resources. Sometimes campus organizations and clubs have offices in the student center. Social event and concert tickets can be purchased there. General information about campus such as bus schedules, campus maps, and event schedules can be obtained. Often, the campus bookstore is located in or near the student center. When you don't know where else to turn, the student center is a good place to start if you need information about your campus.

NETWORKING

Your School's Web Site

Access the Web site of the college or university you are currently attending. Search the Web site for information about some of the services discussed in this chapter such as the Learning Center, Health Center, or Counseling Center. What did you find out about these services that you didn't know before? What other services did you find?

Check your syllabi to see if any of your professors listed their e-mail address. If they did, write a brief e-mail to introduce yourself or to ask a question. Also, some professors have their own Web pages. If any of your professors has a Web page, check it out.

So, college is different from high school in many ways. You must think differently about the expectations, learning conditions, level of responsibility, and studying methods than you thought about them in high school. This is not bad. It simply means you will have to make some transitions in the way you learn and study in order to be successful.

SUCCESS AT A GLANCE
How High School Differs from College

	High School	College
Independence	Less independence	Greater independence
Pacing	Slow	Fast
Level of critical thinking	Less critical thinking	Greater critical thinking

(continued)

	High School	College
Safety nets	Teachers provide many	Professors provide few
Study effort	Limited and sporadic	Greater and effective
Evaluation	Many opportunities	Limited opportunities
Responsibility	Rests on others	Rests on you
Anonymity	Little	Lots
Importance of being proactive	Low	High

What Special Situations Can You Expect to Encounter Sooner or Later?

Now that you have seen some of the ways in which high school and college differ, let's examine this transition from another perspective. We'll present eight situations that most college students will encounter sooner or later, and we'll also examine how you might cope with or handle each situation. All of these situations will be addressed again throughout this text, so you will be able to explore these ideas in greater detail later.

In a perfect world, none of the following situations would occur. All students would go to class every day, distribute their study time over a period of days, stay on top of their reading, and make the Dean's List every term. However, the world of college is an imperfect place. So, let's discuss some of the situations that you might encounter in college, some of which you might not be prepared for. As you read each section, think about how you might handle the situation and what additional information might help you cope better.

- **Professors Who Take Roll.** Someone may have told you that the only time you really *have* to show up in college classes is on test days, or that if you can get the information on your own, professors don't really care whether you are in class. Although many professors don't take attendance, eventually you will run across one who does, and, in reality, most actually do want you present in class. You will eventually come across a professor who truly believes that attending class will help you learn. Of course, even if your professor does not take roll, it's still a good idea to attend class.

- **An Early Morning Class.** Most college students are not morning people. In fact, there's even scientific evidence to indicate that college-age biological clocks are preset to stay up late at night and to sleep late in the morning. However, the college officials who determine the times of class periods evidently are unaware of this research. Unfortunately (for most college students), a time will come when you will have to take an early morning class. If you do have that early class, try to juggle the rest of your schedule so that you can go to bed earlier than usual. Additionally, try to take one that meets only two or three days a week, thus allowing you a little more flexibility on other days.

- **A Course or Professor You Don't Particularly Care For.** It's perhaps sad but true—there will be courses you don't like, and professors with whom you fail to connect. Even if you have a wide range of interests and you can get along well with almost everyone, at some point you'll have to make it through a rough class. You can take one of two routes when this happens.

  Route A: You can think of every excuse imaginable not to do the work or go to class. You can blame your attitude on the professor or the "boring" material that you are expected to learn.

  Consequences of Route A: A poor course grade, feeling bad about yourself, and having to work doubly hard in another course to bring up your overall grade point average.

  Route B: Acknowledge that you really don't care much for the course or the professor. It's one course, however, and you can make it through. Study with someone who seems to like the course. Try to motivate yourself with small rewards. Tell yourself that this is temporary and the course will soon be over.

Consequences of Route B: Perhaps you will not earn an A in the class but you will emerge with your ego and your grade point average intact.

- **Cramming for a Test.** Imagine you have a big test in a couple of days (or worse yet, tomorrow) and you've done very little preparing. Now it's *cram time*! Personally, we've never met a student who didn't have to cram at some time. And cramming occasionally probably isn't a horrible thing, but it shouldn't become the way you live your academic life. If you have to cram occasionally, try to use what time you have left to study to your advantage. And, as soon as possible, regroup so that you don't have to go cram again.

- **Difficulty Maintaining Motivation for Academics.** Most college students experience motivation problems at some time or another. It usually doesn't last long, but for some students the decline in motivation is long enough and severe enough to interfere with their schoolwork. Other students experience a lull in motivation in just one class, generally a class with which they may be experiencing difficulty. Still others begin the term with good intentions, yet quickly develop general motivation problems in every class. If you are having motivation problems, try setting some specific, reachable goals. Whether your lack of motivation is concentrated in one particular course, occurs at a specific period of time, or is generalized across all your academic courses, goal-setting can help you stay focused and improve your motivation to learn.

- **Personal Problems and/or Illness.** No one plans on getting ill or having personal problems and knowing that either of these issues may arise does little to solve the entire problem. However, there are some things you can do to salvage even a bad situation. First, as you plan your schedule for the term, build in some flexibility, just in case. If everything goes according to plan, the worst thing that can happen is you'll have some extra time to study, work, or play. Second, as mentioned earlier, know what services are available on your campus. Third, develop a set of reliable peers who can be there for you in times of illness or other problems. Often knowing that some other person can help you out makes all the difference in the world.

- **Frustration.** It's a given that you will experience frustrations and stressful situations, but it's how you deal with them that makes the difference. Try not to let things build up to the point where you can't emotionally cope. As much as possible, deal with frustrations as they come along. Evaluate all the alternatives. And try not to become stressed by things you have no control over. So . . . take a walk. Go work out. Spend a few minutes venting to a friend. In time it will work out.

COLLEGE CAMPUS TODAY

Creating a Balanced Life

Today's college students can become easily overwhelmed without even realizing it. There are so many things vying for student attention and participation: concerts, speakers, Greek life, intramural sports, athletic events, and community service, to name a few. Although we believe that participation in a variety of social and cultural activities leads to a more well-rounded student, we also know that students can easily become involved in too many extracurricular activities. Try to create a balance in your life. If you find yourself stressed because you don't seem to have time for your class work, take another look at your schedule.

• **Juggling Too Many Responsibilities.** College students tend to be busy people—going to class, studying, attending meetings, working, working out, taking part in athletics, and the list goes on. Add to all of this—family responsibilities, social interactions, and some good old time to play, and you can easily become over-committed. Although you certainly want to get the most out of your college experience, try to think about how new responsibilities will affect you. Remember that your primary job in college is to be a student. Then you can ask yourself: "What other kinds of responsibilities can I take on?" Will you have so much to do a month from now that you will constantly feel stressed out and frustrated? If you can think about this in advance and learn to say "No" when you find yourself maxing out, you will be able to keep all those balls in the air and be a much happier student.

☐ Real College
Wanda's Woes

DIRECTIONS: Read the following *Real College* scenario and respond to the questions based on the information you learned in this chapter.

Wanda was a pretty good student in high school. She earned good grades and "studied as much as she needed" to make As and Bs. She just naturally assumed that she would earn similar grades in college. But here it is, only three weeks into the fall semester, and things aren't going as planned. She didn't do well on her first chemistry test because she had to cram and asked the professor for an extra credit assignment. Her professor chuckled and shook his head no! Then there's the pace. Things seem to be moving so fast. She's having a difficult time keeping up. From her perspective, she's studying about the same amount of time as she did in high school but her efforts don't seem to be paying off. In addition to these academic problems, she feels alone and isolated. She likes her roommate, and would like to get to know her better, but her roommate knows a lot of people already so she's not around much. It seems so hard to make new friends.

1. What advice do you have for Wanda?
2. What could she do to help herself academically? Socially?

☐ Thinking Critically
Something to Think About and Discuss

DIRECTIONS: Now that you have read about some of the differences between high school and college, analyze your own experiences and respond to the following questions.

• What do you think is the biggest difference between high school and college?

- What do you think you should have learned in high school that would better prepare you for a positive college experience?
- Have you been in the situation yet where you were enrolled in a course or had a professor that you did not like? How have you dealt with this situation? How would you deal with it if you haven't already experienced it? What suggestions do you have for others who might be in the same predicament?
- Have you been in a situation in which you had to cram? If so, think back to how you felt. What influence did cramming have on your test performance?
- Think about a time when your motivation to learn was low. What caused you to lose motivation? What did you do to restore it?

☐ Follow-Up Activities

1. Sometimes professors can seem intimidating, especially when you first begin college, but most college teachers are personable people who enjoy interacting with students. In order to get to know one of your professors a little better, make an appointment to talk with her. You might discuss course expectations, ask for studying pointers, or discuss your past successes or problems with similar courses.

2. Find out where you can get help with academic problems. Is there a Learning Center on your campus? If so, what services does it offer? How do you go about making an appointment in the Learning Center?

3. Find out where you can get counseling assistance. Is there a Counseling Center that can help you make the adjustment to college? What if you just need someone to talk with? How do you go about making an appointment to see someone?

CHAPTER 2

ACTIVE LEARNING
What's in It for You?

Read this chapter to answer the following questions:

- How do active learners differ from passive learners?
- What are the benefits of active learning?
- What are the four factors that influence learning?
- What is the holistic nature of active learning?

SELF-ASSESSMENT

DIRECTIONS: On a scale of 1 to 5, with 1 being "rarely," 3 being "sometimes," and 5 being "most of the time," evaluate how active you are as a learner.

1. When I read my texts, I can make connections with what I have read earlier in the course.   1   2   3   4   5

2. After I read my texts, I can restate the key ideas in my own words.   1   2   3   4   5

3. After lectures and when I am finished reading my texts, I can clearly state what I don't understand.   1   2   3   4   5

4. I can take meaningful and organized notes for a full class period without losing concentration.   1   2   3   4   5

5. When I prepare for tests, I use my time wisely. 1 2 3 4 5

6. I seek out help when I am having problems 1 2 3 4 5
understanding the material presented in a course.

7. I use different strategies for learning, depending 1 2 3 4 5
on the course and the type of exams.

8. If information I hear or read fails to fit with 1 2 3 4 5
what I already know, I try to examine the issue
from a variety of viewpoints.

9. When I enter a testing situation, I have a good 1 2 3 4 5
idea of how I will do.

10. I am motivated to learn in most of my classes. 1 2 3 4 5

11. I feel confident about myself as a learner. 1 2 3 4 5

Now, add up your score. The higher your score, the more active you are as a learner. The lowest score you can receive is 11; the highest score you can receive is 55. Your score gives you an overall picture of how much work you have to do and also lets you know which areas of active learning you need to work on.

NETWORKING

Going Online

There is so much information available to you on the Internet that it takes an active learner to be able to sift through it. To practice your skills as an active learner go online to your local newspaper or to a news magazine and use the search function to find a current article that interests you. Try to actively engage in the article to find out the author's intent. Question the author as you read. Does any of the information seem suspect or unsupported? Does it agree or disagree with what you already know about the topic? Use the answers to these questions to help you reflect on the information you find.

What Do Active Learners Do?

You hear it all the time, read about it in magazines and newspapers, and even watch television programs dedicated to one theme: ACTIVITY! Be active, exercise. It's good for your health. It seems as though everywhere you turn there's another piece of research or another claim about the importance of being active. Let's take the premise that you are tired of being out of shape. You take the big step and join a fitness club or gym, so that you can work yourself back into shape. Such good intentions! But what if you went to the gym and merely watched other people exercise? Would you become fit? Probably not, because you would not be an **active** participant. Learning works in the same way. If you are not an active participant in learning, you won't become mentally fit, nor will you maximize your performance in the classroom.

To define active learning, we'll discuss the differences between active and passive learning by examining seven characteristics of active learners and contrasting them with the characteristics of passive learners. Active learners:

- **Read with the Purpose of Understanding and Remembering.** We'd bet that no one deliberately sits down to read with the purpose of *not* understanding the text. However, we're certain that you have been in a situation, probably more than once, where you "read" an assignment, closed the text, and thought, "What in the world was that about?" When you interact with a text in this manner you are reading passively. Active readers, on the other hand, set goals before they read and check their understanding as they read. When they finish, they can explain the main points and know that they have understood what they have read.

- **Reflect on Information and Think Critically.** Being reflective is an important part of active learning because it means that you are thinking about the information. In other words, you are processing the information. You may make connections between the new information and what you already know, identify concepts that you may not understand very well, or evaluate the importance of what you are reading. An active learner reflects constantly. In contrast, passive learners may read the text and listen to lectures, and even understand most of what is read and heard, but they do not take that crucial next step of actually thinking about it.

- **Listen Actively by Taking Comprehensive Notes in an Organized Fashion.** We are always amazed at the number of students who engage in activities other than listening and note taking in their lecture classes. We've seen students reading the campus newspaper, doing an assignment for another class, working crossword puzzles, or chatting with a classmate. Perhaps the all-time winner for passive learning, however, was a student who regularly came to class with a pillow and blanket and fell asleep on his girlfriend's shoulder. Unlike these students, active learners are engaged learners. They listen actively to the professor for the entire class period and they write down as much information as possible. To be an active note-taker, you must be more than simply present. You have to think about the information before you write.

- **Know that Learning Involves More Than Simply Putting in Time.** Most students know about the importance of having good time-management skills and expect to invest time in studying in order to be successful. But just putting time into studying is not enough. It is the quality of that time—what you actually do with it—that makes the difference.

- **Get Assistance When They are Experiencing Problems.** Because active learners are constantly monitoring their understanding, they know when their comprehension breaks down, and they ask for help before they become lost. In addition, active learners often predict the courses (or even particular concepts within courses) that may give them trouble. They have a plan in mind for getting assistance should they need it. Active learners may hire individual tutors, take advantage of free peer tutoring, or seek assistance from their professors. Although passive learners may seek help at some point, it is often too little too late. In addition, because passive learners do not reflect and think critically, they often don't even realize that they need help.

- **Accept Much of the Responsibility for Learning.** Active learners understand that the responsibility for learning must come from within, while passive learners often want to blame others for their lack of motivation, poor performance, time-management problems, and other difficulties that they might experience. When active learners don't perform as well as they'd hoped, they evaluate why they didn't do well, and change those studying behaviors the next time. Passive learners, on the other hand, often approach every course in the same manner and then get angry with professors when their performance is poor. It is only when students accept the responsibility for their own learning that they can truly be called active learners.

- **Question Information.** Active learners question information that they read and hear, while passive learners accept both the printed page and the words of their professors as "truth." Active learners don't question *everything*, but they do evaluate what they read and hear. When new information fails to "fit in" with what they already know, they may differ in the conclusions they draw or in the inferences they make.

SUCCESS AT A GLANCE

Differences Between Active and Passive Learners

	Active Learners	Passive Learners
Reading	Read to understand and remember.	Read but may not understand or remember.
Reflecting and thinking critically	Make connections between what they already know and new information in texts, lectures, and from studying with peers.	Don't think about and process information that they read and hear.
Listening	Are engaged during lectures and take organized notes.	Do not pay attention during lecture and take unorganized or incomplete notes.

(continued)

	Active Learners	Passive Learners
Managing time	Put in quality study time.	May put in a lot of study time but it isn't quality time.
Getting assistance	Realize when they need help and seek it early.	Seek too little help too late.
Accepting responsibility	Understand they are responsible for their own learning, analyze weak performance if it occurs, and change the way they study accordingly.	Blame others for poor performance, approach every course in the same way, and fail to learn from their mistakes.
Questioning information	Question new information that doesn't "fit in" with what they already know.	Accept what they read and hear in lectures as true and don't question.

Benefits of Active Learning

As you can probably tell by reading the last section, being an active learner involves both *skill* and *will*.

- By **skill** we mean that you have the tools to handle the studying and learning demands placed on you. You have a variety of study strategies that you consciously employ, and these strategies change depending on the text, the task, and your own personal characteristics as a learner, as we will further discuss in the next section. In addition, you know how to mange your time, when and where to get assistance if you are having difficulty, and you can monitor and evaluate your learning.

- By **will,** we mean that you have the desire and motivation to follow through. Skill is nothing without will. For example, you may have a friend, relative, or peer who is knowledgeable but not motivated in the classroom. Even though he reads widely and can intelligently discuss a variety of issues, he does little work associated with school and rarely studies. Teachers may say that this person is "bright but lazy," or " . . . isn't working up to his potential." In other words, students such as these may have the skills to do well; for some reason they simply do not have the will. And because skill and will go hand-in-hand, unmotivated students—those who do not have the will—may experience difficulty in college and end up dropping out or being "asked" to leave.

It's much easier to teach someone the skills needed to be an active learner than it is to give them the will. Skill is something that can be developed only if one has the will to do so. Think about the example used earlier in the chapter pertaining to exercise: If you go to the gym to develop skill, and you have the will to put in the effort to persist in developing your athletic skill, you'll be successful. But if you work out for two weeks, then only sporadically, then not at all, you might lack the will to be successful, even though you might have the skills to do so. No one can force you to go to the gym, just as no one can force you to study effectively, to plan your time, or to go to class. That all is a matter of will, no matter how much skill you have.

Active learning, then, has numerous benefits, both in terms of academic and psychological payoffs.

- In terms of **academic payoffs,** active learning leads to higher grades, increased time to pursue extracurricular and social activities, and most importantly, gained knowledge. Active learners tend to earn higher grade point averages, seek more involvement with their professors, and like to learn new things. And while active learners certainly all don't believe that they are studying simply for the "love of learning," they are more apt to find learning new things more of a challenge than a chore or a bore.

- The **psychological payoffs** to active learning may even outweigh the academic benefits. Have you ever heard the saying, "Success begets success"? This saying means that being successful motivates you to do what it takes to have greater success. In other words, once active learners experience academic success, they want to continue along this path. Being successful makes them feel good about themselves, gets positive feedback from family, and often influences future goals. Everyone knows that it's much easier to continue to use the skills you have acquired if you get positive feedback about how you have applied those skills.

Four Factors That Influence Active Learning

As you can see, active learning is a complex process. Part of the complexity of learning is caused by the many factors that you have to consider. Cognitive psychologists, those who study how individuals learn, suggest that there are four key factors that influence learning:

1. Your own characteristics as a learner;
2. The tasks your professors ask you to do;
3. The texts with which you interact; and
4. The strategies you select.

We will briefly discuss each of these factors here, but we will discuss each factor in greater detail in later chapters. In fact, you will notice that the remainder of the text is organized around each of these four factors.

Factor 1: Characteristics of the Learner

As a student, you bring a variety of unique characteristics to each learning situation. These characteristics play a key role in how well you will perform, your interest in the material, and the strategies you will select to learn the course content.

- **Motivation** is one of the most important characteristics you can bring to a learning situation. Without motivation, you would find it hard to get out of bed each morning. And you will probably experience frustration and failure as a student. General interest in the topic being studied helps, but if you are open to learning new things and expanding your interests, you will be more successful. Motivation is discussed in Chapter 5.

- **Background knowledge** plays a role because the more you already know about a topic, the easier it is to learn. This means that it might be a good idea to select at least some courses during your first semester or two that you know a lot about. Using the knowledge you already possess is discussed in Chapter 3.

- Your **ability to concentrate** on what you are reading or studying also affects your learning. Everyone has times when his mind wanders and concentration is difficult. But if you frequently leave class or finish reading a chapter feeling that you got little or nothing out of it, learning may be difficult. There are things you can do to improve your concentration, however. Attention and concentration are discussed in Chapter 12.

- Your **beliefs about knowledge and learning** is a characteristic that is rarely discussed, but is very important. What do you believe knowledge is? Do you believe that knowledge consists of information that is transmitted from your professor to you? Or do you believe that you can be a part of creating knowledge? How you answer questions such as these influences the way you learn. Beliefs about learning are discussed in Chapter 6.

These characteristics and others not only help determine what you will learn, but also how you will study course material. Active learners understand the importance of being aware of these characteristics as they approach learning tasks, whether these tasks are easy or difficult.

QUICK TAKES

Getting to Know You

Figuring out your own characteristics as a learner can help you with more than succeeding in your classes. Once you know yourself, you can begin to make changes regarding relationships with others, how you manage your time, and even how to meet your goals for your future. This is because you

(continued)

are learning all the time—not just in your classes—and the way you handle your learning will follow you outside of the classroom and into your life. As you read *Penguin Academics: College Success Strategies*, think about how you can apply these concepts to your life.

Factor 2: The Tasks

Simply put, tasks are what your professors ask you to do. You can think of them as daily tasks, such as reading your text before you attend lectures; or larger tasks, such as preparing for various kinds of tests or writing papers. Most professors are pretty clear about what the task is. They will let you know the number of tests you will have and the kind of tests they will be (e.g., essay, multiple choice, etc.), as well as their expectations about papers, lab participation, or library work. Some will even let you examine copies of old tests or student papers so that you can see the kinds of questions they will ask or what their writing expectations are. Others will give you example test questions so that you can get an idea of how the questions will be asked.

But some professors aren't so clear in defining course tasks. Some may even give you conflicting messages. Therefore, it is important to try to get your professor to be as clear as possible about the tasks you must undertake. If you don't know what is expected of you, then you can't select the proper learning strategies or the most effective way to approach your texts. We discuss issues relating to tasks in Chapters 8-11.

Factor 3: The Texts

Texts are crucial to learning in college. In fact, it has been estimated that 85 percent of all college learning involves reading. Students often think of texts as simply **textbooks**. Certainly textbooks are a major source of information in many of your college classes, but texts also come in other forms. **Periodicals, newspapers, novels**, and **essays** are printed texts. Another type of text that is being used more often on university campuses is **computer text**, sometimes called nonlinear or hypertext. You may even be required to view films or documentaries, which are **visual texts**.

In addition to textbooks, **lecture notes** are the other most frequent type of "text" with which college students must interact. Strategies for note-taking are discussed in Chapter 10.

Whatever types of text you are expected to interact with, you should know how the particular text is organized. In most textbooks, each chapter is usually organized in the same fashion. In addition, your professor's lectures probably follow the same organization each day. Even visual texts have organizational patterns. Once you have determined how your text is organized, learning the material becomes a much easier task. Like learner characteristics and tasks, texts are an important part of the learning puzzle. Texts are discussed in more detail in Chapters 14 and 15.

Factor 4: The Learning Strategies

The final, and perhaps the most complex, factor that influences learning is the strategies that you choose. It is important to realize that these strategies should be chosen based on your characteristics as a learner, the tasks you have to do, and the texts with which you interact. Thus, a large portion of this text, Chapters 12-15, is devoted to learning strategies.

Strategies for active learning have several features in common.

1. Once you learn them, you can use all of these strategies on your own. Because studying is mostly a solitary activity, it is important to be able to use strategies without guidance from someone else, a professor or a friend for example.

2. These strategies have underlying processes that research has consistently shown to lead to better performance. For example, all of the strategies you will learn have a self-testing component, which immediately tells you whether or not you understand the information.

3. The strategies require participation on your part in the form of critical thinking and reasoning. If the task requires it, they help you to think beyond the text and to analyze, synthesize, and apply the information.

4. The strategies are flexible. You can modify them according to your own learning preferences, the tasks, and the texts.

COLLEGE CAMPUS TODAY

Getting Involved

We believe that active learning stretches beyond the walls of the classroom. Students who get the most out of college are the ones who get involved on campus. You will find lots of opportunities on your college campus to pursue (or find) a hobby. Some examples of organizations you will find include (but are certainly not limited to): fraternities and sororities, intramural sports, religious or political organizations, Zen meditation, and even rock climbing groups. So our advice is to find at least one organization that you find interesting and go to a meeting—we think you'll be glad you did.

The Holistic Nature of Active Learning

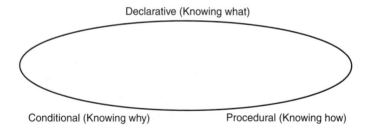

Declarative (Knowing what)

Conditional (Knowing why)   Procedural (Knowing how)

Active learners possess three different kinds of knowledge about the strategies they use during learning. It's not enough just to know how to use a particular strategy; in order to be an efficient and effective learner, you need to have declarative, procedural, and conditional knowledge (Paris, Lipson, and Wixson, 1983).

1. **Declarative knowledge.** Declarative knowledge is *knowing what*— what you need to do and what strategy you need to use. For example, if you were in a history class and the task was to get ready for an essay

exam in which you would need to synthesize information, declarative knowledge enables you to select the proper study strategy that matched the task. You might say to yourself, "I need to begin by predicting some questions, and then I need to practice answering those questions."

2. **Procedural knowledge.** Procedural knowledge involves more than knowing what you should do. It is *knowing how* to do it. Returning to our history example, you would have to know how to go about predicting questions that are likely to be on your test. You might search your lecture notes for hints your professor gave about important ideas, look to see what she spent a lot of time on in class, or look for overlap between your lecture notes and your text. Once you have predicted your questions, then comes the practice. You would need to have a plan—sketch out an outline of the key points you want to include in your answer, say those points to yourself, and practice writing out the answers to one of the questions you predicted. You might even show it to your professor if she is willing to give you feedback. As the name suggests, you have "procedures" to follow once you have identified the appropriate strategies.

3. **Conditional knowledge.** Conditional knowledge means knowing under what conditions to use certain strategies—*knowing why*. Using our history example again, you would know that you would have to use test preparation approaches that would lead to synthesis since that is what the task is. Therefore, you would not want to use strategies that encouraged only memorization.

Becoming an active learner, especially if you have been a passive learner, does take some time and effort. It doesn't happen overnight. Most students, especially first year-students, are located somewhere in the middle of the active/passive continuum. That is, rarely are students totally passive or completely active learners when they begin college. Becoming an active learner is a sort of work in progress.

Look back at your score on the Self-Assessment at the beginning of this chapter. Your score probably was not 11, the lowest possible score, nor was it 55, the highest. You probably fell somewhere in between. Just try to keep in mind that all students can become better learners.

☐ Real College
Maclolm's Malingering

DIRECTIONS: Read the following *Real College* scenario and respond to the questions based on what you learned in this chapter.

Meet Malcolm. Malcolm has a good attitude about being in college, but he's having a little trouble academically. Perhaps Malcolm does not understand that numerous factors all interact in order to be an active learner.

Malcolm decided after the first week on campus that he was made to be a college student! He has signed up for volunteer work, joined two campus clubs, and found several local "establishments" in which to hang out. He has discovered that he loves his freedom—the fact that he can come and go as he pleases. He never knew that a day could go by so quickly. Because he is often up late, trying to study while lying on his bed, he has trouble getting up for his 8:00 A.M. math class. Some days he is late; on other days, he never even hears his alarm. His other classes also present problems. He hates his history class because there is so much to read, and English, well . . . who cares about iambic pentameter? He is stressed out because he wants to do well, but he has already missed two math quizzes because of oversleeping and made a D on the first test. He thought he should have done much better because he did most of the homework, which is about as much as he had in high school, and he made As and Bs in those math classes. In English he made a C on his first writing assignment, which he felt was good for him. In history he has no grades yet since there is only a midterm and a final, but he is far behind on the reading assignments. Right now, things don't look promising for Malcolm!

Based on what you read in this and other chapters in this book, what advice do you have for Malcolm? As you are thinking about this advice, remember what we said earlier about the four factors of active learning that you need to consider: (1) your characteristics as a learner; (2) the tasks you must complete; (3) the texts with which you interact; and (4) the strategies you select. How might Malcolm consider each of these factors in order to become a more active and effective learner?

☐ Thinking Critically
Something to Think About and Discuss

Consider the four factors involved in active learning to respond to the following questions.

- Think about your current level of motivation. How motivated are you to do well in college? When do you think you might experience some problems with motivation?

- How do you think interests and attitudes influence college performance?

- Have you ever been in a class where you were confused about the task? How did you handle your confusion?

- Examine the textbooks you are using this term. How are they organized? What similarities and differences do you see?

- Think about how each of your professors lectures. How do their lecturing styles influence your note-taking?

- Currently, what kinds of study strategies are you using to learn new information? Do you use the same strategies for every class?

☐ Follow-Up Activities

Think of at least two things you can do right now to move toward becoming a more active learner. They can be small things, such as sitting closer to the front of the room in a class you don't like. Sitting closer might help you focus better and take better notes. Or you might try reading a section of one of your text assignments and then stopping to reflect on what you remember. Both are little changes, but if you make two small changes this week and two small changes the next, and so on, you will be well on your way to becoming an active learner.

CHAPTER 3

HOW YOU LEARN

Read this chapter to answer the following questions:

- What role does memory play in learning?
- How do the two major theories of learning differ?
- How can you stretch your memory?
- How can you use your senses to be a more effective learner?

SELF-ASSESSMENT

DIRECTIONS: Respond to these questions to determine your knowledge about how memory works.

1. T F   Researchers know how human memory works.
2. T F   Most people attend to all the sensory information around them.
3. T F   If you want to remember something forever, you should store it in short-term memory.
4. T F   Short-term memory holds only 5 to 9 pieces of information at one time.
5. T F   Usually, to move information from short-term to long-term memory you must rehearse the information.

6. T   F   Information processed at deep levels will be remembered for a long time.

7. T   F   Using mnemonics can hinder memory processing.

8. T   F   Creating acronyms can improve memory processing.

9. T   F   A person with a visual learning style can only learn by seeing things.

10. T   F   To remember more you should learn using all of your senses.

Answers: 1 F, 2 F, 3 F, 4 T, 5 T, 6 T, 7 F, 8 T, 9 F, 10 T. Read the rest of this chapter for a detailed explanation of why these statements are true or false.

Have you ever heard students comment that they don't do well on tests because they simply have a bad memory? Does it seem to you that the older people are, the poorer their memory? And why can you remember some things very easily, while other information needs to be pounded into your head? The answers to all of these questions have something to do with the way memory operates. Because researchers can't actually "see" memory, no one knows for sure exactly how memory operates. But scientists do know that certain sections of the brain are responsible for certain types of memories. Although there are different theories about how information gets into and is retrieved from memory, the theories do have commonalities. As you are reading about the two most common theories, keep in mind that they are just that . . . plausible explanations about how memory works.

The Role of Memory: Two Theories

The "Parts" Theory

According to what we will call the Parts Theory, there are three different types of memories, or what we will refer to as parts. It's easiest to think of memory in sort of a flowchart that might look something like this:

Sensory Store $\longrightarrow$ Short-Term Memory $\longrightarrow$ Long-Term Memory
(STM)   (LTM)

The first part, the **sensory store,** serves as a kind of filter. That is, your senses are often bombarded with information, much of which you can't remember. For example, if you are looking up a number in the telephone book, you don't look at every number. You run your finger down a specific page until you find the number you're looking for and then you interact with that piece of information in some way. For the most part, you probably have no recollection of the other names, addresses, or telephone numbers that were in that column. Your sensory store has filtered that information for you. Likewise, it's very likely that as you walked to class this morning you saw many other students, but can't recollect the faces of the ones that you passed. That's your sensory store at work as well.

Although your sensory store can never be "filled up" it can operate on overload. Think about a situation you have been in where your senses have been overwhelmed. It may have been at a place like Disney World where there are so many sights and sounds that it's difficult for your sensory store to take it in. It may have been a situation where you are trying to study for your history exam but your roommate has the TV on, your next door neighbor is listening to loud music, a fire truck goes by with its siren blaring, and you hear dogs barking in a distance. There's just too much vying for your attention that it's difficult for the filter to function in your best interest.

Under normal circumstances, however, when you identify a piece of information that you need to remember, your sensory store filters out what you don't need and you are actually not even aware of the process. What happens to the information that you need to remember? According to the parts theory, **short-term memory (STM)** takes over. STM is the part where information is held for a brief period of time—less than thirty seconds, unless you do something to retain it. In addition to short-term memory being brief, it can only hold a small number of items, anywhere from 5 to 9 pieces of information, or as it is sometimes referred to 7 ± 2 pieces of information. Let's return to the phone number example. You have just looked up the number of the campus health center. Phone numbers are seven digits so it's right within the capacity of STM. You pick up your phone to make the call just as your roommate walks in with a brief question. You answer her question, and begin to dial the health center. But you can't remember it. Only about a minute has passed, but the number didn't stay in short-term memory long enough for you to use it.

In order to increase the amount of time information can stay in STM you can do two things. You can rehearse the information by saying it several times or writing it down, or you can "chunk" the information to reduce the number of pieces you have to remember. When you **chunk** information, you group it together so that you are learning fewer pieces of information. For example, grouping the numbers in a phone number into two groups—531-2958 rather than thinking of it as seven separate numbers—5-3-1-2-9-5-8 makes it easier to remember and helps hold the information in STM.

QUICK TAKES

The Importance of STM

Although most students rarely think about how memory influences their learning, it is a crucial part of being able to retain information, something that you must be able to do if you are going to be an effective learner. It is interesting to think about the different parts of memory and what would happen if one of the parts failed to function properly, or not at all. That was just the premise of the movie *Memento*. In this film, the main character loses his short-term memory as a result of a head wound. In order to remember things and to track down the individual who raped and killed his wife, he tattooed himself and took photographs as ways of recording what he had learned. Had he not done this, every minute of his life and all information that he "knew" would have been forgotten. This movie certainly drives home just how crucial STM is to learning and remembering.

But what if you need to remember the information longer than a minute? Then your **long-term memory (LTM)** takes over. LTM has an unlimited capacity; it never gets "filled up" which is why you can remember things that happened when you were a small child. In fact, older people can often remember things that happened decades ago but have difficulty remembering things that happened last week because the older the memory, the more firmly it is fixed in LTM. In order to get information into LTM (like information that you study for an exam) you have to rehearse. Just as rehearsal will help you hold information in STM, it also helps you put information into LTM so you can remember it for an indefinite period of time. Therefore, if you write it, repeat it several times, listen to it over and over again, or talk it through with someone, you will be able to remember it later. (You'll learn more about rehearsal in Chapter 13.) According to the parts theory, the more and different ways you rehearse influence how much information you can remember and for how long.

Some things seem to get into LTM without rehearsal. For example, years from now when you're sitting around with friends, the September 11, 2001 date will probably come up. We can guarantee you that you will remember where you were and what you were doing when you heard that two airplanes had crashed into the World Trade Center in New York City. Tragic or personally traumatic events somehow get easily etched into our long-term memories without making any kind of effort.

Think for a minute about how this theory of memory applies when you are taking a test. For example, if you have a multiple-choice exam, your sensory store must filter out all the distractions as you read the questions such as the hum of the air conditioner, the noise from the hallway, or the person behind you with a persistent cough. Then, your STM must hold the question while you think about what the correct answer is. Finally, you must be able to retrieve the information you need from your LTM in order to answer the question. This process repeats for each item on the test.

The Levels of Processing Theory

Not all psychologists agree that the parts theory explains how memory works because they do not believe that there are separate systems in the brain. Another plausible explanation is the Levels of Processing Theory. Scientists who purport this theory believe that the degree to which you can remember and retrieve information depends on the "level" or depth that you have processed the information. Material that is processed at a "shallow" level cannot be remembered very well or for very long. But information that is processed at a "deep" level is remembered considerably better.

According to the levels of processing theory, it's not important to process everything at a deep level. In fact, if we did that we would be wasting our time in many instances. For example, if we return once again to the phone number example, if you simply wanted to remember the phone number long enough to call the health center to get an appointment, repeating the number several times or writing it down in an attempt to process it deeply would be a waste of time. You would still need to rehearse the information a bit, just long enough to make the call. This type of rehearsal is called **maintenance rehearsal**—engaging in just enough rehearsal techniques to process the information shallowly so that you can use it for a brief period of time and then "forget" it. This is not the kind of rehearsal you would want to use when studying for an exam.

On the other hand, if it was important for you to remember that telephone number for a long period of time so that you could retrieve it quickly a few days later, you would need to engage in **elaborative rehearsal**—making the information meaningful and rehearsing to the point where the information is at your fingertips. For example, you might note that the last four digits are the same as your grandmother's address. Usually, when you use elaborative rehearsal, you are engaging in deep processing because you want to use or retrieve the information easily at some time in the future. If you were studying for an essay exam in history, for example, it would be important for you to use elaborative rehearsal in order to have access to the information at test time. Elaborative rehearsal includes writing the information in an organized way, repeating the material, or personalizing it in some way to make it easier to remember.

Stretching Your Memory

Although you will have to do more than memorize in most of your college classes, we are not suggesting that the role memorization plays is trivial. In just about every course you take, you will have to do some memorization of facts. When you are trying to memorize information there are ways to stretch your memory to make it easier to learn and retrieve material. **Mnemonic devices** help you stretch your memory, and you most likely already use them, but weren't aware of their name.

COLLEGE CAMPUS TODAY
Who's Who?

In the past few weeks you have probably met quite a few new people. Have you found that you just can't remember all of their names? You can use mnemonics to help. When you meet someone, repeat the name and form a mental image (Amy—Amy has red hair. I picture a fire on Amy's head.), or use an association (Holly—just like the holly at Christmas time). It might also help to use the method of loci by recalling an object in the place where you have met this new person and associating the name with the object (Mark—dartboard). Try it yourself. As odd as it may sound, it really works.

In general, mnemonics encourage the personalization of information so that you have easy access to it at some future date. They are good for learning lists of items or for learning sequences of events or processes. They can be visual to help you create images or they can be a string of letters or a nonsense sentence—anything that enables you to remember information better. Even if you are unfamiliar with the term mnemonics, you have probably used them without even knowing it. For example, you may have learned the rhyme "use *i* before *e* except after *c* or in words sounding like *a*, as in *neighbor* and *weigh*." This mnemonic is known by almost every elementary school child.

Try out the following techniques to stretch your memory.

- **Acronyms.** You can use mnemonics to learn a list by creating an acronym. This means taking the first letter of each item you are trying to memorize and making them spell something. Your mnemonic device doesn't have to make sense to anyone but you. In fact, the more outrageous the memory device, the easier it generally is to remember. For example, if you needed to remember the parts of the forebrain, you might use this mnemonic: 4brain=TLC. This mnemonic works since you are probably already familiar with the letters TLC being used together, as in *t*ender *l*oving *c*are. In this case, TLC stands for *T*halamus, *L*imbic (system), and *C*erebral (cortex). You could then create other mnemonics that would help you remember the parts of the midbrain and the hindbrain or the functions each of these portions serves.

- **Imagery.** Forming images is another powerful way to help you remember when you review. Like other mnemonics, images can be very personal and don't have to make sense to anyone except the person forming the images. Images work best when the information you are trying to learn is concrete rather than abstract. In other words, it is difficult to make images for concepts such as courage, democracy, or freedom and it is much easier to make images for ideas such as cell division, presidential elections, or chamber music. Images work well because they give you both verbal and visual labels for things. A simple example may help you understand this idea. The three letters d-o-g together form a very familiar word— dog. Few people would have trouble understanding this word when they saw it in print. But what would happen if you asked each person who read that word to tell you his or her image of a dog? Would everyone describe *dog* in the same way? Of course not. Your image of a dog would be based on some experience you have, whether it's a dog you currently own or one who bit you when you were a child.

- **Method of Loci.** In the method of loci technique, you image a place that is familiar to you such as your living room, the street where you live, or your residence hall. Then you walk down this path through your memory. As you proceed, you attach a piece of information you have to learn to different places and objects to help you remember it. Remember the path markers can be as strange as you want (and the stranger the better) because that will make it easier for you to visualize. One of the authors uses a simplified version of the method of loci to remember who attended certain meetings. She visualizes the room and the table where the meeting was held, starts at one end and mentally walks a path around the table, visualizing where each person was seated.

We realize that some of these techniques sound strange, but we guarantee you they help stretch your memory under the right circumstances. And they can be fun to create, which also aids in helping you remember information.

The Role of Learning Styles

When students talk to us about their difficulty remembering information, they often mention learning styles as reason why memory sometimes breaks down. However, when we use the term learning styles, we are referring to how students learn best. Researchers who study this issue suggest that there are three main kinds of learners:

- **Visual learners,** or those who learn best by watching or seeing. Visual learners like to be shown how to do things and often learn best through diagrams or by using imagery. If you are a visual learner, if someone asks you how to spell a word, you probably have to write it down yourself first, rather that simply trying to spell the word in your head or out loud.

- **Auditory learners,** or those who learn best by listening or speaking. Auditory learners can learn easily through listening to lectures or by talking information over with a peer. If you are an auditory learner, you probably rarely miss a class lecture and you may participate in study groups for many of your courses. You may rehearse information by saying it over, either to yourself or out loud.

- **Kinesthetic learners,** or those who learn best by touching or movement. Kinesthetic learners generally learn best through writing or even typing things out. If you are a kinesthetic learner, you may rehearse information by writing it several times. You also may enjoy lab courses where there is a hands-on approach to learning.

Sometimes in study skills classes, instructors will have students take a learning styles inventory to find out how they learn "best." We believe these tests oversimplify the complex task of college learning. These tests also often pigeonhole students into one of these three categories and then give them suggestions for learning and studying based only on this particular style. Students can often feel trapped when their preferred mode cannot be used in a particular course. For example, it is hard to be kinesthetic in a philosophy course. Additionally, even in this day of technology, the fact remains that most colleges offer traditional classroom structure where students must read their texts, listen to lectures, take notes, and take exams. Therefore, you need to tap as many of these learning styles as possible if you are to be successful in college. That is why we suggest that rather than relying on one particular learning style, which may actually impede your learning, you use strategies that incorporate them all. We call this learning through your senses.

NETWORKING

Learning Styles Inventories on the Web

The Internet is loaded with learning styles assessments. You can find questionnaires that assess learning styles the way we have mentioned above (visual, auditory, kinesthetic), you can find out about multiple intelligences, you can take a personality inventory designed to help you figure out how you learn best, or you can even find out about the learning style of your dog. If you have never taken a learning styles assessment, you might want to. But, remember to take the results with a grain of salt. Don't try to base your entire approach to college on your score.

Using Your Senses to Learn

Many first-year students are "one trick ponies." That is, they prepare the same way for all of their classes, regardless of the type of test they'll have. They study biology the same way they study history. However, in college, it's important to use a variety of strategies and all of your senses to learn. In history, for example, you would want to read your text, listen actively to the lectures, and take a good set of notes. In that way, you would be using your senses to begin to get the information into your memory. You have a record of the important information to study from and you are actively engaged. As test time approached, you might study with a group of other students, make time lines as a way of outlining major historical events, and predict and answer essay questions. You would be listening, reading, discussing, and writing as a way of engaging all of your senses. Contrast that approach with simply attending all the lectures. Which student do you think would remember more come test time?

Although we encourage you to use all of your senses to learn, we also realize that many students prefer one mode of learning over another.

That's fine. We always encourage students to go with their strengths at the same time realizing that they can use strategies and approaches that are related to their weaker mode. In fact, most students have to approach learning in college by using a multiple sense approach. For example, in the sciences, there are generally diagrams to learn and understand. You can't ignore that task just because you aren't a visual leaner. Likewise, just because you learn best visually, you still must be able to attend and listen actively to lectures.

In Chapter 13, we will present a variety of strategies that will assist you in learning and remembering information. We have divided these strategies according to the three major types of learners:

- Visual learners learn best by seeing information. When they read their texts, they often visualize what the page looks like. They like to create diagrams, flowcharts, concept maps, or concept cards. They also tend to use imagery to remember information.

- Auditory learners learn best from listening or hearing information. They may be able to actively listen to lectures, but they may take horrible notes. They like to study with others where they can hear what others say. They also like to say information out loud.

- Kinesthetic learners learn best by doing. They learn best through writing and may write information in an organized way as a method of rehearsal. They like to be shown how to do things rather than figuring it out through reading or listening.

☐ Real College
Leo's Learning (Style)

DIRECTIONS: Read the following *Real College* scenario and respond to the questions based on what you learned in this chapter.

Leo knows he is a kinesthetic learner. He loves to work on cars and learned everything he knows by having hands-on experience at his uncle's body shop. Now that he is in college, he finds that he is having a lot of trouble remembering the material in his classes. The professors talk so fast, and he has never been a good note-taker. Although he is not sure how this would work in some of his classes, he wishes there were more opportunities to try out some of the things his professors were presenting—to use his kinesthetic abilities.

To try to remember what was discussed in class, Leo tries to memorize all of the key terms. He writes the information on cards and repeats it over and over again until he thinks he has it down cold. However, he sometimes finds that he can't remember even the simplest definitions on exams. Although Leo finds this really disturbing, he chalks it up to a bad memory.

Using what you have learned about how memory works, how to stretch your memory and using your senses to learn, how would you suggest Leo modify his approach to maximize his learning?

☐ Thinking Critically
Something to Think About and Discuss

- Think about the way you currently study. Do you tend to be one of those "one trick" ponies" or do you learn using variety of strategies? Share the strategies you use and discuss why you use those particular strategies with a friend.

- Think about something other than September 11, 2001 that became part of your long-term memory with little or no effort. Why do you think this happened? Why are some events more memorable than others?

- Why do you think it is often difficult to get course information into long-term memory? What are some steps you could take to help the process along?

☐ Follow-Up Activities

1. Try some of the mnemonic methods for stretching your memory the next time you prepare for an exam. Evaluate the effectiveness of each method. What worked and what did not work for you?

2. Examine several Web sites devoted to how memory works. What other theories did you find? Which theory sounds most plausible to you? Why?

PART TWO

YOUR LEARNING CHARACTERISTICS

Part II discusses how your characteristics as a learner affect your success in college. In Chapter 4, you learn strategies for managing yourself and your time. You learn how to create a schedule so that you can keep track of your college and personal obligations.

Chapter 5 discusses motivation, attitudes, and interests. You learn what motivates people as well as some strategies for maintaining your own motivation for learning. You also learn how your attitude toward college, your instructors, the topic, and toward yourself as a learner affect your learning. We also discuss ways to maintain a positive attitude.

Chapter 6 introduces five components of beliefs that influence learning. These components are discussed and you answer questions that assess your own beliefs about learning.

In Chapter 7, you learn about sources of stress in college and some strategies for reducing your stress levels. You also learn about strategies for coping with specific types of academic stress such as writing, math, and test anxiety.

CHAPTER 4

GETTING ORGANIZED
Managing Yourself and Your Time

Read this chapter to answer the following questions:

- Why do I need to manage my time?
- What is self-management?
- How can I create a schedule I can live with?
- How do I plan time to study for finals?

SELF-ASSESSMENT

DIRECTIONS: On a scale of 1 to 5 with 1 being "not at all effective," 3 being "somewhat effective," and 5 being "very effective," respond to each of the statements below. This evaluation should give you a good idea of your current time-management system.

1. How effective is your current system for managing time?   1 2 3 4 5

2. How effective is your current system for balancing your school, work, and social obligations?   1 2 3 4 5

3. How effective is your ability to get things done in an organized way?   1 2 3 4 5

4. How effective is your use of short periods of time   1 2 3 4 5
   (such as the time in between classes) to get
   things done?

If you scored mostly fives, then you are already finding success in your ability to manage yourself and your time. However, if your scores indicated that your current system is less than stellar, read on for some great time-management strategies.

Managing yourself and your time may be one of the most difficult challenges for you as a college student. If you are a returning student who has been in the workforce for a while, or you are raising a family, or holding a full-time job while attending college, you will face new challenges in juggling your many responsibilities. If you are a recent high school graduate, you are probably used to having most of your time managed for you. Your teachers and parents were responsible for setting a good deal of your daily schedule—you were in classes most of the day and after school you probably had some family obligations that were planned for you or perhaps you had a part-time job.

But in college, you are in class for fewer hours each day, which leaves you with big blocks of time to manage. The trick is to start out with a plan and not have to scramble to make up for lost time once you are already behind. What you want to be able to do is to create a plan that will help you maximize your time so you can get everything done without falling behind.

Managing Yourself

Before you can manage your time effectively, you have to be able to manage yourself. We believe that the key to self-management is being able to organize and keep track of all the things that you have to do. College life is very hectic; you have class assignments, roommates to deal with, tests to prepare for. You may also have a job to help pay your way through college or you may have daily family obligations. The secret to getting organized is to create a balance among school, home, work, and social life. In the past you may have been taught about time management with an approach that suggested giving up your social life to focus only on studying. However, we believe that you should have fun in college, too.

We want you to be able to hang out with your friends, but we also want you to be able to get the work done for your classes so that you can be academically successful and **stay** in college as well.

In order to create a balance between all the things you have to do and all the things you want to do, consider the following points:

- **Treat College Like a Full-Time Job.** If you are a full-time student, academic work should take up about 40 hours each week. So for the next several years, consider college your full-time job. You might be in class only 15 hours per week, but the other 25 hours should be spent studying and preparing for class. If you break it down, it is really not so bad. You will spend 3-4 hours in class and 4-5 hours reading, studying, and preparing for your assignments each day. The rest of the time is left for other activities that you want to participate in or a part-time job. The good news is that unlike a full-time job, in college you have more control over when you want to schedule your classes and your study time. No one says that your studying must take place between 9:00-5:00 Monday through Friday—you are free to study whenever you want.

- **Schedule Your Classes for Your Most Alert Times.** Are you a morning person? A late afternoon person? An evening person? Are you up with the sun or are you lucky to be awake by noon? If you know you will never make it to an 8:00 A.M. class, don't schedule a class for that time if possible. Likewise, if you are totally useless in the afternoon, try to schedule your courses before lunchtime. Many students don't consider their class times as an issue to think about when making their course schedule, but because you have the luxury of creating your own schedule, you should try to tailor it to your needs as much as possible.

- **Go to Class.** Although many professors don't take attendance, most still believe that going to class is a very important part of learning. Students who skip a lot of classes miss out on the important information that they can only get in class. For example, some professors consider their syllabus a work-in-progress and modify it throughout the term. Suppose a professor assigned a paper that was mentioned only in class but was not on the syllabus. You would be responsible for turning in the paper, but the only way you would know it was assigned is if you attended class. Also, as an added bonus, by going to class each day will you know what the professor emphasized, which will help you know what to focus on when you study. So do yourself a favor and **go to class** every day.

- **Don't Procrastinate.** Procrastination is intentionally and continually putting off work that needs to be done. This problem may actually be the toughest part of self-management for some students. Because you are in control of your own time, it is tempting to put off work until later. It's just human nature. But you can become quickly overwhelmed by all you need to do when you continually neglect your work. Almost everyone has a friend who has procrastinated until the last minute and must read an entire novel and write a five-page English paper all in one night. Procrastination tends to become a bad habit and a way of life for some students. Once you start procrastinating, it is difficult to get back on track. However, the strategies in the next section should help you avoid procrastination by helping you determine what you need to do each day.

COLLEGE CAMPUS TODAY

Financial Management

Many campuses offer financial management workshops for students who are often bombarded with offers for credit cards the first month they hit college. We believe this is another way to help learn to self-manage as you are beginning to learn the complexity of money management. Check out what your college offers before you break in that new credit card.

Managing Your Time

Effective time-management strategies can help you organize your responsibilities and reach your goals. To manage your time effectively you will need to determine three important pieces of information:

1. **What do you need to accomplish?** Consider the classes you must attend each week, your work schedule, social commitments, class

assignments, and so forth. One of the hardest problems to figure out is how much time an assignment will take. For example, when writing a paper you have to know if it will take you one hour to find what you need in the library or on the Web, or if it will take considerably longer. Will you be able to write your paper in two days or will you need a full week? Some of the ability to know how long things will take comes with experience, but the following general rule may help you plan your time:

THINGS ALWAYS TAKE LONGER THAN YOU THINK THEY WILL.

Given this basic rule, try to plan more time than you think you will need. When you rush to get an assignment completed, you probably feel frustrated or angry when things take longer than planned. You may even give up without completing the assignment. So plan for things to take longer to avoid this problem.

2. **What things do you currently do that waste your time?** Before you can figure out how to spend your time effectively, you need to find out if and how you are wasting time. To do this, think about how you currently spend your days. Are there some things you do that simply waste large amounts of time? For example, are you playing video games, watching TV, surfing the net, napping or hanging out with friends for hours on end? How might you restructure your days so that less time is wasted?

3. **How can I keep track of what I need to do?** Most people who manage their time successfully say that they can't live without their schedule book or daily planner. It helps them keep track of appointments, assignments, social commitments, and even important phone numbers. If you don't already use some kind of schedule book, invest in one today. Take your schedule book with you to class and be sure to mark down your assignments. But writing things down is only half the battle—you have to make a habit of checking your schedule book every day to see what you need to do. To be really effective, plan to schedule in exactly when you will study for your classes. You have so many things to juggle in college that sometimes it is hard to find the time to study. Planning your study sessions along with the rest of your responsibilities helps you stay on top of your school responsibilities.

NETWORKING

Managing Your Time

There are many Web pages devoted to helping people organize and manage their time. Find at least three such Web sites. What kind of useful information did you find? How much overlap was there in the information about time-management? What differences in time-management advice did you find? What changes will you make based on their suggestions?

Creating a Schedule You Can Live With

Creating a schedule that works is a challenge. Many students start out with good intentions, but ultimately end up with an unworkable schedule for a number of reasons. Some students create a schedule that is too rigid, so they don't have the flexibility they need. Others create a schedule that is not detailed enough to be of any use. Still others create a good schedule, but don't consult it regularly, so they forget what they need to do. In order to avoid falling into one of the time-management pitfalls, consider the following tips as you create you own schedule:

SUCCESS AT A GLANCE

Characteristics of Good and Poor Time Managers

Good Time Managers	Poor Time Managers
Study when they are most alert	Study whenever the mood strikes (even when they are dead tired)
Spend some time every day on each course	Study the night before each exam

(continued)

Good Time Managers	Poor Time Managers
Create a schedule that is specific	Do not schedule study times or do so only in a very general way
Make a reading schedule for each class	Read the night before the exam
Prioritize their work	Do the things they like to do first and put the rest off
Make "to do" lists to stay organized	Often find that they don't have assignments completed because they did not write them down
Use the time in between classes to get work done	Don't use small pockets of time wisely

Timely Tips for Following Your Schedule

- **Plan to Study When You are Most Alert.** If you find that you are tired or you can't concentrate when you study, you probably are not studying at your most alert time. Try to find some blocks of time that are naturally best for you. Some students study best at night, others study best first thing in the morning. Test several times of the day to find out when you are the most ready to study. Experiment with times that you might not initially think are your best times of day—you just may surprise yourself and be a morning (or night) person after all.

- **Spend Some Time Every Day on Each Course You are Taking.** Even when you don't have an assignment due, plan some time each day to read the text, review your notes, and prepare for the next class. If you are taking classes that require problem solving such as math or chemistry, it is a good idea to work some problems each night. If you are taking a language class, plan to review new vocabulary or work on verb conjugation every day. By spending some time every day you won't have to cram for exams because you will always be caught up.

- **Be Specific.** The more specific you can be when planning your study schedule, the better because you will know exactly what you need to do each time you study. When you create your schedule, don't just write down "study." Instead, write "Read psychology text pgs. 219-230." By creating a schedule that lists each specific task, you are more likely to remember to get everything done.

- **Make a Reading Schedule for Each Class.** One of the simplest, yet most effective, ways to manage your time and to stay on top of your reading assignments is to make a reading schedule for each class. To make a reading schedule simply add up the number of pages you need to read in the next week (some students prefer to add the pages in-between each exam rather than weekly) and divide that number by five (or six or seven if you will read during the weekend). For example, Robert has the following reading assignments this week:

History	Read Chapters 3-4	65 pages
Statistics	Read Chapter 5	27 pages
	Complete 15 practice problems	
Music	Read Chapters 4-5	39 pages
Literature	Read 6 chapters of novel	90 pages
Biology	Read Chapters 8 and 11	29 pages

This equals 250 pages of text reading, which according to several college surveys, is about average. Thinking about reading 250 pages can be overwhelming, but when he divides the reading over 5 days he sees that he has only 13 pages of history, 6 pages of statistics (and 3 practice problems), 8 pages of music, 18 pages of literature, and 6 pages of biology to read each day. And that sounds a lot more manageable. If he reads over 6 or 7 days, his daily load is cut even more. To create you own reading schedule, survey your reading assignments (usually found on your syllabus) and divide up the reading in a way that makes sense. Use section breaks or headings to help you determine how to divide the readings so that you are not stopping in the middle of a concept.

- **Prioritize.** When you make your schedule, it is helpful to prioritize what you have to do. You might want to label your assignments as "high," "medium," or "low" priority. For example, reading your biology text before the lab might be high priority, but starting on your history research paper that is due in three weeks might be lower. In general, start with high-priority tasks first so that you are sure to get them done. But don't ignore the medium and low priorities. That history research paper may be low priority now, but if nothing gets done in the next three weeks it will become high priority fast.

- **Make "To Do" Lists.** Sometimes when students begin to study they start to think about all the other things they need to do—call home, get a haircut, cancel a dental appointment. All of these thoughts are very distracting. To keep yourself on track and to avoid procrastination, keep a "To Do" list next to you when you study. Write down all the things you think of including course work, household chores (such as laundry), phone calls, e-mails to answer, and so forth. Cross items off as you complete them. Your To Do list might look something like this:

Date: Oct. 2	What do I need to do?	Priority (high, medium, low)
1.	Finish revising English paper	High
2.	Do Laundry	High
3.	Read Math pp. 81-97 and do the problems	Medium
4.	Call home	Medium
5.	Plan spring break trip	Low
6.	Think about topic for final history paper	Low

- **Borrow Time—Don't Steal It.** If you decide to go out for a pizza instead of spending an hour reading your psychology chapter—great. But remember that it's important to just borrow that time. If you decide to go out instead of following your schedule, be sure to add the activity you missed (that is, reading your psychology chapter) to your schedule (or To Do list) for the next day so that you can make up that time. By having a schedule that is very specific, you'll know exactly what you have to do to catch up and you can easily make up for the lost time.

- **Use the Time Between Your Classes.** Many times students don't know where all of their time goes—an hour in-between classes, two hours between school and work, 15 minutes before classes begin—all of this time adds up and it is useful for getting your work done. You can read for class during hour breaks, review your notes while you are waiting for class to begin, use the time between lunch and class to review, or even meet with a study group in the laundromat. Plan to use short periods of time when making your schedule so this time does not get "lost."

- **Schedule Studying Breaks.** If you plan to study for more than an hour or so at a time, schedule a 10-15 minute break for each hour and a half to two hours of study. You should also plan short breaks when switching from one topic to another so you can give yourself some time to refocus. But be careful that your short breaks don't turn into long breaks.

- **Take Some Time Off.** Many students feel guilty when they take time off because they are always thinking about the things they "should be doing" such as working on that chemistry lab assignment. But when you have a good schedule, you will be able to reward yourself by taking time off without guilt because you know that you have planned time to get all of your assignments done. So after you have completed your work—relax and enjoy yourself, you deserve it. In fact, you should plan some free time when creating your schedule.

- **Don't Spin Your Wheels.** If you are having trouble in a course, get some assistance. Seek help from a tutor, a professor, or a friend, anyone who might be able to help. There is nothing that gets in the way of managing your time more than wasting it worrying, rather than doing something productive so that you can be on top of things in a course that is difficult for you. It's important to get help if you need it and get back on track before you fall too far behind to catch up.

QUICK TAKES

Creating a Workable Schedule

Learning to manage your time is a skill that will help you in college and beyond. Start now, and by the time you enter the world of work, you will be a time-management veteran. Start this week. Consider the tips you just read to create a schedule. Use your schedule book to fill in your plan for the upcoming week in the following order:

1. Enter your class and lab times

2. If you commute, enter the time it takes to travel to and from campus

3. Enter your work schedule

4. Enter your meal times

5. Enter all of your weekly personal activities (clubs, athletics, exercise)

6. Schedule your study times for each class. Include time for the following:

   • Reviewing your notes
   • Reading the text
   • Preparing for exams, writing papers, working on projects, etc.

7. Keep some time open so that your schedule is somewhat flexible

8. Add any other things that you have to do this week

Planning for Midterms and Finals

Every principle of time- and self-management discussed in this chapter usually goes into warp speed when you are preparing for midterms and finals. Generally, you will need to rethink your entire schedule to cope with the added pressures. In fact, you might even need to put in a few hours of overtime on your 40-hour workweek, but don't despair. By following the techniques outlined in this chapter you should get through it.

In addition to the strategies we have already discussed, we add the following suggestions to help you cope with crunch exam time:

- **Plan Ahead.** Start to rehearse and review your notes and the texts *before* exam week so that you can cut down on your workload for the week. Starting early is essential for classes that have cumulative exams (exams that hold you responsible for topics covered over the entire term) because there is so much information to review.

- **Cut Down on Work or Other Commitments.** If you work part-time, ask for some time off or for fewer hours at your job and make sure that your family and friends understand that you will be extra busy. Try not to add any new commitments during midterm and final time.

- **Get Enough Sleep.** Pulling all-nighters for a big exam rarely pays off. Instead try to create your schedule for exam week in a way that leaves you adequate sleep time (try for at least 6 hours each night). You won't do well on an exam if you are falling asleep while taking it.

- **Study with a Partner.** Misery loves company and this is never truer than during midterms and finals. Hopefully by the time midterms roll around you have found a study group that works. Study with your group or study partner to keep each other on schedule and motivated to work.

- **Don't Panic.** This point will be further discussed in Chapter 7, but to put it simply—midterms and finals are really just exams. The world will not stop and does not end because of midterms and finals. If you find that the pressure is getting to you, readjust your schedule to allow more break time and try to really relax during those breaks. If you find that you have excessive anxiety, get some help before it becomes a stumbling block to doing well.

In this chapter you have learned some strategies for managing yourself and your time. Try to make a schedule and follow it strictly for one week. Then make adjustments to suit your needs. Even if you do not consider yourself a "schedule person," you should find that keeping track of what you need to do really helps you organize and take control of your college career.

☐ Real College
Janice's Jam

DIRECTIONS: Read the following *Real College* scenario and respond to the questions based on the information you learned in this chapter.

Janice is a college freshman. She loves her new freedom. A new town, her own place, new friends, and a great social life. Gone is the 10 o'clock curfew that her parents had enforced in high school. Janice is living it up and having the time of her life, but she can't seem to make it to all of her classes and is falling way behind on her work.

Janice is taking five courses this term— American literature, accounting, sociology, history, and a chemistry course that involves lab projects. Her reading load is about 240 pages each week and she has at least one exam every other week. She never seems to be able to keep up with her reading or to find time to study. In addition, Janice is having trouble making it to her 8 A.M. accounting course. In fact, she missed both class periods last week. She has also missed several of her chemistry classes, even though she really enjoys them, but she just can't seem to make it to class on time.

Another concern is Janice's part-time job at a local video store. Although her hours are somewhat flexible, she always works at least two weeknights and one weekend day. She thinks that the 15 hours spent at her job each week is really getting in the way of her studying, but she needs the money so she can't quit or cut back on hours.

She also finds her new social life to be a problem. It seems that no matter when she tries to study, someone is calling or stopping by her dorm room to ask her to go out. Janice really has a hard time saying no and ends up procrastinating on her work every time. She never had trouble in school before, but now she is failing several courses including chemistry, which she wants to major in. She knows that she needs to do things differently, but she just can't seem to find the time to get everything done.

Using the strategies you learned about time- and self-management, what advice would you give Janice to help her manage her time?

☐ Thinking Critically
Something to Think About and Discuss

- How do you think your current time management system is affecting your performance in college?
- Do you find yourself with a lot of time during which you do not get anything accomplished? If so, how can you adjust your current schedule to account for this wasted time?
- What kinds of obstacles currently make it hard to manage yourself as a college learner?
- How do you think your schedule will change when you are preparing for midterms and finals? How do you plan to make those changes successfully?
- If you have taken midterms or finals in the past, what obstacles did you find to managing yourself and your time? What do you plan to do differently this term?

☐ Follow-Up Activities

Follow the schedule you created in this chapter for one week and then evaluate it by asking yourself the following questions:

1. Did you find that you accomplished more work?
2. What adjustments would you make to your schedule?
3. Have you left enough flexibility in your schedule for emergencies?
4. Are you studying during your most alert times?

CHAPTER 5

ACADEMIC ENERGY
Motivation, Attitudes, and Interests

Read this chapter to answer the following questions:

- What motivates people?
- How do you get and stay motivated?
- How do attitudes and interests influence learning?
- How can you change your attitude and develop interest for topics you dislike?
- How can you maintain a positive attitude?

SELF-ASSESSMENT

DIRECTIONS: On a scale of 1 to 5 with 1 being "not at all true of me," 3 being "somewhat true of me," and 5 being "very true of me," respond to the following statements as honestly as you can. This assessment should give you a good idea of your motivation, attitudes, and interests.

1. I am not very motivated for college learning.   1 2 3 4 5

2. It seems like other students are more motivated to succeed in college that I am.   1 2 3 4 5

3. I have trouble setting and reaching my goals.   1 2 3 4 5

4. I am often unsure of when my goals have been achieved. 1 2 3 4 5

5. I don't have a good attitude about attending college. 1 2 3 4 5

6. I don't have a good attitude about many of the courses I am taking this term. 1 2 3 4 5

7. I tend to have a limited range of interests. 1 2 3 4 5

8. I have trouble getting motivated in courses I find uninteresting. 1 2 3 4 5

9. I am not sure why I am attending college. 1 2 3 4 5

10. I am motivated to learn in courses where the professor is interesting. 1 2 3 4 5

If you scored mostly ones, you probably have a positive attitude and are motivated for college learning. If, on the other hand, you scored mostly fives, you may want to pay extra careful attention to the strategies discussed in this chapter.

You may have already noticed that motivation, attitudes, and interests are tied together. It just makes sense that for courses in which you are interested or have a positive attitude about, you will be more motivated to learn. But let's try to separate these three important factors related to active learning to define what they are and how they interact to promote active learning and success in college. We'll begin with motivation.

What Influences Motivation?

Motivation is a combination of several factors including choice, desire for learning, and value of learning. Motivation is influenced by:

1. **The amount of choice** you have about what you are learning. Sometimes your professors will offer you several projects to choose from, or sometimes they will even ask you to choose what topics will be covered. Choices like these will help to increase your motivation. However, even if you are not given choices about the class content, college offers you many choices about what you will learn. You choose your major, and to a certain extent you choose the courses you will take, and your course schedule.

2. **Your desire to learn.** It's likely that because you are currently enrolled in college you do want to learn, but sometimes you might be required to take courses that you are not particularly interested in. For example, most colleges have a liberal arts requirement for all students, which means that regardless of their major, students must take courses in humanities, mathematics, and the sciences.

3. **How much you value the subject** to be learned. The more you believe the subject to be worthwhile, the easier it will be to become motivated. For example, many colleges require students to take at least one foreign language course. If you believe that it is valuable to learn another language you will feel motivated—perhaps even enough to take a second course. However, if you do not, you may have a harder time motivating yourself to learn in your language course.

In an ideal setting you would have all of the components of motivation. However, you can learn successfully without choice, desire, and value, but learning will take more of a conscious effort from you.

What Motivates People?

You may not realize it but you are always motivated. No matter where you are or what you are doing, *you are always motivated to do something* even if it's just sleeping. Focusing your motivation on learning, however, may be challenging sometimes.

It's important to understand right from the beginning that you are responsible for your own motivation, even in courses that you don't like. Although an interesting instructor makes it easier for you to stay motivated, no one can directly motivate you to learn. But given that you are always motivated to do something and that you are primarily responsible for your motivation, there are some differences between students who are motivated to learn and students who are not.

You may have heard the terms **intrinsic** and **extrinsic,** especially as they relate to motivation. Intrinsic motivation occurs when the activity is its own reward. For example, some people read for the sheer enjoyment, others like to calculate numbers for the pleasure of it. Still others like to conduct experiments for the thrill of discovery. Think of intrinsic motivation as being curious about something or doing something you choose to do.

Extrinsic motivation, on the other hand, occurs when your incentive is a reward, such as grades or praise. Think of extrinsic motivation as trying to "get it done" rather than for the sake of learning. For example, you may be failing organic chemistry, but when the professor offers an extra credit assignment, you decide to do it even though you are not motivated to learn in the course. In this case, you are extrinsically motivated to earn extra credit points that can boost your course grade rather than by learning organic chemistry for the sheer pleasure of it.

The more you are intrinsically motivated to learn, the easier learning will be for you. The key to becoming intrinsically motivated, even in classes you don't particularly like, is to find *something* about the course that you find motivating and try to focus on the positives about the course rather than the negatives. It also helps to focus more on understanding the concepts to be learned rather than focusing solely on grades.

QUICK TAKES

Motivation After College

Whether you have a part-time job as a student or a full-time job after graduation, motivation makes a big difference in how satisfied you will be with your work, and ultimately how successful you will be in your career. If you show up at work just to bring home a paycheck (extrinsic motivator) and don't have much motivation to do anything beyond what is required, you probably won't rise to the top of your profession. Alternatively, if you are motivated to go to work because you like what you do and work hard to be the best you can be, you will reap positive rewards, both in your paycheck and in life.

Getting Motivated Through Goal Setting

Getting motivated is the first step toward staying motivated. One of the best ways to become motivated is to set learning goals. Your goals should be more than just "I want to make an A in the course," because grades are an extrinsic motivator. In fact, students who focus only on grades to motivate themselves usually have a harder time maintaining their motivation as the term goes on. Students who set goals that focus on learning rather than grades tend to be more successful.

You probably have set goals before without even realizing it. For example, think about some New Year's resolutions you have made—to exercise more, to stop smoking, or to increase your GPA. How many of your resolutions have you kept? If you are like most people, your resolutions are long forgotten by Valentine's Day! That's because most people do not set themselves up for achieving their New Year's goals. People tend to be unrealistic when they make New Year's resolutions. Although a goal of exercising more and getting in shape is a good resolution to make, it is unrealistic to expect to be in great shape right away if you have not been exercising regularly. Individuals who do not set short-term goals on their way to reaching long-term goals will soon find that their resolutions are not easily achievable and will give up on reaching their goals.

In order to set goals that can be achieved, your goals should be:

- **Realistic:** Can the goal be achieved? If not, how can the goal be divided into smaller goals? You should try to have short-term, intermediate, and long-term academic goals. A **short-term goal** is one that you will achieve within the next few days, such as "I will read chapter 10 of my biology book tonight." **Intermediate goals** are ones that you will achieve within the next few weeks or months, such as " I will compare my notes to the text material each night to prepare for my next psychology exam, which will be in three weeks." A **long-term goal** is one that will take longer still, perhaps a few months or even years to achieve, such as "I will begin to learn Spanish this year" or an even longer-term goal is " I want to graduate with a degree in marketing." Most people make the mistake of making only intermediate and long-term goals, but short-term goals are also important because they help you follow the progress you are making and they help you stay on track.

- **Believable:** Do you feel that you will be able to achieve your goal? Being confident about your ability to learn is crucial to your motivation. If you feel that a task is too difficult for you to achieve, your motivation will decrease and you might give up before you even try. Some students believe that they can succeed only in certain topics. Students will say, " I'm good at math, but I'm terrible at English" or " I can learn history really well, but not science." These statements tell us that the students are motivated to learn one topic, but not another. If you find yourself making these kinds of statements, take a minute to reflect on how they are negatively affecting your motivation to learn in those courses.

- **Desirable:** How much do you want to reach your goal? In order to succeed in reaching your goals, they should be goals that you really desire. Then, learning will be particularly rewarding or enjoyable to you and it will be easier to achieve. Your goal may be to graduate from college within four years and to land a good job in your field, but you must have the desire for success to reach that type of goal.

- **Measurable:** How will you know whether or when your goal has been met? Some goals are easy to measure. If your goal is to lose 10 pounds, you will know whether your goal has been met when you weigh yourself. However, sometimes learning goals are not so easy to measure, so you need to set some standards to help you measure your progress. This may be as simple as taking a few minutes to think about what you have learned after each study session or it may include a more in-depth assessment. In general, you will need more checks of your progress for long-term goals than for short-term goals.

NETWORKING

Finding Motivation

Many sites on the Internet feature tips for getting and staying motivated. Some good sources include college counseling centers or freshman-year experience sites. Try the following keywords to find at least three motivation sites: motivation, college motivation, student motivation, or learning motivation. What kind of information did you find that will help you become more motivated or to maintain your motivation?

Staying Motivated

Getting motivated is one thing; staying motivated is another. In order to stay motivated you should give yourself checkpoints on the way to reaching your goals. These checkpoints might include:

- Monitoring your motivation for learning just as you monitor your comprehension when you read. Each time you sit down to study, ask yourself about the level of motivation for what you are doing. You have an internal "body clock," which means that you will find that certain times of the day are more conducive to learning than others. (This idea was discussed in Chapter 4.) Listen to your body clock to find out when you are most motivated (first thing in the morning, late afternoons, evenings) and try to plan your study sessions around those times.

- Studying the subjects you find the most difficult, or are least motivated to learn, first. Then move to the subjects that are easier, or those that you enjoy more. In that way you will be more likely to stay motivated to study the subjects you find the most interesting.

- Planning some breaks in your study time—don't try to study for more than one hour without a short break because you will find it difficult to maintain your motivation.

But what if you find yourself losing motivation? It's important to have strategies to follow in this scenario as well. It might help if you:

- Take a break and come back to what you were doing at a later time.
- Switch topics every hour or so.
- Work with a study group. Misery loves company and others can often remotivate you.
- Plan to study in the library or another quiet place if you find that your social life is interfering with studying because your friends are calling you or dropping by. Find somewhere to study where you will be free from distractions and temptation.

Sometimes students find that they lose motivation as the term goes on. Some of this is natural—people are generally more motivated at the beginning and at the end of a term. So, if you experience a slight dip in your motivation toward the middle of a term, or during the first nice spring day, you probably shouldn't be too concerned. Set some new goals to get back on track. However, sometimes losing motivation can be a sign of a bigger problem. If you think your loss of motivation may be a problem, reflect on the source of your lack of motivation. Can you pinpoint a reason for it? Or are you unsure why you are unmotivated? Sometimes students become unmotivated by poor grades in a particular course, or sometimes outside influences (for example, family, roommates, social situations, or health concerns) cause students to lose their motivation.

Another way to maintain your motivation is to figure out all of the tasks that you need to complete in your courses. By listing this information, you should be able to find something in the course that is motivating for you. You will also be able to determine the tasks you find unmotivating, which can help you psych yourself up to maintain your motivation in advance. Before each exam (or paper, or project) for each of your courses this term, complete this chart to monitor your motivation.

Any method you find to renew your motivation is great! Try a few techniques to find out what works best for you instead of giving up entirely. The motivation checkpoint chart that follows should help you monitor your motivation in many different situations in all of your courses to help you discover the kinds of tasks you find particularly motivating and the kinds of tasks that you find less motivating. Once you know the kind of tasks that unmotivate you, you can be prepared with some of the techniques discussed above.

SUCCESS AT A GLANCE

Motivation Checkpoints

When you are setting your goals, remember that achievable goals are:

Realistic

Believable

Desirable

Measurable

(continued)

DIRECTIONS: For one of your courses this term answer the following questions.

What do I need to learn? What is the task (exam, paper, presentation, discussion, etc.)?

What sources will I need to use (text, labs, lecture, discussion, etc.)?

What is my level of motivation for beginning the task (high, medium, low) and why?

What are my goals for completing this project (include short-term, intermediate, and long-term goals)?

What is my level of motivation for completing the task (high, medium, low) and why?

(continued)

DIRECTIONS: For one of your courses this term answer the following questions.

What, if any, adjustments do I need to make to reach my learning goals?

Changing Attitudes and Interests

Now that you understand the role that motivation plays in active learning, let's turn to attitudes and interest. As you read this portion of the chapter, reflect on how they relate to one another.

How many times have you dealt with a clerk in the grocery store, a family member, your advisor, a server in a restaurant, or even your best friend and walked away thinking, "Now there's a person with a bad attitude"? Everyone probably has a bad attitude about something at some time, which suggests that attitude, like motivation, is situational. Rarely are people positive about everything, nor are they negative about everything.

Likewise, interest is situational. Students generally aren't interested in everything. In most cases, individuals tend to show great interest in a limited number of areas, moderate interest in a greater number of topics, and low or no interest in many more. Everyone knows people who have a strong passion for something—computers, fly fishing, travel, photography, writing, basketball, history. And more often than not, these passions are reflected in majors that students select. Interests can't help but influence academic decisions students make and how actively they pursue certain goals.

Like motivation, attitudes and interests help define who you are as a learner. Moreover, each of these factors is either directly or indirectly a part of your personality, thus making them a bit more difficult to change than basic study habits.

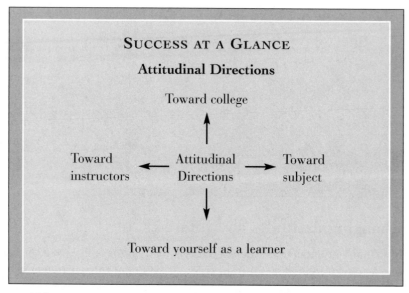

SUCCESS AT A GLANCE

Attitudinal Directions

Toward college

Toward instructors ← Attitudinal Directions → Toward subject

Toward yourself as a learner

Although everyone seems to know someone who, in general, has an overall bad or good attitude, attitudes can actually be thought of as emotional reactions to specific situations. Think of attitudes as:

- **Reflexive, Meaning You Experience Them Without Even Thinking About It.** For example, if your professor assigns you two extra chapters to read before a quiz on Friday and you already have every minute of your schedule between now and Friday planned, you may have an immediate negative reaction. However, that attitude may not be permanent. Perhaps a professor in another class cancels a test that was scheduled for Friday, or a date that you really didn't want to go on in the first place begs off, causing your initial bad attitude to mellow. The bottom line is that most students' attitudes about things change. What you have a bad attitude about on Tuesday may be seen in another light by Wednesday.

- **An Influence on Your Motivation.** It makes sense that if you are motivated in a particular course that your attitude would be more positive than if you were unmotivated.

- **Characteristics that Match Your Behavior.** For example, if you have a bad attitude toward learning a foreign language and feel that no matter what, you can't succeed, your behavior will follow suit. You won't interact with the material on a daily basis, you won't say much in class, and you even may display a poor attitude toward your professor, even if she is a good teacher.

As a college student, you will often experience four attitudinal directions: (a) attitude toward college; (b) attitude toward your instructors; (c) attitude toward the subject and learning environment; and (d) attitude toward yourself as a learner. As you read about each one, think about yourself as a learner and the attitudes that you have.

Attitude Toward College.   Students begin college with different attitudes for many different reasons. Some are happy with their school choice, others aren't, and still others don't care. Obviously it's better to begin on the right foot—with a positive attitude about the college you are attending—but also remember that attitudes change. We've known many students who started college having one perception about what they would experience only to be either disappointed or elated later on. For whatever reason you chose to attend your current college, know that your general attitude about being in college and your expectations of what that college experience will be strongly influence the attitudes you will have. In turn, these attitudes influence your academic performance. Sometimes college just isn't what students expected it would be. Factors such as large class sizes, classes that are difficult to get into, long lines, roommate problems, and homesickness are just a few of the many problems that can turn initially good attitudes sour.

Attitude Toward Your Instructors.   Your attitude about your instructor also influences your academic performance. This is especially true for disciplines you don't particularly like. If you go into a mathematics course "hating" math and project that feeling onto your professor, you are probably going to have some problems. On the other hand, if you try to have the attitude that each instructor has something unique to offer to your education you may have a totally different experience. We suggest that students try to get to know their professors and not to feel intimidated about talking with them. We know of a student who, at the beginning of every term, makes an appointment to see all of his professors. He takes only about 15 minutes of their time introducing himself and talking with each of them about how to study in their courses. He says it helps him see his professors in a different light, and although he still has a better attitude toward some professors than others, the experience makes all his professors "human." Rarely does a professor turn down his request for an appointment, and in many cases, this initial contact makes it easier for him to approach a professor if he is experiencing problems with a course.

Attitude Toward the Subject and Learning Environment. When we think about attitudes toward subject matter, it's difficult to separate attitude from interest and motivation since most students have a more negative attitude toward subjects in which they are not interested and less motivated. For example, if you are strong in mathematics and science and have been successful in those courses in the past, you will most likely enter into these courses in college with a positive attitude toward learning the material. However, if you have little interest in math and science and fail to see any relevance in these courses to your future career choice, then you are much more likely to have a bad attitude toward these classes. In fact, some students try to avoid subjects they dislike until the very end of their program. We know students who have delayed taking their lab science, history, or mathematics requirements until their senior year, only to find out that the course wasn't as bad as they thought it would be. It's also important to try hard not to have preconceived notions about a course. Even though you may have had an unpleasant experience in a similar past course, try to begin each course with an open mind. An open mind can go a long way in changing your attitude, helping you develop your interests, and maintaining motivation.

Attitude Toward Yourself as a Learner. The attitude that you have toward yourself as a learner may be the most important of the four attitudinal directions because it is the sum total of the educational experiences you have accumulated in your 12+ years of schooling. If you have had teachers who encouraged you, if you have experienced academic success, and if you have parents who have been actively involved in your learning at home, you probably have a positive view of yourself in learning situations. That's not to say that students who have a positive attitude never doubt themselves. They do. But they know themselves well enough to realize what they will have to change and how they will have to change it to make things improve.

On the other hand, if school was not challenging, if you experienced only moderate academic success, and your family had little involvement with your learning, you may have a more negative view of yourself and lack confidence academically. Students who fall into this category may initially have a more difficult time adjusting to college, but we have seen such students continue to gain confidence in themselves when they begin to experience academic successes.

Maintaining a Positive Attitude

Few students begin college with a totally negative attitude. Thus, we suggest that your first step is to evaluate what it is you like about college. You may have a great roommate, you may have at least one class and professor that seems to be enjoyable, or maybe you are simply positive about having a new beginning. Whatever excites you and makes you feel positive should be what you concentrate on, especially during those first few days of a new term. Yes, things will go wrong. The computer might "crash" just when you finally were making some progress in adding a class you wanted, the registrar may have "lost" proof that you paid your tuition, and the lines in the bookstore may go on forever. But you have no control over these things. Take a deep breath, count to 10 (or 50, if need be), and try not to let all of these negative happenings get in the way of your excitement and positiveness. We realize that this can be difficult, but it's important to learn early on that you have little or no control over many things in life. Don't let those things bring you down. Save your energy for staying on top of what you can control and do something about.

Another suggestion that students find helpful in maintaining a positive attitude is not to dwell on past mistakes. For example, if writing has always been a struggle for you, telling yourself "I'm a terrible writer" will do little to help. Rather, concentrate on the positives such as "I'm a good learner in general, so writing should not be impossible. I can get help at the Writing Center if I need it, so I know I can do it." Everyone has strong points and weak points. The secret of maintaining a positive attitude is one of balance. If you lack confidence in writing, for example, be sure to balance that writing course with another course that you will like and that will be less of a struggle for you. Also, try to give each course and each professor a chance. Enter each course with the attitude that you will do your best. In some courses, this may mean that you will not earn the best grade. There's nothing wrong with *earning* a C in a course that is particularly difficult for you. There is something wrong, however, in *settling* for a C because your attitude in that course was negative and you simply did not put in the necessary effort.

In addition, expect to learn something valuable in every course you take. We know that's often a difficult suggestion to follow, but if you try to think that parts of a course might be interesting and valuable, both your attitude and your motivation will be better. It's particularly difficult to follow this suggestion when you are a first-year student because we know that first-year students often get stuck taking "leftover" courses or core courses in which they haven't developed much interest. But no matter how uninteresting or boring you might find a course, look toward the positive. Think how you might use some of the information at a later date or how it might be related to other areas that do interest you and for which you already possess a positive attitude.

The Role of Interests

As we mentioned earlier, attitudes and interests go hand-in-hand. Whatever you have an interest in, you also probably have a good attitude toward. Likewise, when you're not interested in a topic or course, you may not have a very good attitude about having to learn it.

We have found that many students lack interest in a wide variety of areas, which puts limitations on the courses that they want to take. But not having a wide variety of interests doesn't mean that you can't develop them. As we suggested, every course has *something* interesting about it or people wouldn't spend their lives studying it. Students who have the most focused interests are usually those who have the most difficult time developing new interests. We have had conversations with students that go something like this:

Student: Why do I have to take this stuff—history, sociology, and drama, for goodness sakes! I'm a computer science major and none of this is important to me. I just want to be able to work with computers.

Professor: Well, I understand that, but you also have to take a series of "core courses"—courses that help you have a well-rounded education. Besides, they can help to develop other interests. One of the reasons for a college education is to give you a broader view of the world.

Student: (rolling her eyes) Maybe so, but I don't care about any of this. I'll do it because I have to, but I'm not going to like it.

The student shuffles off, unhappy, determined to get nothing from any courses, unless they are in some way computer-related. Chances are that she will get into academic trouble simply because she is already convinced that there is nothing about these courses that could possibly be of interest. How different the scenario might have been if she thought about courses as a chance to develop new interests and learn new things.

COLLEGE CAMPUS TODAY

Effects of Alcohol on Motivation

On most college campuses, the issue of alcohol abuse among students has become a point of much discussion. Everyone knows the obvious results when students abuse alcohol: automobile accidents, unwanted sexual advances, hospitalization, and in some cases even death. But what students often don't understand is how the use of alcohol or drugs can affect motivation to learn. Students who drink heavily (binge drinking)

(continued)

skip class, get behind, can't concentrate, and lose motivation to study. Some research even indicates that binge drinking impairs cognitive functioning for up to 30 days after it happened. Many campuses sponsor programs to make students more aware of the unpublicized results of alcohol consumption.

There are also students who enter college with no overriding interest in any one particular area. Many of these students have not yet selected a major and hope to find something that interests them as a result of enrolling in general core courses. The best advice we can give to these students to develop interest is to keep up with assignments. Do the reading, participate in discussion groups, study with others, and seek assistance when the going gets rough. Often a class that starts out slowly turns into an interesting course if you keep on top of things. It particularly helps if you create study groups to talk about the information, and it helps even more if at least one person in the group has more than a superficial interest in the course. What starts out as a way to try to earn a decent grade in a class can turn into an experience that creates an enormous amount of interest in a course.

A final suggestion about developing and maintaining interest in courses: Don't save up all the courses you think you'll hate because they're uninteresting and boring until the end of your college career. Intersperse the good with the bad. In other words, try to balance a course you know you'll be interested in with those that you think hold little interest for you. And for those less interesting courses, try to select your instructors carefully. A good instructor can make or break your interest toward and attitude about a particular course.

It is easy to see that motivation, attitude, and interest are related to one another and difficult to separate. Unfortunately, lack of motivation, a poor attitude, and few interests usually go hand-in-hand. But everyone can make a conscious effort to develop interests, improve their attitude, and work on motivation.

☐ Real College
Martin's Misery

DIRECTIONS: Read the following *Real College* scenario and respond to the questions based on the information you learned in this chapter.

Martin is a first-year student. Because Martin did very well in high school and also earned high entrance exam scores, he had his pick of colleges and was courted by some of the top schools in the county. Martin's parents, who were very proud of their son's accomplishments, persuaded him to attend a large prestigious Eastern school. Martin wanted to go to a smaller school that had a good reputation in the sciences, because he had a strong interest in majoring in biology. In fact, although he had been successful in all of his courses in high school, he really didn't want much to do with anything that wasn't in some way related to science. His career goal is to become a veterinarian.

When Martin arrived on campus, he immediately felt overwhelmed. The campus was too big, he didn't know anyone, and his classes were extremely difficult. He had no choice in his courses for the first term since his schedule was set for him. He was enrolled in five courses: World Literature I, Political Science, Calculus, Anthropology, and Computer Applications I. Martin became miserable—fast! For the first couple of days, he tried to maintain a positive attitude and a high level of motivation, but he kept asking himself "Why am I here? Why did I let my parents talk me into this?" Before he knew it, he found himself with a general bad attitude about being in college and zero motivation. He knew if he didn't do something fast, he was going to dig himself in a hole he couldn't get out of.

Martin is bright and has long-term career plans. But it is also obvious that he's not motivated to do the work and has a bad attitude about school and his classes that may influence him negatively if he doesn't do something fast. Based on what you have read and what you know about the role that motivation, attitudes, and interests play in learning, what advice would you give Martin?

☐ Thinking Critically
Something to Think About and Discuss

DIRECTIONS: Discuss the following questions about your motivation, attitudes, and interests to learn in college with a partner or a small group. Summarize your answers to present to another group or the entire class.

- What do you want to get out of college?

- What do you want to get out of your courses this term (other than a good grade)?

- Why do you think you have to take courses that are outside your major?

- How would you describe your general level of motivation for learning in college?

- Why do you think some students have more developed interests than others?

- We stated that motivation and attitudes were situational. In what kinds of situations are you more motivated? In what kinds of situations do you have a poor attitude?

☐ Follow-Up Activities

1. In each of your courses, monitor your motivation throughout the term. What activities do you find particularly motivating? What do you find unmotivating? What strategies do you find helpful in regaining your motivation? How can you use these strategies in other situations to help you get or stay motivated?

2. As you plan your schedule for next term consider your motivation to learn in each of the courses you select. Remember to balance courses you don't feel particularly motivated about with those that greatly motivate you to learn.

3. It's always interesting to find out how people become interested in things. Students ask us all the time: "How did you ever become interested in writing about and doing research in the area of studying?"

or "How in the world could you be interested in cooking?" We usually have pretty long and detailed answers to these questions. Think about your own interests. How did those interests develop? Did you used to have interests in something that no longer interests you at all? Why did you lose interest?

4. Think about small steps you could take to improve your attitude in a course this term. Could you get help from a tutor if you are having problems with the class? Could you join a study group? Would it help to talk things over with the professor? If these suggestions won't work, brainstorm some that will.

CHAPTER 6

JUST WHAT DO YOU BELIEVE ANYWAY?

Read this chapter to answer the following questions:

- How is your learning affected by your beliefs?
- What are the five belief components that influence learning?

SELF-ASSESSMENT

DIRECTIONS: Read the following scenario and answer the questions honestly to find out your personal theory of beliefs. The purpose of this scenario is to get you to think about your beliefs. Remember that there are no right or wrong responses.

Chris is a student in Introductory Biology. He studies hard for the class, but he has failed his first two exams. When he studies, he tries to focus on the material covered in the lectures, but really doesn't read the text. He does try to memorize almost all of the bold-faced terms in the text by writing them on 3 x 5 cards and flipping through them until he has memorized the definitions. After the last exam, he tried studying with friends, but he didn't find it helpful because his friends were explaining the information in a different way than the professor, so he was not sure if they knew what they were talking about and didn't want to get confused.

Chris believes that science is really just memorization and that most science problems have only one answer, so if he looks at the material enough he should do fine. Even though he doesn't spend a lot of time studying, he feels that he puts in hard work and effort and, therefore, he should be receiving high grades, but this has not been the case. Chris thinks his poor grades could be due to the new professor teaching the course. Professor Smith tries to have class discussions, despite the fact that there are 250 students enrolled in the class. Professor Smith also tries to tell the class about all sides to each issue. When there are competing scientific theories, she is sure to inform the class and discuss each one, because she wants to give an unbiased lecture each time. However, Chris knows that science is based on proven facts and finds all these theories confusing. When Chris went to her office asking which theory is the right one, or which one he needed to know for the exam, she told him that all of the theories have some merit and that he must decide for himself what he will believe. Chris believes that it is the professor's responsibility to make sure that the students learn in class. However, this professor often asks exam questions over topics that were covered in the text but not during the lectures. Chris is beginning to believe that he is failing the class because he is not able to learn science.

	Strongly disagree ⟷ Strongly agree				
1. I agree with Chris that science is based on proven facts.	1	2	3	4	5
2. I agree with Chris that the students should only be responsible for the scientific theories that the professor discusses in class.	1	2	3	4	5
3. Like Chris, I believe that there must be one theory that is more correct than others.	1	2	3	4	5
4. I agree with Chris that the professor is responsible for student learning.	1	2	3	4	5
5. I agree with Chris that if I don't do well on my biology exam it is because I am not able to learn science.	1	2	3	4	5
6. Like Chris, I believe that I don't have to read the text as long as I listen in class because the professor goes over all of the important information.	1	2	3	4	5
7. I agree with Chris that learning competing science theories is too confusing for students.	1	2	3	4	5

8. I agree with Chris that there is usually only one right answer to a science problem. 1 2 3 4 5

9. I believe that some people will do fine in Chris's class because they are good learners, but others have a limited ability to learn science. 1 2 3 4 5

10. Like Chris, I believe that I will only do well in this class if I can learn information quickly. 1 2 3 4 5

11. Chris's plan of taking good notes and trying to memorize facts should be all it takes to get a good grade in Introductory Biology. 1 2 3 4 5

12. Chris will be able to understand the complex processes involved in biology if he memorizes definitions. 1 2 3 4 5

13. If Chris tried to understand every theory it would take him too much time to read a chapter. 1 2 3 4 5

14. Like Chris, I believe that no matter how much time and effort is put in to it, some people will never be able to learn biology. 1 2 3 4 5

15. I believe that if I am going to understand my biology text, it will make sense the first time I read it—rereading will not help me understand any better. 1 2 3 4 5

Source: Adapted from Holschuh, J. L. (1998). *Epistemological beliefs in introductory biology: Addressing measurement concerns and exploring the relationship with strategy use.* Unpublished doctoral dissertation, University of Georgia, Athens.

To find out your personal theory, add your scores to the following questions together.

Component 1: Certain Knowledge	1 ___ + 3 ___ + 8 ___ = ___
Component 2: Simple Knowledge	7 ___ + 11 ___ +12 ___ = ___
Component 3: Responsibility for Learning	2 ___ + 4 ___ + 6 ___ = ___
Component 4: Speed of Learning	10 ___ + 13 ___ +15 ___ = ___
Component 5: Ability	5 ___ + 9 ___ +14 ___ = ___

Assessing Your Personal Theory

Your score on each component can range from 3 to 15. Take a look at where your scores fall on each component. The way the scale is structured, the higher your score on a component, the more strongly you hold a belief that may get in the way of your academic success. The lower your score on a component, the more strongly you hold a belief that research has been shown to lead to academic success. Because no person is completely consistent in his or her beliefs, chances are you hold a strong belief on some components (as indicated by either high or low scores), but are more in the middle on other components.

The Five Components of Beliefs That Influence Learning

Many different kinds of beliefs affect your life everyday. People have different religious beliefs, moral beliefs, political beliefs, and so on. You may have thought a lot about those kinds of beliefs, but have you ever thought about your beliefs about learning? Have you ever considered how you gain knowledge or what knowledge is? If you are like most students, you probably haven't thought much about where knowledge comes from, but your beliefs about knowledge do impact what and how you learn.

As you read this chapter, consider your own beliefs about learning. Where do your beliefs fall? How might these beliefs affect your learning in college courses? Remember that to get off on the right foot in college you may need to reevaluate your beliefs and the role they play in your academic success.

SUCCESS AT A GLANCE

The Five Components Of Beliefs

Component 1　Certainty of Knowledge　Can range from the belief that knowledge is fact, to the belief that knowledge is continually changing

(continued)

Component 2	Simple Knowledge	Can range from the belief that knowledge is made up of isolated bits of information, to the belief that knowledge is complex
Component 3	Responsibility for Learning	Can range from the belief that it is the professor's responsibility to ensure that students learn, to the belief that it is the individual's responsibility to learn information
Component 4	Speed of Learning	Can range from the belief that learning happens fast or not at all, to the belief that learning is a gradual process that takes time
Component 5	Ability	Can range from the belief that the ability to learn is fixed, to the belief that people can learn how to learn

- **Component 1: Certainty of Knowledge.** Some students believe that knowledge is continually changing based on current information. When they are in class, they think about what they already know about the topic and may change their beliefs about the topic by adding new information to what they already know. For example, a student might enter a physics class believing that when a bullet is shot from a gun, it falls to the ground faster than a bullet that is simply dropped. However, that student might change her beliefs based on the new information after learning about the laws of gravity. Other students believe that there are absolute answers and there is a definite right or wrong solution to every problem. These students approach learning by trying to find the truth in all situations. In the same physics class, another student may have trouble understanding that scientists believe that physics is based on theories, not truth, and that these theories are in a constant state of change based on new research. Even though experts are continually reassessing what they know, students are often encouraged only to look for the facts in their textbooks. They may approach reading history by looking strictly for names, dates, and places because that was what was important in their previous experience. But most college courses expect you to do more than learn "facts." Professors tend to view their disciplines as constantly changing. Therefore, to memorize only "facts" would be a waste of time. Instead, most professors not only want you to be able to understand what is currently known, but also want to prepare you for future learning. Professors expect students to question what they read and be willing to live with the notion that there may not be a solution or definite answer to every problem or question.

- **Component 2: Simple Knowledge.** Some students believe that knowledge consists of highly interconnected concepts, but other students believe that knowledge consists of a series of unrelated bits of information. Students who believe that knowledge is complex look for relationships between ideas as they learn. They try to see the "big picture" and the relationships among the small piece of information within that big picture. On the other hand, students who have a strong belief that knowledge is simple tend to break information down into very small isolated parts and never put it back together again. Although breaking information into smaller chunks is a great strategy for some tasks, for example when learning something you must memorize (like the periodic table of the elements), a student who learns *only* isolated pieces of information will miss the big ideas. If a student in history class only memorized dates and names, she would be unprepared for an essay question that asked her to compare and contrast ideas about the larger concepts. Because most of the assignments you will experience require you to apply what you have learned, you need to go beyond memorizing small bits of information and begin to see how the information is connected.

QUICK TAKES

Taking Responsibility for Learning

The ability to take responsibility for your own learning is a good skill to learn in college because when you enter the workforce you will be expected to draw on your ability to direct your own learning (look at the number of help-wanted ads looking for a "self-starter"), which includes making decisions and creating new solutions. So the next time you find yourself putting the responsibility on others ("I can only learn when I have a good professor," "I didn't do well on the test because my roommates made too much noise for me to study"), think about ways to take responsibility for the situation.

- **Component 3: Responsibility for Learning.** Beliefs about knowledge also depend on your beliefs about who is responsible for your learning in college. Some students believe that it is the professor's responsibility to be sure that all students learn the information. Other students believe that although the professor guides their learning, they are ultimately responsible for their own learning. In high school, your teacher probably took a lot of the responsibility for your learning in class. You most likely had little choice in the subjects you studied, what you learned, or the way you were assessed (e.g., tests, papers, labs, etc.). In fact, the teacher may have even gone over all of the relevant information in class, which left you little to learn on your own. However, you probably have already noticed that college professors have different assumptions about who is responsible for learning. Professors expect students to take responsibility for a good deal of their own learning. They expect students to be able figure out information on their own, and they also may expect students to be able to pull together information from a variety of sources.

- **Component 4: Speed of Learning.** Some students believe that learning is a gradual and on-going process, but other students believe that if learning is going to happen, it happens quickly or not at all. In other words, some people believe that most things worth knowing take a long time to learn, but other people think that if they don't "get it" right away, they never will. Students who believe that learning takes time are better prepared for college tasks. However, students who believe that learning should happen quickly are often frustrated in college when they are faced with complex information. Many college students believe that learning should happen quickly because of their experiences in high school (and elementary and middle school, too). In fact, research has shown that in high school mathematics classes, most problems that students answered could be solved in less than two minutes! It's no wonder that many students are unprepared for more difficult tasks in college and why some students get frustrated or just give up when faced with challenging problems.

- **Component 5: The Role of Ability.** Some students believe that people can learn how to learn, but others believe that the ability to learn is fixed and that they are naturally good at some things but will never be able to do other things. For example, a student may say, "I am good at math and science, but not history or English." Students who believe that the ability to learn is fixed tend to talk to themselves in a negative way. For example, a student may say, "I will never be able to do this" or " I am too dumb to learn this" when in fact this student may be just giving up too easily. On the other hand, students who believe that people can learn how to learn tend to view difficult tasks as challenges that can be met. Instead of giving up, these students will try different strategies for learning and will ask for help from the professor or their friends if they need it. There are probably people in your classes who make learning look easy, but students who appear to learn "naturally" probably spend time and effort in activities that promote academic success, such as reading and reflecting.

Based on what you have read about beliefs you probably have figured out that students who believe that knowledge is changeable, that knowledge consists of interrelated concepts, that learning is under the control of the student, and that learning may take time and effort will be expected to have more success in college than students who hold the opposite beliefs.

NETWORKING

Deciding What to Believe

You may have noticed that some of the information you find on the Internet seems to contradict other information. Your personal theory of beliefs will influence how you decide which information to believe. Find three sites that give you different perspectives about the same topic. For example, you might look at three reviews of the same movie, or three political essays about an issue from a democratic, republican, and independent perspective. Think about how you will decide which one to believe. How do your beliefs about knowledge affect your decision?

Changing Your Beliefs

After evaluating your personal belief theory using the scale at the beginning of this chapter, you may have found that you have some beliefs that need to be changed because they may negatively affect your success in college. This section will present some strategies for promoting change.

Your beliefs about learning influence the strategies you use to study, which is part of the reason why beliefs are related to college performance. For example, if you believe that knowledge is simple, then you will select a strategy that reflects your belief, such as making flash cards to memorize definitions of key terms even when your professor expects you to integrate ideas. Thus, when you have all of the terms memorized, you will feel that you have prepared enough for the exam. If you do not pass the exam, you may not understand what you did wrong, because according to your beliefs about learning, you were adequately prepared. The question, then, is: If you currently hold beliefs that may make academic success more difficult, how do you go about changing those beliefs?

- **Be Aware of Your Beliefs.** If you have beliefs that are getting in the way of your learning, consider changing them. However, before you can change a belief, you must first be unsatisfied with your current beliefs about learning. When you find yourself giving up on a task too quickly or trying to merely memorize when you need to understand and apply difficult concepts, you can reflect on your beliefs, rethink your approach, and take the time to really learn the information.

- **Look for the "Big Picture."** Instead of memorizing a lot of separate facts, make a conscious effort to relate ideas to what you already know and to other ideas discussed in class. Many of the strategies presented in *College Success Strategies* will help you learn to integrate and synthesize ideas as you read.

- **Learn to Live with Uncertainty.** It is sometimes difficult to accept there there are no right answers to some questions. For example, in a statistics class, you may want to know the "right" way to solve a problem, and although there are some ways that are better than others, chances are that if you ask three statisticians how to solve the problem you will get three different answers.

- **Don't Compare Your "Ability" with Others.** Worrying that you are not as good as your roommate in math will not get you anywhere. Focus instead on how to improve your ability to learn in the subjects that you find difficult. You can find a tutor to work with or form a study group to help you learn. It may take you longer to get there, but remember that college learning is more like an endurance sport than a sprint.

- **Realize That Learning Takes Time.** If you begin your assignments with the expectation that they will take time to fully understand and complete, you are likely to experience less frustration and more understanding. Don't expect to learn complex concepts the first time that you encounter them. Instead, plan to spread out your study time so you can review difficult material several times.

COLLEGE CAMPUS TODAY

Broaden Your Horizons

Student beliefs change through experience. One great way to help change your beliefs about learning is to take a course that will make you think about things in a different way. For example, you might sign up for a philosophy, religion, or ecology course just to broaden your horizons. There is a speech communications professor on our campus who begins the term by telling students that he believes that there is no truth. The students then spend the entire semester debating this issue by using real life situations. What a great way to consider beliefs about the certainty of knowledge.

Now that you know about how your beliefs affect your learning, you can begin to examine your beliefs in the many learning situations you encounter. Your beliefs about learning are continually changing based on experience, but by being aware of what those beliefs are you can help yourself learn more effectively by not letting your beliefs get in the way of your learning.

□ Real College
College Knowledge

DIRECTIONS: Read the following *Real College* scenario and respond to the questions based on what you learned in this chapter.

In this section, you will read about the beliefs of four college students. Use what you know about beliefs about knowledge to consider the following students' beliefs.

Pat is taking history mostly because it is required. In this history class, he finds that the professor often asks exam questions about topics that were not covered in class. Pat doesn't think that is fair because he doesn't know how he is supposed to figure out what to study if the professor doesn't tell him what is important.

Amy believes that she will be successful in biology, because she has always done well in science class. She believes a scientist, if he or she tries hard enough, can find the truth to almost anything. One problem she has is that her professor tries to tell the class about too many science theories, which Amy finds confusing.

David was a good English student in high school. He was always able to quickly understand the concepts and didn't need to spend a lot of time on homework. When he started his literature class, the readings were familiar and he didn't really spend much time outside of class reading or studying. However, he found that he did not do well on the first essay exam and that the new concepts were confusing. He still believes that he should be able to learn the information quickly and is unsure why he is having so much trouble.

Lisa believes that she is the type of person who can't do math. She sees that some students just seem to "get it" because they are naturally good at learning calculus. She wishes that the university would understand that some people just can't learn math and that it shouldn't be a requirement for all students.

Answer the following questions then discuss your responses with a partner or small group.

1. How are these students' beliefs similar to yours? How do they differ?

2. How do you think these beliefs will affect the students' performance in their classes?

3. What advice would you give these students?

☐ Thinking Critically
Something to Think About and Discuss

- What have you observed about your own beliefs that may make learning easier for you?

- What have you observed about your own beliefs that may make learning harder for you?

- How are your beliefs affecting how you approach and carry out the tasks in your courses?

- Are your beliefs leading you toward academic success? Why or Why not?

☐ Follow-Up Activities

1. As you read your texts, think about how the authors' beliefs are affecting how and what they write. For example, is your history text presenting the information as fact, or are you encouraged to think about multiple viewpoints? Does your science textbook try to point out connections between concepts, or are they presented as isolated bits of information?

2. At the end of this year retake the self-assessment (found on pages 78–81). How have your beliefs changed in the past year? What do you think you still need to work on in the future?

CHAPTER 7

DEALING WITH STRESS

Read this chapter to answer the following questions:

- What are common sources of stress?
- What is academic stress?
- How do you control or reduce stress?

SELF-ASSESSMENT

DIRECTIONS: Take the following assessment of stressful situations to determine your current stress level. Check the events you have experienced in the past six months or are likely to experience in the next six months. This assessment will help you determine whether you are currently experiencing an unhealthy amount of stress. Remember, some stress is necessary for everyday life, but if you are experiencing an overwhelming amount of stress, look for ways to reduce it and seek help if necessary.

Student Stress Scale*

1. Death of a close family member   ✓ 100
2. Death of a close friend   ____ 73
3. Divorce between parents   ____ 65
4. Jail term   ____ 63
5. Major personal injury or illness   ✓ 63
6. Marriage   ____ 58

7. Fired from job   ____ 50

8. Failed important course   ✓ 47

9. Change in health of a family member   ✓ 45

10. Pregnancy   ____ 45

11. Sex problems   ____ 44

12. Serious argument with a close friend   ____ 40

13. Change in financial status   ____ 39

14. Change of major   ____ 39

15. Trouble with parents   ✓ 39

16. New girl or boyfriend   ✓ 38

17. Increased workload   ____ 37

18. Outstanding personal achievement   ____ 36

19. First quarter/semester in college   ✓ 35

20. Change in living conditions   ____ 31

21. Serious argument with instructor   ✓ 30

22. Lower grades than expected   ✓ 29

23. Change in sleeping habits   ✓ 29

24. Change in social activities   ____ 29

25. Change in eating habits   ✓ 28

26. Chronic car trouble   ____ 26

27. Change in number of family get-togethers   ✓ 26

28. Too many missed classes   ✓ 25

29. Change of college   ____ 24

30. Dropped more than one class   ✓ 23

31. Minor traffic violations   ____ 20

TOTAL 537

handwritten calculations: 100, 63, 47, 45, 39, 38, 35, 29, 29, 28, 26, 25, 23 — 537

SCORING: A score of 300 or higher indicates an extremely high stress life; a score of 200–299 indicates a high stress life; a score between 100–199 indicates a moderate stress life; and a score below 100 indicates a low stress life. If you find that you are having a very high stress life, you might want to seek help from a counselor, friend, or family member.

*The Stress Scale was adapted from:

DeMeuse, K. (1985). The relationship between life events and indices of classroom performance. *Teaching of Psychology*, *12*, 146–149.

Holmes, T. H., & Rahe, R. H. (1967). The social readjustment rating scale. *Journal of Psychosomatic Research*, *11*, 213–218. Insel, P., & Roth, W. (1985). *Core concepts in health*, 4th Edition. Palo Alto, CA: Mayfield Publishing

Believe us when we say that as a college student you will experience many different types of stress including social pressures, financial burdens, and academic competition. In fact, stress levels in college tend to ebb and flow—you might feel more stress at the beginning of a term when everything is new, less stress in the middle of the term (until midterms, of course), and more stress again at the end of the term when you have to take final exams. Usually we think of stress as something to be avoided, but actually that's not always true. Stress is a normal part of life and at least some of the stress you experience in college is helpful and stimulating—without stress we would lead a rather boring existence. The problem comes when you have an extremely high stress life.

Sources of Stress

Although at times it may feel as if there are infinite sources of stress, generally college stress can be broken down into six categories: prior academic record, social influences, family, finances, career direction, and situational problems (such as illness or drug problems). Most students think that stress is caused by outside factors. They might say that a test, a professor, or a paper is "stressing them out." But stress is really an internal process. Therefore, it's important to have some strategies for dealing with stress in order to put your reactions to it in perspective. As you read about the six categories of stress, remember that stress is natural, it is internal, it is often an overreaction to a specific situation, and *it can be controlled.*

1. **Prior academic record.** Students who have a "shaky" academic past may feel that they can't succeed in college. On the other hand, students who have a 4.0 average may feel stress to keep their stellar grade point average. Either way, your past history as a learner affects your stress level.

2. **Social influences.** You probably have realized that dealing with your friends can often be stressful. A fight with your roommate, breaking up with a boyfriend or girlfriend, meeting new people—all of these situations can be stressful. In fact, even situations we would consider to be positive social factors, such as falling in love or socializing with really good friends, can cause a stressful reaction. Overall, however, having good friends and social support will actually reduce your stress levels because you have someone to confide in.

COLLEGE CAMPUS TODAY
Social Stress

Although you may not realize it, you may feel stress in social situations because you find yourself in an atmosphere that is very different from your high school or your hometown. Because college campuses tend to be very diverse, you will be interacting with students who look different, have different cultural and ethnic backgrounds, possess different values, and think differently than you. This can cause a level of stress, particularly social stress. Try to remember that an important part of the college experience is to broaden your horizons and open your mind, so think of campus diversity as a positive influence (rather than a stressful one) that will help you grow as a person.

3. **Family.** You may feel pressure to do well in college in order to make your family proud, you may feel stress because you have moved away from your family, or because of family crises that arise. But like social influences, your family can also be a source of support to help you when you experience a lot of stress.

4. **Finances.** Financial stress usually begins in college because students take out loans to attend college, get jobs to help pay for college, or have to maintain a certain grade point average to keep their scholarships. Many college students are also responsible for paying bills and are gaining responsibility for their financial security. In addition, college

students get their own credit cards, which can lead to great financial stress if used inappropriately. We know numerous college students who graduate not only with a diploma, but also with student loans and a stack of credit card debt. All of these things can cause stress, especially for students who are handling their own finances for the first time.

5. **Career direction.** "So what's your major? What the heck are you going to do with a degree in that?" You may have heard similar comments from friends and relatives. Everyone (perhaps yourself included) wants to know what you will do with your life after college. The less sure you are about your career direction, the more stress you might feel about it. You may even be concerned that you'll never find your direction. On the other hand, students who have already decided on a career might also feel stress because they are concerned about achieving their goals.

6. **Situational problems.** Certain stresses are unexpected and sometimes devastating. You may become ill during the term, experience the death of someone close to you, realize you have a drug or alcohol problem, or an eating disorder. As with all of the categories of stress you feel overwhelmed by situational problems, seek help from a counselor on campus or someone you can talk to about these concerns.

Strategies for Reducing Stress

Now that you know what stress is and what causes stress for most students, you will be happy to know that there are many ways to control or even reduce your stress levels. Before you start feeling overwhelmed, consider the following strategies for reducing your stress.

- **Relax.** You should make relaxation a regular part of your day. If you don't know anything about how to go about relaxing, there are numerous paperback self-help books available that actually offer some great techniques and advice. At the very least, try deep breathing or meditation for a few minutes each day to help you unwind. If you find yourself "stressing out," stop whatever you are doing, close your eyes, and focus on your breathing for a few minutes. This should help you relax so that you can return to what you were doing, feeling in more control of the situation.

- **Exercise.** Working out daily is a great stress buster. Physical activity helps take your mind off of your stress and the chemicals your body releases during exercise actually boost your ability to handle stressful situations. If you are feeling especially "stressed out," try taking a walk or a jog to clear your head.

- **Take Charge.** You are in control of your own situation and you have to accept that responsibility. By taking charge, you can control the amount of stress you feel by remembering that stress is an internal reaction to situations and it is often really an overreaction. However, if stress gets out of control, you can also take charge of the situation by seeking help.

- **Put Problems in Perspective.** Sometimes it helps to talk to a good friend or a family member who has been in a similar situation to help you put your problems in a more realistic light. Don't allow yourself to get carried away imagining all the things that could go wrong in a situation—instead, focus on the positives.

- **Be Flexible.** Everyone makes mistakes, and learning from your mistakes will help reduce your stress levels. But if you are too set in the way you do things or the way you view the world you may end up causing yourself additional stress. It pays to have an open mind and to try new approaches.

- **Develop Interests.** Join a club on campus, meet with others who share similar interests, or find some new interests on your own. By having interests outside of schoolwork, you will be able to enjoy yourself and relax during your time off from studying. Developing new interests also helps you in the classroom because you tend to do better in subjects that interest you.

- **Seek Help.** Seek out campus resources to help you through stressful times. In fact, it is a good idea to seek out the people and places that can support you **before** you need them. Often problems can be solved easily if you ask for assistance before a small problem balloons into a major one.

- **Enjoy Yourself.** Take a walk, read a good book, see a movie, call a friend. Do something you like to do before you start feeling overwhelmed. Remember, if you manage your life appropriately, you should have plenty of time for studying and engaging in activities for fun.

SUCCESS AT A GLANCE

Strategies for Reducing Stress

Relax

Exercise

Take Charge

Put Problems in Perspective

Be Flexible

Develop Interests

Seek Help

Enjoy Yourself

Academic Stress: Anxieties

The stress students feel in college, or what we refer to as academic stress, is due to many different factors and is a part of the general stress you feel every day. You want to do well in your classes, you want to gain valuable experience, and you want to be a success in life. However, four common types of academic stress or anxieties that some students experience can actually get in the way of these goals—public speaking anxiety, writing anxiety, math anxiety, and test anxiety. If you have experienced one of these stresses you know how harmful it can be. In this section we will discuss the four types of academic stress and strategies for coping with each of them.

> ## QUICK TAKES
> ### College Stress Yields Workplace Stress
> Individuals who never learned how to manage their stress in college tend to carry this over into the workplace once they graduate and get a job. This is particularly true in jobs that tend to be high stress in the first place. That's why it's important to learn how to manage your stress early on. Many of the things you do to control academic stress can also be used later on: relaxation, deep breathing, exercise, and brief periods of meditation can make your life considerably less stressful. And less stress leads to a healthier lifestyle.

Public Speaking Anxiety

Public speaking causes people to react in strange ways. They may find that their hands get sweaty, that their mouth is dry, or that they forgot what they were going to say. In fact, research has found that some people fear public speaking more than death. In college, there will be many times when you are required to speak in public, whether it is making a comment in a large lecture class or giving a presentation or speech to a class.

Coping with Public Speaking Anxiety   The best way to cope with a fear of public speaking is to be prepared. Practice your presentation out loud several times before presenting it to your class. Practice in front of a mirror, or better yet, recruit some friends to listen to your speech. Have them record your time to be sure that you are on track and ask them to critique your speaking style using the following questions:

- **Are You Speaking Too Fast?** Sometimes when people are nervous they talk very fast, which makes it difficult for the audience to follow. Don't rush through your talk. Instead, try to use a conversational tone.

- **Are You Using Good Inflection?** When people are nervous they sometimes speak in a monotone, which is difficult to listen to for an extended period of time. Try to speak confidently and with enthusiasm.

- **Are You Jittery?** You may find yourself moving from side to side or wringing your hands when you are nervous. It is good to move around a little, such as using hand gestures or walking around to include the audience, but too much nervous movement can be distracting to your audience.

- **Are You Making Eye Contact?** When you are giving your presentation it may help to focus on one or two friendly faces in the room and "present" to them. You should be sure to make eye contact with the other people in the room, of course. But concentrate mostly on those two people. This strategy should help calm your fear of speaking in front of a large group.

- **Have You Jotted Down Some Notes?** Making some notes to follow during your presentation makes you feel more secure and confident. Even though you have rehearsed your talk and have a good idea of what you will cover, you should have notes of your presentation with you just in case you need a reminder of what you are going to say.

Writing Anxiety

Many students experience a great deal of stress when asked to write something for a class, especially if they are asked to write during class under the added pressure of time limitations. Students might be anxious about having to think up a good idea, flesh the idea out, and then have their writing evaluated by their instructor. They sit staring at a blank page waiting for the words to come. This is sometimes called writer's block and it is a very frustrating experience. Just about every writer, the authors of this book included, has had an experience when finding the words to write has been difficult. However, writing anxiety becomes harmful when students experience writer's block almost every time they try to write. When students are anxious about writing, they try to avoid it as much as possible because they find it such a stressful activity. The problem is that in college (and in most careers after college) you are often asked to express your ideas in writing.

Coping with Writing Anxiety   We offer the following suggestions for dealing with writing anxiety.

- **Write Often.** Like any skill, your ability to write will improve with practice. You may want to keep a daily journal where you record you experiences. Or you might want to do some "freewriting" by giving yourself a fixed amount of time (like 5 to 10 minutes) to write about whatever you want. Another alternative is to sit on a bus or in a coffee shop and write some character sketches about the people you see.

- **Work from a Plan.** It's helpful to make a list of the points you want to make and then use your list to guide you when you are writing your paper. If you are having trouble organizing the points you want to make, talk to a classmate or a tutor about your ideas. Most campuses have a writing center or a place where students can talk to a tutor about their papers at any stage—from choosing a topic, to reading rough drafts, to critiquing final drafts.

- **For Essay Tests, Predict Questions.** This idea will be covered in greater detail in Chapter 17, but in brief, use your class notes and topics emphasized in the text to predict the kinds of questions that might be asked. You might want to look at some of the professors' old exams to help you predict good essay questions.

- **Start Early.** Because students who experience writing anxiety try to avoid writing, they often procrastinate until the last minute. Sometimes these students believe that they can write only under pressure, but they are fooling themselves because they are actually making their stress level greater by waiting until the last minute. If they do not make a good grade on the paper, they blame it on the fact that they have trouble writing instead of the fact that they churned it out quickly.

Mathematics Anxiety

As with writing, some students feel stress when they encounter anything that has to do with numbers. Students who experience math anxiety usually try to avoid taking math or math-related courses. For most students, math anxiety usually results from previous experiences in math classes. You may have had some trouble with a particular topic (word problems in algebra maybe) and have told yourself "I can't do math" ever since. For some reason math anxiety seems to be the most traumatic and widespread. However, just like any other type of stress, math anxiety is an overreaction to a situation and, therefore, you can change your response to mathematics.

Coping with Mathematics Anxiety   The following suggestions will help you deal with mathematics anxiety:

- **Face it Head-On.** Don't wait until your senior year to take your math courses—take them early and overcome your fears.
- **Take a Class That is at Your Level.** Don't try to get into calculus if you have never had a pre-calculus course.
- **Spend Some Time Each Day Reading the Textbook and Doing the Practice Problems.** Going to class is not enough, because you must be able to apply what you have learned to new situations.
- **Talk the Problems Through.** One of the best strategies for learning math is to solve problems with words. That is, explain in words how to solve the problem rather than just trying to plug in numbers.
- **Get Help Early On.** If you find that you are having trouble learning math concepts, seek help as soon as you need it. Get help from a classmate or the instructor, and plan to work with a tutor weekly if necessary. In math classes, the information you are learning usually builds on itself so if you don't understand what you learned in Chapter 2 you will have even more trouble learning the material in Chapter 6.
- **Use Positive Talk.** Don't say, "I can't" or "I'll never" to yourself because these thoughts can be self-defeating. Instead, try to focus on the positives. Reward yourself for figuring out a tough problem and keep trying to do your best.

General Test Anxiety

Test anxiety is similar to writing and math anxiety except it is a feeling of stress when studying for or taking an exam, regardless of the subject. You might worry about the types of questions that will be on the test, forgetting about and missing the test, or studying the wrong material. Students who experience test anxiety are often paralyzed with fear when faced with a test situation and they end up missing questions they knew.

Many different experiences can lead to test anxiety. It might be caused by past test-taking experiences, such as blanking on answers, or failing an exam. It could also be caused by inadequate test preparation. If you know that you are not really prepared to take an exam, it's natural to be anxious about it. Test anxiety can also be caused by competition with your friends or classmates. If you are focusing on how others are doing, you might cause yourself undue stress. In addition, test anxiety can be caused by a lack of confidence in yourself as a learner. When students feel that they are not good learners, they tend to become more anxious about testing situations. If you find that you are talking negatively to yourself about your ability to learn, you may actually be causing yourself greater anxiety.

Coping with Test Anxiety   To cope with general test anxiety, try the following suggestions:

- **Be Prepared.** If you monitor your learning to the point where you know which concepts you understand and which concepts are giving you problems, you will feel more confident. Allow enough time for studying, but also have all of the things you need ready for the test. Do you need a pencil, calculator, notes, or anything else? You don't want to be tracking these things down right before the test, so be ready to go the night before.

- **Understand the Task.** Talk to the professor about what the exams will be like. Even better, try to look at some of the professor's old exams. Examining retired tests will give you an idea of what kinds of questions the professor asks and will also help you become familiar with the professor's questioning style. It is also a good idea to talk to the professor or to students who have taken the class about the content and format of the exams.

- **Arrive to Take the Test a Bit Early.** Get organized and practice some deep breathing techniques to relax. Take a few deep breaths; think of something you find comforting—the sound of the ocean, a walk in the woods; concentrate on and relax each of your muscle groups.

- **Have an Approach in Mind.** If you find you blank out on exams, try to make jot lists as soon as you get the test. Read each question and just jot down everything you know about it in the margin of the test. Don't look at any answers if it is a multiple-choice type test, just write everything you know before you blank out.

- **Focus on You.** Ignore other students who finish the exam before you. Just because they finish before you does not mean that they know more than you do. It might be that they are done so early because they *don't* know the answers. But either way, don't worry about what other students are doing.
- **Get Help in Controlling Your Anxiety.** There are usually several resource areas on campus that can help you. You might need some tutoring on course content, or some counseling to deal with your anxiety, or you might be eligible for alternate testing situations such as increased time for tests.
- **Visualize Your Success.** Think about how well you will do before you walk into the test and remind yourself that you are well prepared and ready to go as the test is being handed out. The more positive you can be, the less anxiety you'll feel.

NETWORKING

Help on the Web for Stress

Many colleges and universities offer advice for stressed out college students. Use the following keywords to search for at least three Web sites dealing with stress management: stress, stress management, college stress, student stress, test anxiety, math anxiety, writing anxiety. What kind of useful information did you find about the causes of stress or about stress management? How will this information help you cope with your own stress?

Three Important Tips for Reducing Academic Stress

In addition to the ways to cope with math, writing, and test anxiety, here are three tips for coping with the general academic pressures that you experience every day.

1. **Don't procrastinate.** This sounds simple enough, but probably most of the academic stress students experience comes from waiting until

the last minute to get their assignments done. As we discussed in Chapter 4, you are much better off starting early and doing some work each night rather than letting it wait until it is due.

2. **Don't listen to other students cram right before the test.** If your classmates are discussing something you have forgotten it will just make you more nervous. Simply take your seat, gather your thoughts, take a few deep breaths, and wait for the test to begin. Many students who experience academic stress madly rush through their notes as they are waiting for the exams to be passed out, but this too can make you more stressed if you find a topic that you don't remember. It is much better to use the time before the exam to relax.

3. **Learn to say no.** Many students experience academic stress because they have too much to do. Don't take on too much added responsibility beyond your classes. Even though you might be offered some interesting opportunities, if you wind up with too much to do, your grades and your health could suffer. Learn to say no to some things if you find you have too much to handle.

☐ Real College
Andrea's Anxiety

DIRECTIONS: Read the following *Real College* scenario and respond to the questions based on what you learned in this chapter.

Andrea is a first-year college student. She is the first person in her family to attend college and she is trying hard to make her parents proud, but she is worried that she won't make it. Every day she wakes up with a pounding headache and sometimes she even has trouble sleeping because she is so stressed out. Part of the problem is that she feels very homesick for her family and her friends. She is also worried about her relationship with her boyfriend who still lives at home—6 hours away. He gets upset if she doesn't come home every weekend and it seems likely that they will break up soon. In addition, although Andrea is starting to meet new friends in college, they are not like her old friends from high school—she just doesn't have anyone she can really confide in yet.

Another problem is that Andrea was forced to register for a math class because it was the only course open and she hates math. Every time she studies for an exam, she gets so nervous that her palms get sweaty and she can't really concentrate on what she is doing. She just knows that she will fail the course, but she doesn't know what to do about it because she believes that there is no way she will ever be able to learn math. She is thinking about dropping out of school because she's afraid that she is not smart enough to make it.

Use what you have learned about coping with and reducing stress to help Andrea figure out what to do.

1. List 3 to 5 strategies Andrea should use to reduce her general stress about her social and family relationships.

2. How do you think these strategies will help Andrea's situation?

3. List 3 to 5 strategies Andrea should use to reduce her math anxiety.

4. How do you think these strategies will help Andrea's situation?

☐ Thinking Critically
Something to Think About and Discuss

- What kinds of academic tasks (e.g., essays, mathematics, standardized tests) cause you to feel the most stress? Why do you think you experience anxiety when faced with those tasks? What can you do to reduce your anxiety in those situations?

- How can you tell the difference between being really stressed out and having normal, productive stress?

☐ Follow-Up Activities

1. Think about your general stress level. Are you stressed out all the time? Or do you find yourself stressed out in specific situations? Keep

a stress diary where you record your reactions to stressful events. Use the strategies presented in this chapter to help you cope with those stressful situations.

2. Find someone you know who seems to handle stress well. Interview that person about the ways he or she deals with stress. What strategies does that person use? How does that person plan for stressful situations ahead of time? What advice can he or she give you about dealing with the stresses of college life?

PART THREE

YOUR TASKS IN COLLEGE LEARNING

The chapters in Part III discuss the different tasks you experience in college. Chapter 8 presents effective ways to interact with your professors. It gives you tips for approaching and talking with professors as well as general information about why it is important to get to know your professor.

Chapter 9 introduces the concept of "task." You learn what the term *task* means and strategies to figure out what professors expect from you.

One of the major tasks you have to accomplish in college is to take effective lecture notes. In Chapter 10, you learn about the importance and characteristics of good lecture notes. You also learn strategies for taking lecture notes more effectively and strategies for note-taking in alternative kinds of learning situations such as discussion groups.

Chapter 11 discusses how technology is used in college classes today. You learn how to use technology to help you study as well as some strategies for evaluating Internet information.

CHAPTER 8

INTERACTING WITH YOUR PROFESSORS

Read this chapter to answer the following questions:

- How are professors ranked?
- How can you make a positive impression on your professors?
- How can you approach a professor to ask for help?

SELF-ASSESSMENT

DIRECTIONS: On a scale of 1 to 5, with 1 being "extremely uncomfortable" and 5 being "extremely comfortable," respond to each of the statements below. This should give you a good idea of how comfortable you will be interacting with your professors.

How comfortable do you feel

1. asking a question during class about something   1   2   3   4   5
   you don't understand?

2. approaching your professor to make an   1   2   3   4   5
   appointment to see her?

3. confronting your professor about a grade you made on an assignment?   1 2 3 4 5

4. disputing an answer to an item on a multiple choice test?   1 2 3 4 5

5. answering questions in class?   1 2 3 4 5

6. interacting with your professor in a social situation?   1 2 3 4 5

If you would feel very uncomfortable in the majority of these situations, you would probably benefit from learning new strategies for interacting with your professors. So, read on.

College can be intimidating at times. Sometimes it's easy to find yourself in situations where you want to initiate conversations with classmates or professors but you are simply just too scared to follow through. This uncomfortable feeling can be especially painful if you are overly shy or feel like the new kid on the block. One situation that seems to make many college students uneasy, particularly first-year students, is approaching professors. Whether it's to ask for assistance, to clarify a reading assignment, or to discuss a grade on a paper or an exam, talking with your professor doesn't have to be so threatening. Just try to keep in mind that professors are people, too.

What Is a Professor?

Take a minute to think about the characteristics that you believe define a professor. Did you think about words or phrases such as smart, well educated, reads a lot, well informed? When college students are asked to complete this task, they generally write down descriptors that have to do more with the education a professor has rather than terms that focus on other traits. For example, when we carry out this activity with our students at the beginning of the term, we rarely get comments such as fair-minded, cares about students, helpful, or energetic, nor do we get comments such as mean, unapproachable, distant, or unfair. The point that we want to make here is that most students seem to lump all professors in the same bag . . . professors are smart, they have a considerable amount of education, and they are *the* source of knowledge in the classroom.

Some research suggests that students at various stages of knowing and reasoning interact with and respond to their professors in very different ways (Baxter-Magolda, 1991).* Professor Baxter-Magolda suggests that there are four different "ways of knowing": absolute, transitional, independent, and contextual.

- **Absolute knowers** tend not to question what their professor says and believe that the professor is the authority. They believe that it is the job of professors to communicate knowledge to students.

- **Transitional knowers** realize that there can be two different sides to a story and that the role of the professor is to guide students. Professors are still seen as authority figures whose opinions supercede those of classmates. They may argue with their classmates, but rarely with their professors.

- **Independent knowers** believe that knowledge is open to a variety of interpretations and believe that the professor should promote the sharing of opinions and should allow students to define learning goals. Independent knowers like to discuss issues with their professors, not just look to them for answers.

- **Contextual knowers** believe professors should promote the application of knowledge in a specific context and that students and professors should critique each other. Contextual knowers believe that knowledge is a shared experience and that they are on more or less equal footing with the professor.

This research is important because it indicates that how students view the professor's role in the classroom is based on where they are on the knowing continuum. Interesting, and perhaps not very surprising, was that most first-year students are primarily absolute knowers, and as students progress through college they move more toward being independent and contextual knowers. It is also important to think about how absolute knowers would interact with their professors versus how contextual learners would interact with theirs.

Students are often unsettled by talking with professors because they believe that the professor is the one who determines their grade. Many students fail to acknowledge that grades are earned, not given, and therefore they see the professor as the power person in the classroom. Because they

*Baxter-Magolda, M. B. (1992). Knowing and reasoning in college. San Francisco, CA: Jossey-Bass.

view the professor as having all of the control, they see little they can do in the way of talking to professors as being very influential on their grade. What they don't realize is that knowing how to interact in a positive way with their professor can go a long way in helping students *earn* a better grade. Notice that we didn't say that just because the professor knows who you are and gets the impression you are trying he will *give* you a better grade. No professor that we know gives a student a grade just because the student has gotten to know him. But knowing how to talk with your professor can go a long way in making a positive impression and in helping you feel more relaxed with that professor and other professors in the future.

SUCCESS AT A GLANCE
Rankings of College Professors

	Degree held	Years in rank
Assistant Professor	Masters or Doctorate	4-7
Associate Professor	Masters or Doctorate	5-7
Full Professor	Masters or Doctorate	Until retirement

Most professors have what are called advanced degrees. The degree required generally depends on the type of post-secondary institution in which an individual teaches. For example, a community college may require each of their teachers to have a minimum of a master's degree, while a large college or university would expect a doctorate degree. It is becoming more and more common for colleges to prefer or require the professors they hire to have a terminal degree—a doctor of philosophy, or Ph.D. for short. A person can have a doctor of philosophy in botany, English literature, history, or just about any other discipline you can think of. Usually, it takes an individual three or more years after he or she has completed a master's degree to earn a doctorate.

QUICK TAKES

What's in a Name?

Many students have problems knowing just what to call their professors. Do you call her Professor Jones, Dr. Jones, or Ms. Jones? We think you are always safe in referring to your professor as Professor Whomever until she makes it clear what she wants to be called. It's interesting to note, however, that students are more apt to refer to their male professors as Professor or Dr. and their female professors as Ms. or Mrs. A word to the wise: be particularly careful about using the proper title.

When a professor is hired who has a brand new Ph.D. under her belt, she will normally begin at the **Assistant Professor** level. Each new assistant professor receives guidelines from her institution that outline what she must do in order to get promoted to the next level, which is an **Associate Professor.** Depending on the type of post-secondary institution, the criteria for promotion may be weighted heavily on the professor's ability to teach, but it might also be on the research she publishes, the committees she serves on, and the service projects in which she participates. Often, faculty must be evaluated as having superior accomplishments in two of these areas—teaching, research, service—in order to get promoted. It takes anywhere from four to seven years to reach the Associate Professor level.

The next rank, **Full Professor,** is reserved for those who are able to sustain exemplary teaching, research, and/or service records for another several years, since college teachers usually must hold the rank of Associate Professor at least five years before being promoted to Full Professor. Full professors generally have high status because they have an extended track record.

The ranking system of professors is quite complex and unlike that of any other profession. One of the more interesting aspects of the promotion system that college faculty go through is that at every level they are judged by their own peers. That is, a committee of faculty who already have been promoted to the Associate Professor level examine the credentials of those who are trying to advance to this level. Those of us who are part of this unique system often wonder how and why it has become that complicated.

We believe that students should be somewhat familiar with this ranking system so that they can better appreciate how much work their college professors must invest in order to be promoted. Some college students believe that all professors have to do is to sit in their offices and wait for students to come and ask them questions. Nothing could be further from the truth. Certainly, most professors enjoy interacting with students and enjoy teaching, but the majority have other expectations and responsibilities that extend beyond the classroom. Even if professors are at colleges where they are not expected to conduct research, publish in professional journals, or write books, they usually have a heavy teaching load, serve on numerous committees, and are expected to stay abreast of developments in their discipline. The point here is that college professors, no matter where they teach, are busy people who can't afford to waste time.

Some General Tips About Interacting with Professors

"The first impression is a lasting one" holds true when interacting with professors as much as it does with others with whom you come in contact. Recall the first time you met someone with whom you eventually became friends. What was your first impression of him? Chances are that you liked that person right from the beginning. You didn't become best friends overnight, but there was something about the person that made a good impression on you and made you want to get to know him better. Because first impressions don't change dramatically, it's important to make a good impression on your professor right from day one. How can you do that? Several general tips may help you out.

- **Sit Up Front in Class.** When you are up front, you are more likely to stay alert and focused on the lecture, especially if you are in a class with lots of other students. If you can't get a seat up front, at least try to sit in the professor's line of vision.

- **Ask Questions.** Professors may begin or end each class with a question and answer period. Others will tell students to raise their hands at any time during the lecture if they have a question. And more and more professors are taking questions over e-mail. When you ask *well thought-out questions*, you make a good impression because professors sense that you are interested and that you are keeping up with the course material.

- **Ask for Help Sooner Rather than Later.** Nothing makes a worse impression than waiting until the day before the test, or worse yet, five minutes before the test, to ask a question about course material that was presented a week earlier. As soon as you realize that you are having trouble, make an appointment to see your professor, a tutor, or some other person designated to provide assistance.

- **Read the Syllabus.** The syllabus contains a wealth of information and should always be your first source when you have questions about grading, course pacing, or expectations. Therefore, it's important not to waste time by asking questions whose answers are outlined on the syllabus. For example, if your professor hasn't discussed how your course grade is determined, before you ask him to explain it, check your syllabus. If the information is not on there and he hasn't explained it in class, then ask.

- **Know and Follow the Class Rules.** Most professors have pet peeves about something. It's important for students to know what rules are in place (i.e., what happens if you miss a test) and to follow them. Don't be the student in the class that the professor uses as an example of inappropriate behavior.

- **Talk with Your Professors Via E-mail.** As we briefly mentioned above, more and more professors are encouraging students to communicate with them through e-mail. In fact, we know of some professors who require students to interact with them using e-mail at several points over the term. In addition, more professors have Web pages where you can view the syllabus, download class notes, and obtain additional information about both the course and the professor.

NETWORKING

Locating Your Professor's Web Page

As a way of learning a little more about one of your professors, check to see if he or she has a Web page. You can begin by looking at the professor's departmental Web page. For example, if you want to see if your botany professor has a Web page, you could first find the Web page for the botany department. Department Web pages generally list each faculty member with links to their individual Web pages. At smaller colleges, which may not be large enough to have a botany department, look for the science department instead, or perhaps life sciences. Once you have found the Web page for your professor, look to see the information that is included. After you have checked it out, consider sending your professor an e-mail if you have any questions about the syllabus or course.

Talking with Your Professors

Like it or not, at some time in your college career, you will probably have to interact with one of your professors. Of course, not all professors are easy to talk with and some can make you more ill at ease than others, but if you can answer a few questions and use some common sense, you should be able to get through the situation. It can even be a positive experience if you follow a few simple guidelines.

Question 1: Why are You Going to See Your Professor?

This question should be an easy one to answer. Do you need clarification about a project that is due? Are you having trouble understanding how to do the assigned chemistry problems? Do you have to explain to your professor about a specific learning disability that you have? Are you trying to get clarification on why you received a low grade on your essay test? Did your professor request a conference with you? Whatever your reason for seeing your professor, the answer to this question should be very evident. You may be going to see your professor just to get to know him a little better as did the student we mentioned in Chapter 1. That's fine. Just make sure you have a reason in mind and that you begin your conversation with something such as "Good morning Professor Carter. I am here to see you this morning because . . . " Beginning on this note shows your professor that you do have an overarching reason for showing up in his office. We realize that this advice is basic and that you might be reading this asking yourself "Why would anyone go to see a professor without having a clear purpose in mind?" but you would be surprised at the number of students who have sat in our offices without a clear notion of why they were there.

Question 2: What Are the Logistics of this Meeting?

We assume that if you need to see your professor you have approached her either before or after class about setting up a time that would be convenient for both of you. Some professors list office hours on their syllabi and announce that you can drop by during those hours without an appointment. In our opinion, however, it never hurts to check out a time with your professor in any case. When professors post office hours at the beginning of the term, they often don't realize that there will be days and times when conflicting meetings, conferences, or personal obligations necessitate them not being available during their normal office hours. It is always appropriate to ask the professor something such as the following: "I noticed on the syllabus that your office hours on Friday are from 9:00 to 10:30. I just wanted to check with you to be sure that you would be in around 9:30 so that I could ask you a couple of questions."

After you know what time your appointment is, find out where the meeting will take place. We have often assumed that students would know to meet us in our offices only to find out that they went to the classroom instead. If there is any question at all in your mind about where you are supposed to meet your professor, be sure to get clarification. Once you know the building and room number, make certain you know the location. This is especially important on larger campuses where getting across campus for an appointment can take 15 or 20 minutes, and it might take another 10 minutes to find the office once you have found the building. Whatever you do, don't show up late. Showing up late indicates that you don't think your professor's time is worth much, and that's not the impression you want to make.

Question 3: How Do I Talk with My Professor?

Before you go to see your professor for the first time, you need to think about the approach you are going to take and what you are going to say. Depending on why you are going to see your professor, this can be an easy task or one that is a bit more difficult. In the two examples that follow, John goes to see Professor Thomas knowing full well that writing has always been a problem for him. Harry, however, usually did well in high school English, but he did poorly on his first college composition paper and goes to see Professor Thomas with somewhat of an attitude.

John's approach: John has made an appointment to see his composition professor, Professor Thomas, because he did not do well on his first paper. Writing has always been difficult for John, but with the help of his past teachers he has managed to do fairly well. Professor Thomas seems like a fair-minded person and he said he was willing to talk with students about their writing problems. During his appointment with Professor Thomas, John acknowledges that he has weaknesses in writing and states that he feels his low evaluation on the first paper was pretty accurate. He takes out his paper and begins to ask the professor questions about the comments written on his paper. He takes notes on the suggestions that Professor Thomas gives and asks for clarification if necessary. At the end of the appointment, he thanks Professor Thomas, and tells him that those suggestions should help him do better on the next assignment. John leaves feeling positive about the conference. Professor Thomas has similar feelings and enjoys having students like John in his class. Although John isn't the best writer, he's working hard and taking advantage of the available assistance. Professor Thomas is sure John will improve on the next paper if he follows the suggestions they discussed.

Harry's approach: Harry also is in Professor Thomas's composition class. Harry made good grades in English in high school but he has somehow forgotten that he actually did very little writing in those English classes. He really doesn't like to write that much, but he always thought he was pretty good at it. So, he was quite surprised and, in fact, downright upset when he got his first paper back with such a low score. "Doesn't Professor Thomas know that I made excellent grades in English and that my teachers rarely commented on any problems I might have had writing? What's up with this guy?" thought Harry.

Harry talked with the professor after class and made an appointment to find out if Professor Thomas made a mistake in grading his paper. Harry arrives about 10 minutes late for his appointment with the excuse that he had trouble finding the office. He sits down, puts his paper down on Professor Thomas's desk, and says "So, can you fill me in here? I have never got a grade like this on an English paper! My high school teachers never gave me less than a B and I even worked on the school newspaper for a while." Professor Thomas reads through Harry's paper, pointing out some of the more apparent problems. Harry only tries to justify his writing and seems not to be paying attention to Professor Thomas's suggestions for improvement. Professor Thomas asks Harry if he has any questions. "Not really," mutters Harry as he picks up his paper and leaves.

It's pretty obvious which of these students used the better approach. Even if you *feel* the same as Harry did—that there must be some mistake, that you've never been evaluated this low—Harry didn't get much out of this meeting because of his approach. Although students have been rewarded for "trying hard" ever since kindergarten, college professors rarely award students higher grades simply because they are giving it all they've got. However, they do remember students who have been respectful and those who have not.

In addition, all things being equal—let's say that John and Harry had similar grades on all of their papers and John's average was a 79.2 and Harry's a 79.3. On his syllabus, Dr. Thomas stated that his grading scale was the traditional 90–100 = A, 89–80 = B, and so forth. But he also stated that he had the right to raise someone's grade but they would never receive a lower grade than they had earned. Therefore, although some might view grading such as this as subjective, Dr. Thomas could ethically award John a B and Harry a C.

Perhaps the biggest problem students have when they go to talk to their professors about concerns they are having with the course material is that they don't go in with specific questions prepared. For example, if you are in a mathematics or chemistry course and you find yourself totally lost, it's often difficult to know the questions to ask. You may sit in class and have no idea what the professor has been talking about. But when you go to see your professor, you need to be prepared to ask specific questions. Going in and stating "I don't understand the material" is

COLLEGE CAMPUS TODAY

Faculty Mentors

It is quite common on campuses of all sizes for faculty members to socialize with their students as a way of forming mentorships. Some campuses even provide small amounts of money for faculty to invite students into their homes for meals or other types of social functions. This type of socialization has sprung up because of an abundance of research that has shown that students who are mentored by faculty outside the classroom persist at higher rates and tend to develop long-term bonds with their institutions. So, if you happen to get invited to your professor's home for dinner and a movie, by all means go.

only going to get you the response "Okay. So what concepts are unclear?" In order to be able to articulate your questions as clearly as possible, use the following suggestions:

- Go back to your notes or your homework problems and see where your understanding broke down.
- Show the notes or homework to your professor so that she can try to get an idea of what happened.
- Talk through how you have been thinking about the information. Saying something such as "I understood everything up to this point, but then when we had to add this step, I became lost. Now I don't even have the slightest idea of how to solve these types of problems. This is what I know . . . "

If you open your conversation with your professor with a general statement such as "I don't understand any of this" you're probably going to get a response such as "Are you reading the text? Are you coming to class? Are you doing all the homework problems? Well, you'll just have to work harder (or more)." None of these suggestions will be very help-ful to you. When you can state as specifically as possible what your prob-lems are, you and your professor will walk away from the meeting with a much better feeling and more concrete advice.

Interacting with your professor is often not the easiest thing to do, especially if you are frustrated about your performance in the course, if the professor is distant and seems not to want to have to deal with students, or if you believe that you are being treated unfairly. On the other hand, most students find it enjoyable to talk with their professors and find that getting to know them better helps when they need rec-ommendations for jobs, scholarships, or even admission to graduate or professional schools.

☐ Real College
Marsha's Mistake

DIRECTIONS: Read the following *Real College* scenario and respond to the questions based on what you learned in this chapter.

Marsha rolled over, opened her eyes, and saw the bright sun stream-ing in her window. She jolted straight up like a bolt of lightning. "What time is it? What time is it?" she yelled jumping out of bed. She looked at her digital clock only to see 12:00 flashing over and over. She knew she was in trouble. She was supposed to be in class for a midterm exam at 8:00 and she knew that it wasn't anywhere near this light when she usu-ally got up. She grabbed her wristwatch off the dresser . . . it was 9:30. The test was already over. "What am I going to do?" she thought. She liked her professor, Dr. Luther, but she also knew that he was a stickler for rules and that if you missed a test without some sort of major docu-mentation as to why, you couldn't make up the exam.

Marsha's intentions were good. She had been studying for the test for several days, but she still felt that she wasn't ready. So she made the mistake lots of students make—she studied until 3:30 A.M. and set her clock for 5:30 thinking that would give her time to have one more hour to review. She was really tired when she finally went to sleep, but thought her alarm would wake her up. She didn't count on a power failure at 4:30! Now she was in real hot water. Dr. Luther would never let her make up the test with a lame excuse such as "My alarm didn't go off."

She knew she would have to make an appointment to talk with Dr. Luther. But how should she handle this situation?

1. Think about what you would do if you were in Marsha's shoes. Explain how you would handle the problem and why you would handle it that way.

2. Discuss solutions with your classmates. Are some solutions better than others? What are some factors you think Marsha should consider before she goes in to talk with Dr. Luther?

☐ Thinking Critically
Something to Think About and Discuss

Think about the approaches that John and Harry used to approach Professor Thomas. Then with a classmate, compare and contrast how they interacted with the professor. How much of someone's individual personality do you think enters into the picture when thinking about how students interact with professors? How about past experience? For example, if Harry had had more writing experiences in high school where he received feedback that his writing was problematic, might he have approached Professor Thomas differently?

☐ Follow-Up Activities

From the information we have presented in this chapter and from your own interactions so far with professors, which of the following do you think are positive things to do when interacting with a professor and which are negative? Discuss your responses with your classmates.

1. You call two weeks in advance for an appointment to see your professor so you can be sure you have an appointment with him the day after the second exam.

2. You go ask the professor if you missed anything important during the three days in a row you were out sick.

3. You are having a hard time taking notes from your professor so you raise your hand during a lecture and ask her to slow down.

4. You send an e-mail to your professor to try to set up an appointment time.

5. You made an appointment to talk to your professor about a couple of concepts that were giving you trouble. You ask him "Is this important to know for the test?"

CHAPTER 9

WHAT IS IT I'M SUPPOSED TO DO, ANYHOW?

Read this chapter to answer the following questions:

- What do we mean by task?
- How can you figure out what your professor expects?

SELF-ASSESSMENT

DIRECTIONS: Rate the following tasks. Place an *E* beside the tasks you consider the easiest, an *M* beside the tasks you consider a middle level of difficulty, and a *D* beside the tasks you consider the most difficult.

1. _____ Taking a matching exam in history

2. _____ Analyzing a chemical process for a chemistry lab

3. _____ Writing a persuasive essay for English class

4. _____ Evaluating and drawing a conclusion about several articles presenting conflicting accounts of an event in political science

5. _____ Taking a multiple-choice exam over two psychology chapters

6. _____ Taking an exam over the bold-faced terms for a biology class

7. _____ Debating a controversial issue in sociology class

8. _____ Giving an informational speech for speech communications class

9. _____ Solving calculus problems on a mathematics exam

How you rated these tasks probably had something to do with your own personal background and interests. For example, if you love mathematics you might have thought solving calculus problems was easy. However, there are some overarching ideas (which you will learn about in this chapter) that make numbers 1 and 6 the easiest, numbers 2, 5, 8, and 9 somewhere in the middle, and numbers 3, 4, and 7 the most difficult tasks.

In Chapter 2, when we introduced the idea that there are four factors that impact learning, we briefly discussed the role that task understanding plays in being an active learner. Because much of your success as a college student rests on your ability to interpret the task, we will talk about it here in greater detail.

There's more to studying and being a successful student than meets the eye and "studying hard" is not always "studying smart." Your ability to understand what your professor wants you to do and the way you are supposed to do it goes a long way in making you a more efficient and effective student. Why? To answer this question, we'll explore two important aspects of task—What do we mean by "task"? and How can you go about figuring out what the task is?

What Is a Task?

The task for any course consists of two parts:

1. The type of activity in which you engage.
2. The level of thinking required as you engage in the activity.

NETWORKING

Using the Web to Understand Task

Find the Web page of one of your professors and look for information concerning task. For example, if you have multiple-choice exams, look to see whether your professor has put any example test items on the site. Also check out online information about the course. Sometimes rather than putting material concerning tests and other course requirements on their own personal Web page, professors will have a separate page for each course they teach. These pages can provide a wealth of information to help you better understand the task.

Part One: The Type of Activity

The activity you will be asked to engage in is usually a test, a paper, or a project by which your instructor will evaluate you. But knowing that you have to take a test is not enough information to be able to carefully select an appropriate approach to studying. You need to know the *type* of test you will take.

- Is it an objective exam, which includes multiple-choice, true/false, or matching items?

- Is it a more subjective exam that requires answering essay, short answer, or identification questions?

- Is it a combination of both types?

Because you should not approach studying for multiple-choice tests in the same way you approach studying for essay tests, it's very important to know right from the beginning the basic type of test you will have. As we will discuss in greater detail later in the book, the kind of reading you do, the way you think about the material, and the strategies you select all have a bearing on the kinds of tasks you are asked to complete in a course.

It is important to reiterate and alert you to the importance of precisely knowing the task by describing a situation that occurred to students enrolled in a large, lecture history course. For each test, students were told that they would have "objective items" and two essay questions. On the first four exams, these objective items were always multiple-choice. When it came time for the final exam and the professor told students that they would have a test that was part objective and part essay, they assumed that they would once again have multiple-choice questions. Imagine their surprise when the tests were distributed and the objective items were fill-in-the-blanks! Many students were outraged and went to see the professor when they discovered that they had done poorly on the test. But the professor wouldn't budge. His definition of task for objective items included fill-in-the-blank as well as multiple-choice. The point here is clear: Get as much specific information as possible about the test. Ask the right questions. Just knowing that you will have an objective test is obviously insufficient information.

Likewise if the task in a course consists of papers or projects rather than exams, the same advice holds true. Talk with your professor about specific aspects of the paper, especially if they seem unclear. In political science courses on our campus, for example, students must do a project that consists of several different pieces. First they select a political issue to follow throughout the term. They must subscribe to and read the *New York Times* daily and find a minimum of 30 articles concerning their issue. For each article they must write a brief summary. At the end of the term, they complete two additional tasks. First they write a policy statement and then they write a memo to an influential political figure about this issue. Students who fail to understand how to carry out the numerous pieces involved in this task have severe problems in doing well on a long-term project that is 30 percent of their grade.

SUCCESS AT A GLANCE

Thinking About the Task

Type of Task + Level of Thinking = Task Knowledge

- Matching exam   **Memorization**
- Multiple choice   **Analysis**
- Essay/Short answer   **Synthesis**

Part Two: The Level of Thinking

Once you have identified the specific activities your professor expects, you're halfway there. The other part of task identification, and perhaps the more important part, is knowing what level of thinking is required to carry out that task. There are many types of thinking that a professor may want you to engage in.

Have you ever heard of Bloom's taxonomy? This classification provides a way to categorize the kinds of questions that students typically encounter in their classes. Knowing the level of questions your professor asks can help you choose appropriate learning and study strategies.

Bloom discusses six levels of questioning:

1. **Knowledge**—This includes knowledge of dates, events, major ideas, bold-faced terms.

   Question Words: list, define, describe, identify, match, name, what, who, when, where

   Examples: When did "black Thursday" occur?

   What is the role of gray matter?

   Define *artificial concepts.*

2. **Comprehension**—This includes grasping the meaning, explaining or summarizing, grouping, predicting outcomes, or inferring.

   Question Words: summarize, describe, interpret, distinguish, defend, explain, discuss, predict

   Examples: Which of the following is an example of *formal reasoning?*

   Summarize the outcomes of the Treaty of Versailles.

   Explain the process of meiosis.

3. **Application**—This level requires the ability to use the material in a new context, to solve problems, or to utilize rules, concepts, or theories.

   Question Words: apply, demonstrate, calculate, illustrate, show, relate, give an example of, solve

   Examples: If a plant with the genotype of BbCcDd was crossed with a plant that was BBCcdd, what are the chances of producing a plant with the genotype of BbCcDd?

Illustrate the changes in the use of flower imagery using at least five poems contained in our class readings.

4. **Analysis**—This involves understanding organization of parts, clarifying, concluding, or recognizing hidden meaning.

Question Words: analyze, explain, compare and contrast, select, arrange, order

Examples: Compare and contrast the characteristics of short-term memory and long-term memory.

Select the most appropriate method for solving this calculus problem.

5. **Synthesis**—This involves creating new ideas, relating knowledge from several sources of information, predicting, drawing conclusions.

Question Words: combine, create, design, formulate, compose, integrate, rewrite, generalize

Examples: Rewrite the play *The Cherry Orchard* as if it were written by Ibsen.

Design a solution to the current parking problem on campus.

6. **Evaluation**—This relies on the ability to make choices based on evidence, to support stance with reasoning, to recognize subjectivity, to assess value of theories.

Question Words: support, judge, discriminate, assess, recommend, measure, convince, conclude

Examples: How successful would the proposed federal income tax cut be in controlling inflation as well as decreasing unemployment?

Do you agree with President Johnson's decision to enter the Vietnamese Conflict? Why or Why not?

Most objective exams will have questions at each of these levels. Many students fail to think about this part of the task, which often results in lower test grades and frustration. Another mistake that students, primarily first-year students, often make is that they believe that objective exams don't involve higher-level thinking. That is, they think that multiple-choice and true/false tests are basically memorization tasks. However, on most objective tests, some of the questions will be factual in nature, some will ask for examples, and some will require you to synthesize and analyze. Most essay questions require the highest level of thinking, but other subjective exams, such as identification items, could ask for just factual information. Remember, unless you know the task, you will have a difficult time selecting the appropriate study strategies. In the next section, we will give you some hints about how to get more information about the task.

QUICK TAKES

Tasks After College

There are many tasks that college students have to do in addition to doing well in their courses. For example, to prepare for life after college, many career centers suggest that first-year students do the following three tasks:

1. **Visit the career center.** The staff can help you with choosing a major, planning for the future, exploring job options, and more.

2. **Start a résumé.** Many students struggle with creating a good résumé of their experience. By starting early, you can update it every term and graduate with a great tool for your job search.

3. **Find a summer internship.** These opportunities can be a great way to learn more about your field and can set you apart from other applicants in the future.

How Can You Get Information About the Task?

Now that you understand how important it is to know the task for each of your classes, you might ask the obvious question: How do I figure out how to carry out the task? Because few professors will state the task precisely and completely, it becomes important for you to be able to piece together bits of information from a variety of sources in order to paint the picture for yourself.

1. **Attend class every day.** The best place to begin, of course, is with what your professor says in class, especially in the early part of the term. Some professors spell out the task very neatly and clearly on the first day when they go over the syllabus. Others will give you a big picture of the task early in the term and then fill in the details as the course moves along. Still others, and perhaps most college professors fall into this category, give you a combination of implicit and explicit cues and expect you to pick up on those cues.

2. **Write it down.** It's just as important to take notes concerning what's expected of you as it is to take notes on the content. Students often think that they will remember how to structure an essay, or the types of questions that will be on their exams. However, they discover two or three weeks later that there's only a faint recollection, or worse, no recollection at all of some important piece of information that the professor had discussed in class. Go to class, listen carefully, and write down what your professor says about the task in your lecture notes.

3. **Consult your syllabus.** Read your syllabus carefully at the beginning of the course and then return to it on a regular basis. Look for any statements that tell you about course expectations. Examine your syllabus for the following information:

   - The number of tests you will have or papers you will have to write, and the approximate dates tests will be given or papers will be due.

   - Your professor's office hours and phone number (or e-mail address) so that you know how to make an appointment to talk with her.

   - Your professor's policies on make-up work or the consequences of missing an exam or another deadline.

   - Your professor's attendance policies (if any).

   - Your professor's philosophy on the course, which can give you insight into how your professor will approach the content and can go a long way in helping you define the task.

- The course objectives. Reading these statements will tell you what the professor hopes you will learn in the course.

All of these factors either directly or indirectly relate to task. Thus it is important not only to read your syllabus carefully at the beginning of the term, but also to refer to it often as the term progresses.

4. **Look at old exams.** Even if you think you have a clear understanding of what the task is, it's always a good idea to look over old exams as a way of confirming course requirements. Many professors routinely make old exams available to students, while others will provide example questions only when asked. Looking at old exams gives you lots of information, especially about the level of thinking required. You want to use these exams as ways of gathering information about the level of thinking, not about the actual content that you should study. Chances are your professor will write the same *types* of questions on future exams but probably will not ask the exact same questions.

COLLEGE CAMPUS TODAY

Exploring Interests Outside of Class

One of the most important tasks of any college student is exploring and maybe even changing their views about many issues that impact society such as racism, women's right to choose, cloning, and so on. Your campus may hold debates about these issues, present lectures, or even have social organizations that explore ways of correcting social ills. We suggest you find a topic that interests you and explore it over the next year. You'll probably make some friends and learn more than you ever would inside a classroom.

5. **Ask former students.** Students who have already taken the course will be able to give you details about a course and a professor. But make sure that you ask former students the right questions. For example, asking someone "Are Professor Smith's tests difficult?" is

not the best way to pose the question because what is a difficult test to one person may not be difficult to another. Better questions would be: "What kind of tests does Professor Smith give?" "Can you remember examples of some questions?" "What kinds of structure does he expect for essay questions?" "Does he give you much guidance?" Questions such as these give you answers about the task.

☐ Real College
Tina's Task

DIRECTIONS: Read the following *Real College* scenario and respond to the questions based on the information you learned in this chapter.

Tina decided that she could no longer put off taking a required history class, even though she "hates history with a passion," so she reluctantly registered for the course. It's not that she hasn't done well in history. On the contrary, her grades in high school history classes were quite good. She sees herself as a good memorizer and since her high school history experience involved lots of memorization of names, dates, events, and the like, she tended to make good grades. She just doesn't like history, plain and simple.

As Tina looks over her class schedule for the term, she thinks about skipping the first class or two, because from her perspective, two less history classes to go to would be a good thing. But her roommate, who has already taken this course, advises her to attend every class—even the first one. Tina reluctantly takes her advice and actually thought the professor was engaging and humorous.

Obviously, in order to earn a good grade in this course, Tina is going to have to figure out what the tasks are. On the first day, the professor said that there would be three essay exams as well as a cumulative final, but he didn't say much else about the tasks. Think about Tina's situation and respond to the following questions:

1. What additional information do you think Tina needs so that she can have a clearer idea of the task?

2. How should she go about gathering the necessary information?

☐ Thinking Critically
Something to Think About and Discuss

Most college students do not consciously sit down at the beginning of the term and say to themselves, "Gee, before I start doing my reading and studying for this class, I'd better figure out the task!" For students who intuitively understand that it is important to figure out the course demands, it's more of an unconscious effort. Think about yourself as a learner and then respond to the following questions:

- Have you taken time this term to figure out the task in each of your classes? If not, how might you begin to gather that information this term and in future terms?

- Have you ever been in a class where you had a very difficult time understanding what the professor's expectations were? How did you handle that situation? What might you do differently now?

- Can you think of any other sources that might be able to give you task information? (We have mentioned your professor, syllabus, copies of old exams, and students who have already taken the course.)

- How might you organize your notes to draw attention to task information that your professor gives you?

☐ Follow-Up Activities

1. Think about the four factors that influence learning introduced in Chapter 2. How does task definition fit into this model?

2. What influence does task definition have on the study strategies you might select in a particular course?

CHAPTER 10

TAKE NOTE! LECTURES

A Different Kind Of Text

Read this chapter to answer the following questions:

- Why is it important to take good lecture notes?
- What should I do before class, during class, and after class to take good notes?
- How can I use my notes to self-test?

SELF-ASSESSMENT

DIRECTIONS: Examine your notes from one of your classes and evaluate them on a scale of 1 to 5, with 1 being "hardly ever" to 5 being "almost always."

1. My notes are organized.	1	2	3	4	5
2. My notes distinguish main points from details.	1	2	3	4	5
3. My notes include examples.	1	2	3	4	5
4. I take notes over class discussions.	1	2	3	4	5
5. I test myself over my notes.	1	2	3	4	5
6. My notes accurately reflect the content of the lecture.	1	2	3	4	5
7. My notes contain abbreviations.	1	2	3	4	5

8. I review my notes as soon after class as possible.   1   2   3   4   5

9. I read my text assignments before lectures.   1   2   3   4   5

10. I compare my notes to the text when I study.   1   2   3   4   5

The more fives you've marked, the better. Many students find that they need more efficient strategies for note-taking. Read on to find out how to improve your note-taking skills.

The Importance and Characteristics of Good Lecture Notes

In college, a large percentage of information will be transmitted to you through lecture. In the traditional lecture format, professors explain information that they feel is important for you to learn in the class. Most professors expect you to take notes in an organized fashion so that you can study and review the notes throughout the course. Note-taking isn't too difficult if you have a professor who speaks slowly, clearly, and lectures in an organized fashion. But many more professors aren't the world's most top-notch, engaging lecturers. Therefore, it's important for students to be able to supply their own organization, to get down the important points, and to fill in the gaps when necessary.

It's important to be able to take good lecture notes for a variety of reasons:

- They serve as a record of what goes on in class each day. Without a complete record, it's difficult to have all the information you need to prepare for subsequent classes or exams.

- If your notes are organized, they can help you to identify patterns in your professor's lectures. Once you see patterns, you get a better idea of what your professor feels is important.

- Your notes will also help you to spot overlap between your text and the professor's lecture. These overlaps are fertile ground for test questions.

What distinguishes good notes from poor notes? As you will see, good notes are more than just readable. As you read about the characteristics of good notes, look at the following examples. These examples show good, bad, and ugly lecture notes related to a text excerpt entitled "Prototypes." We will refer to these examples throughout the chapter.

Example 1: Good Lecture Notes

	Prototypes
	Nov 10

What is a prototype?	Prototype
	Def. The most typical example of a category or concept
	  Ex. Prototype of veggie = carrot (not rutabaga)
	  Ex. Prototype of a bird = robin (not ostrich or penguin)

Give an example of prototype	

2 Char. of proto	Characteristics
	  1. Play role in thinking-stereotypes (will discuss more fully next class)
	  2. Play role in behavior-Blanton et al research study

Explain research on proto and drinking	Research on prototypes and drinking Found relat when asked teens to describe the type of person who drinks alcohol frequently.

Results?	Results
	  1. Teens with + proto of drinkers reported drinking more
	  2. + proto was a consequence of students' peer group-if their friends drank, they were likely to drink
	  3. teens with poor relationship with parents were more likely to associate with drinking peer group

Conclusions?	Conclusions
	  • prototype came from social experience-interactions with parents led some teens to favor a drinking peer group, which fostered a + proto for drinking
	  • the proto affects behaviors because events interact-by becoming a drinker, a person will hang out with drinkers which will further shape prototype

	NOTE: Exam next Thurs (4/17) 40 mult choice, 3 short ans. HINT: Know researchers and focus on theories

Example 2: Weak Lecture Notes

Prototypes

The most typical example of a category. Ex-veggie, bird
thinking-stereotypes
behavior-drinking. Drinkers hang out with other drinkers and have poor
relationship with parents
Research-found relationship between proptotype and alcohol use

Example 3: Very Weak Notes

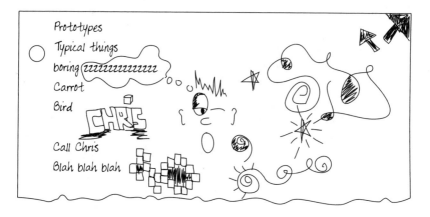

Prototypes
Typical things
boring zzzzzzzzzzzzzz
Carrot
Bird
CHRIS
Call Chris
Blah blah blah

- **Good Notes Are Organized.** When you look at the three examples of lecture notes, it is easy to see which one is better organized. The notes in the first example use organizational strategies such as underlining the main points, indenting details, noting examples, and numbering reasons. This differs dramatically from the notes in the second and third examples. In the second example, it's difficult to tell where one idea stops and another begins or what is a main point and what is a detail. Much of the information written in the notes in the second example is lost or difficult to link together. And what can we say about the notes in example three except that some students actually have notes that are this bad! Incomplete notes—those that are inadequate as well as imprecise—occur most frequently in courses that students find uninteresting or for students who have not yet mastered the art of active learning.

- **Good Notes Distinguish Main Points from Details.** Every lecture has both main points and details. The main points might be reasons, characteristics, or theories. Details include information that supports or explains the main points. It's important to write your notes in such a way that the main points are distinguishable from the details. If the information runs together or if you have only written down the main points and excluded the details, your notes will be less useful to use for studying.

- **Good Notes Include Examples.** Often when professors get to the point in the lecture at which they are giving examples, students are nodding off or thinking about what they plan to have for lunch. But examples often surface on exams, so it's crucial to write down every example of a particular main point that the professor provides. These examples should stand out in some way so that as you study, you know what they illustrate.

- **Good Notes Clearly Indicate Lecture Patterns.** Most professors use the same pattern in all of their lectures. The two most common are the **inductive** pattern and the **deductive** pattern. **Inductive** lectures progress from the specific to the general. For example, an inductive lecturer would provide a series of reasons or characteristics and conclude with a statement such as "So, all of this means . . . " This concluding statement is the generalization that helps make sense of the lecture. **Deductive** lecturers do the opposite. They begin with the generalization ("There are three main reasons for . . . ") and then fill in the reasons, details, and examples. It is generally easier to follow lectures when they are presented in a deductive manner. The style your professor uses should become apparent to you after the first few class sessions and your notes will need to reflect this lecture pattern.

- **Good Notes Allow for Self-Testing.** Students don't usually think about how the way they take notes will influence the way they study. Most students merely "read over" their notes. However, this approach often gives you a false sense of knowing the information when, in fact, you do not. Writing questions or key words, called annotations, in the margin of your notes can help you test yourself. Note the difference between the notes in the three examples on pages 136–137. The notes in example one have questions in the margins that you can ask yourself, which will help you determine your knowledge of the material. (We will discuss self-questioning of lecture notes, or self-testing, in more detail later in the chapter.)

- **Good Notes Stand the Test of Time.** Because your notes are a daily record of what is said in class each day, they should make sense to you long after class is over. You should be able to read through your notes two days, two weeks, or two months later and find they are still understandable. Because of the way memory works, you will be unable to remember everything your professor says in class every day. That's why you take notes to begin with. It's important, then, to be sure that your notes are organized in such a way that they will make sense down the line and that they include as much detail as you can reasonably get on paper.

- **Good Notes Use Abbreviations.** Because most professors speak faster than you can write, it's important to use abbreviations that make sense to you. For example, if your professor is lecturing on the Industrial Revolution, it would be too time consuming to write both words out every time they were mentioned. Using *Ind. Rev.* or even *IR* saves a considerable amount of time. It is also a good idea to develop a series of abbreviations for common and high-use words. Here are some suggestions:

SUCCESS AT A GLANCE
Abbreviation Examples

&	and
b/c	because
/	the
=	means, definitions, is equal to

(continued)

w/i	within
+	in addition to, positives
−	negatives
$	money, wealth
<	less than
>	greater than
↑	increased
↓	decreased
∴	therefore
#	number
*	very important

It is becoming more common for professors to put their notes on the Web or to have students purchase copies of their notes to follow during the lecture. These alternatives are useful as long as you continue to take a good set of notes yourself. We know that simply using someone else's notes (even if they are the professor's) rather than taking your own does not maximize your learning. The better approach is to take notes yourself and then compare them with the Web notes.

Taking Good Lecture Notes

Taking good notes involves active listening, attentiveness, and the ability to synthesize and condense a considerable amount of information on the spot. Effective note-takers know that a lot of thinking goes on during note-taking. Most students probably enter the lecture situation with every intention of staying alert, paying attention, and taking good notes. But for a variety of reasons, many students do not prevail.

From our observations, it seems that several factors enter into students' abilities to take good notes:

1. **Class size.** The larger the class size, the easier it is to become unconnected with what the professor is saying. In addition, the further back or to the side that students sit in a classroom, the worse the problem tends to become. That's why it's important to stay in the professor's line of vision.

2. **Professor's lecture style.** When professors are not entertaining, or if they tend to speak in a monotone, it is hard to stay focused. Professors who are difficult to follow, or those who tend to speak rapidly, can cause students' minds to wander rather than to stay actively involved in listening. We have also found that students tend to pay less attention when the professor has put notes on the Web (we discuss strategies for using Web notes later in this chapter).

3. **Time of day.** Interestingly, students are most likely to fall asleep in an early morning class, presumably after they have had several hours of uninterrupted sleep. Granted, many students would consider themselves as "night people" whose body clocks resist going to bed before the wee hours of the morning, and also resist getting up prior to noon. If you count yourself in these numbers, try to avoid scheduling an early morning class. Some students also seem to have trouble paying attention right after lunch (because they are full and sluggish) or during the late afternoon hours (when they feel hungry and tired). If you have a class immediately after lunch, try to eat a light meal; if a late afternoon class is on your schedule, try eating a snack before class to keep your energy level up.

4. **Health (both emotional and physical).** Breaking up with your boyfriend or girlfriend, family problems, sick children, illness, or taking prescription medication all can influence your attentiveness in class. Everyone experiences problems at one time or another and no one can expect to be perfectly attentive all the time. But when emotional or physical problems become constant barriers to learning, it's time to think about a course of action to get back to health.

QUICK TAKES

Note-Taking After College

Our former students have told us that they were surprised that they needed to use their note-taking skills even after they graduated from college. They have said that the ability to quickly and accurately write down notes during meetings or even informal discussions in an organized way has helped them keep track of information in their careers. So consider good note-taking a life skill. If you can perfect it in college, it will serve you for a lifetime.

General Note-Taking Guidelines

Let's begin our discussion of how to take good lecture notes with some general guidelines. These guidelines tend to work for every type of lecture, regardless of class size:

- **Sit Up Front.** As we mentioned above, students who sit in the front of the classroom tend to be more attentive and listen more actively than those who sit in the back. This holds true in both larger and smaller classes. In small classes, students who sit in the front tend to ask more questions and get to know their professors better. Also, research indicates a significant relationship between students' grades and seat location. That is, the closer they sit to the front, the higher their grade tends to be.

- **Adjust Your Note-Taking to the Professor.** Every professor lectures a bit differently. Some are well organized and taking notes from them is a breeze. Others are unorganized, provide few transitional cues, and get off the topic very easily. Whatever your professor's lecturing habits seem to be, you need to figure them out early in the term and make the appropriate adjustments in your note-taking.

- **Listen, Think, and Write.** Students who try to copy down everything the professor says tend to miss many key points because they can't keep up. Rather than trying to write down every word, listen first, think about what the professor is saying, and then write that thought, as much as possible, in your own words. Because professors tend to repeat information or say it a couple of times in different ways, it's important to listen and think before you write. Your intent should be to understand the concepts rather than get down every word.

- **Paraphrase.** Sometimes professors speak so quickly and try to cram so much material into a lecture that it is virtually impossible to get down all of the key points. If you find yourself getting more "half-thoughts" than complete thoughts in your notes, or if you read over your notes and find that you can't piece together the important parts of the lecture, then you probably need to begin to do some serious paraphrasing. Paraphrasing, in this case, means getting down key concepts in your words and then filling in the details after class with information from the text. The example below shows the notes a professor might use for a lecture on the topic of the Cuban missile crisis. Then, in the same example, you will see how a student's paraphrased notes might look.

Example of a Professor's Notes and a Student's Paraphrased Notes

Professor's lecture notes

October 1962 was the climax of Kennedy's crusade against communism—the Cuban missile crisis. Throughout the summer and early fall of 1962 the Soviets engaged in a massive nuclear arms buildup in Cuba. The Soviets sought to use these weapons to protect Castro from a US invasion. Needless to say, this was an extremely tense situation.

Kennedy and his advisors ruled out diplomacy or an immediate attack and instead decided on a two-step response to the situation. First, JFK would proclaim a

Student's paraphrased notes

Cuban Missile Crisis
Oct. 1962—climax of JFK crusade against communism

- Soviets send nuclear arms to Cuba
- Said these were to protect Cuba from US invasion
- Kennedy—no immed attack or diplomacy—two step response

1. naval quarantine of Cuba—prevent new missiles from arriving
2. threatened nuclear confrontation (war!) if missiles not removed.

(continued)

Professor's lecture notes

naval quarantine of Cuba to prevent the arrival of any new missiles. Second he would threaten a nuclear confrontation with the Soviets if the missiles were not removed from Cuba.

For the next six days the world was on the brink of nuclear war. Finally, Soviet ships halted their approach. Khrushchev sent Kennedy a long and rambling letter, which offered a face-saving way out. Russia would remove the missiles in return for a promise that the US would never invade Cuba.

The fallout from this crisis was considerable. Shaken by the close call, a hotline between Washington and Moscow was installed to allow direct communication in an emergency. The democrats also did better than expected in the November 1962 elections. In addition, after long negotiations with the Soviets, a limited nuclear test ban treaty was passed in 1963. Khrushchev was ultimately ousted from the Kremlin and hard-line Soviets began a tremendous military expansion that greatly increased their nuclear arsenal. This stimulated a vast US military expansion to catch up. However, Kennedy's peaceful resolution of the crisis became a personal and political triumph. In a

Student's paraphrased notes

6 days of tense waiting. Soviets halted approach of ships and Khru proposes that Russia remove missiles in return for promise the US never invade Cuba.

Fallout

1. emergency hotline between DC and Moscow

2. democrats do better in 1962 elections

3. limited nuclear test ban treaty signed 1963

4. Khru ousted

5. Soviets begin military expansion

6. personal and political triumph for Kennedy

7. JFK's Amer. U speech-détente-peaceful coexistence with Soviets called for

(continued)

Professor's lecture notes

speech at American University in
1963 he tried to lay the foundation
for peaceful coexistence with the
Soviets—this was the origin of the
policy that later became known as
'détente.'

Student's paraphrased notes

■   ■   ■

Learning how to take good lecture notes is an integral part of being a
successful college student and an active learner. Like approaching
textbook reading, taking good notes and using them as a successful
study aid involves preparing to take notes, being an active listener
during the lecture, and then rehearsing and self-testing after the lecture.

COLLEGE CAMPUS TODAY
Attending Guest Lectures

Many colleges (and even local bookstores) offer lectures on a
variety of topics. Even though you might not take notes on
these lectures, attending a few lectures a semester is an interesting way to enhance your college experience. On our campus we have seen famous politicians debate, humorous
authors, playwrights discussing their work, researchers presenting their findings, and many other fascinating lectures.
Look in the local paper or on campus flyers for information
about what is available at your school.

Getting Ready to Take Notes

You need to do some preparation before you begin to take notes.
Engaging in pre-note-taking activities can make the difference between
being an active and a passive listener. In order to get ready to take
notes, you should:

- **Do the Assigned Reading.** Most professors expect you to be somewhat familiar with the topics they will lecture on by reading the appropriate text chapters before you come to class. Reading before the lecture gives you the advantage of making connections between the text and lecture. You will also be able to follow the "listen, think, write" rule better, because being familiar with the lecture topic will allow you to take down the key points in a more organized fashion. If you run out of time and can't read the text in its entirety, at least skim the chapter(s) using the techniques described in Chapter 12. That will at least give you some idea of the key points that will be covered in the lecture.

- **Review Your Notes from the Previous Lecture.** Take five or ten minutes before class to read through your notes from the previous lecture. By reviewing, you are refreshing your memory and getting your mind ready to become actively involved in learning. In addition, when you review, you can be sure that you understand the information that has been presented. Because many professors begin each class by answering student questions, you can get unclear information explained.

- **Have the Extra Edge.** Try to get to class with plenty of time to spare. Plan to use this time to review. Get out your notebook, get your paper ready (we'll talk more about this later), and of course, sit in the front.

Staying Active During Note-Taking

In this section we will discuss not only the format and organization of good notes, but also the kinds of information that you should include in your notes. By following these suggestions, you will be able to remain alert and active throughout the class.

Format and Organization

If you were to examine the notes of five different college students, you would probably see five different formats. Perhaps none of these formats would match up with the method we recommend, the split-page method. We will concentrate on this particular method because it allows for self-testing, which we believe is crucial for active learning. Look again at the first note-taking example on page 136. You can see that a line has been drawn down the left-hand side of the paper, creating a 2 to 3 inch margin. During note-taking, you take your notes on the wider right-hand side of the paper and then after class you use the margin to pull out the key points. You should have your lines drawn on several sheets of paper, your paper dated, and several pages numbered before your professor begins to lecture.

As you take notes, use the following guidelines:

- Use a 3-ring binder rather than spiral-bound notebooks. A binder allows you to include class handouts, easily remove your notes, and insert notes easily if you are absent from class.

- Take notes in simple paragraph form, rather than as a tightly structured outline. Outlines cause many students to get hung up on the outline format rather than the content of the lecture.

- Leave spaces between ideas and underline key points. This enables you to see where one idea stops and another begins and helps to distinguish between the key points and the details.

- Indent and mark details and examples. Indenting helps you know what information is related. If your notes all run together, it's difficult to tell what is a key point and what is supporting information.

- Number lists—reasons, characteristics, types, and so forth. Numbering lists enables you to know at a glance how many factors on the list you need to remember.

- Use abbreviations whenever possible. Abbreviating saves time and can distinguish certain kinds of information, such as indicating an example by "ex.," a definition by "def.," important information with a *, and so forth.

Active Listening

It's not only important to know how you should take and organize your notes, but also the kinds of information you should include. Of course, the kinds of information you should put in your notes vary from class to class. For example, although you may include names, dates, and events in your history notes, your psychology notes will probably be more focused on research and theories than on key events. Listen for the following cues that your professor may give as a way of figuring out what is important to note:

- **Lists.** Lists of things begin with cues such as "There were three major reasons why President Johnson committed more troops to Vietnam." "Short-term memory has five characteristics." "Mitosis progresses through eight stages." Anytime you hear a number followed by several factors, stages, characteristics, etc., make sure you write the number of things along with the explanation. In other words, just don't write the stages of mitosis in your notes. Write down what happens in each stage as well.

- **Cause/Effect.** When you hear your professor discuss causes and effects, be sure to write it down. Cause/effect cues are common in history and political science. For example, there might be an event that caused a president to make a certain decision and this decision, in turn, had numerous effects on other events and decisions. In science, cause/effect can deal with concepts such as diseases or the food chain.

- **Definitions.** Perhaps one of the most frequent types of information your professor will give in a lecture is definitions. Your professor might cue you by saying something as basic as "*Covalent bond* can be defined as . . . " It's a good idea to get definitions written in your notes precisely. If you only get down a portion of a definition or aren't sure that you have it exactly right, check your text or with your professor as soon after class as possible.

- **Examples.** Definitions are quite frequently followed by examples, yet often, students will see "example time" as an occasion to tune out. But examples discussed in class make for prime test questions. If you have to choose, we believe that it's actually more important to get examples in your notes than it is definitions (you can get the definitions from your textbook).

- **Extended Comments.** When the professor spends a lot of time explaining something, you can be sure that it is important information. Try to stay connected with the lecturer during extended comments and take down as much of the information as possible. Essay, short answer, and higher-level multiple-choice items often come from these extended comments.

- **Superlatives.** Anytime a professor uses words such as "most important," or "best explanation," "least influential," be sure to write it down. For example, there may be many explanations for how memory works, but your psychology professor might believe that one explanation is the "best." These are the kinds of things professors love to ask about on exams.

- **Voice or Volume Change.** When professors think something is important or they want to stress it, they generally speak louder and slower. A change in voice can be a clear indication that something important is being said.

- **Process Notes.** Process notes consist of information the professor gives about tests, how to study, when study or review sessions are held, how to think about the information, or how he wants an essay structured. They can also include clues about what information might be on the exam. Process notes often come right at the beginning of class, before some students are ready to take notes, or at the end of class, when some students are packed up and ready to leave. Sometimes professors will even comment after a particular lecture something to the effect "Hmmm . . . Wouldn't this make an interesting essay question?" This is all vital information that should be written down in your notes.

Becoming an active listener takes time, especially for classes in which you have little interest. It's not too difficult to stay connected with the lecturer in classes that you like or in classes where you have a professor who is dynamic. It's much more difficult in those courses that are, in some way, less appealing. But try to think about the bigger picture. If you are an active listener and take organized notes for the entire class period, studying and learning the course material will be a much easier task.

NETWORKING

Using Web Notes

Some professors are putting their lecture notes on the Web daily. If any of your professors do this, check out their Web site. There are advantages and disadvantages to Web notes,

(continued)

however. Students who simply print out the notes and study them right before the exam tend to score lower than students who use the Web notes as a supplement. If your professor supplies the notes for you, take them to class and follow along during the lecture. You'll be able to add more details during class.

Annotating and Self-Testing After Note-Taking

You have gotten ready to take notes before the lecture, you remained active and took notes in an organized way during the lecture, but you still aren't finished! Interacting with your notes after the lecture is perhaps the most important phase of note-taking. As soon as possible after the lecture, it's important to read over your notes to be sure that you understand all the major concepts presented. This is when you use the 2 to 3 inch margin on the left-hand side of your paper. As shown in Example 1 at the beginning of the chapter (see page 136), this margin can be used to write in the key points or pose questions. (This is called annotation and it will be discussed in more detail in Chapter 12.) The annotations or questions are used to self-test as you study the course material.

Good annotations or questions have several features. They

- focus on the major points or broad topics
- get at higher level thinking by asking "how," "why," or "for example"
- are brief

Annotating your lecture notes as soon after the lecture as possible helps get the information into your memory and helps you remember it better. In addition, when you go through your notes, you can determine if you have questions about what was presented in class. Writing questions or annotating gives you immediate feedback about what you understand and what you need clarification about.

When it comes time to prepare for the exam, follow these steps to use your annotations or questions to self-test:

1. Read through your notes, trying to get the information fixed in your memory.

2. Fold your paper back, exposing only what you have written in the left-hand column.

3. Ask yourself the question or explain the concept.

4. Flip your notes over to see how much of the material you have remembered.

5. If you knew it *accurately and precisely*, go on to the next concept. If you had problems, read your notes another time or two and try again.

6. As you learn the concepts, check them off in the margin.

7. When you begin the next study session, review what you know, but concentrate your efforts on what you don't know.

Self-testing by using annotations or questions in the margin of your notes should give you confidence as you enter a testing situation. When you self-test, you have a fairly accurate idea of the concepts you know and understand very well and those that may still be somewhat unclear or fuzzy. As with other rehearsal strategies, self-testing of lecture notes has a tremendous payoff.

SUCCESS AT A GLANCE

The Forgetting Curve

The forgetting curve describes the amount of information we forget once it is heard. It is based on a one-hour lecture.

(continued)

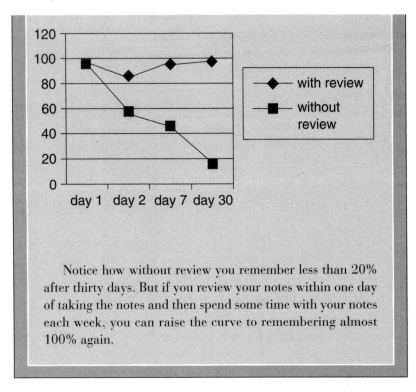

Notice how without review you remember less than 20% after thirty days. But if you review your notes within one day of taking the notes and then spend some time with your notes each week, you can raise the curve to remembering almost 100% again.

Note-Taking Myths

We end this chapter by discussing some myths—information that students tend to believe about note-taking that aren't necessarily so.

- **Myth 1: If You Can't Keep Up with the Professor, Tape Record the Lectures.** The truth is that when students tape lectures, they generally don't listen to the tapes. It's easy to understand why. If you are taking five classes, you hardly have time to do all your reading, studying, and other learning activities, let alone sit and listen to lectures for a second time. In addition, students who tape lectures find it much easier to tune out to what the professor's saying and will miss information written on the chalkboard or overhead. Our advice to you is to go to class, take the best notes you can, and supplement those notes with information from the text, or by forming a study group that has as one of its goals to share notes with everyone. Unless you have a disability that necessitates recording class lectures, tape recording in your courses simply is not an efficient and active way to learn.

- **Myth 2: Copying a Classmate's Notes who is a Better Note-Taker than You Is Better than Struggling with it Yourself.** Think back to sometime in your distant past when you may have actually copied someone's homework. How much did you learn from that experience? We would guess not much. You won't learn much from copying someone else's lecture notes either. A better plan is to compare your lecture notes with a classmates. That can be a very positive and active strategy and you just might learn from your classmate some ways to take better notes.

- **Myth 3: It's Impossible to Take Notes in a Class That Involves Discussion.** When we have observed students in classes that involve a lot of discussion, we see very little note-taking going on. Students seem to think that only information presented by the professor has any merit and fail to write down any comments made by their peers. However, if you think about the purpose of classes that involve discussion, you'll realize that the professor's role is generally just to initiate the discussion. It's the students who actually generate the ideas and these ideas often find their way to the exam. We recommend that for a discussion class, you modify the note-taking process somewhat. Rather than dividing your paper into a narrow and a wide margin, divide it into three equal columns. In the first column, write the question that is being posed or the theory that is being debated. In the second column, take notes on what the professor has to say about it. In the last column, take notes on what your classmates say. Then when you are studying, you can evaluate your classmate's comments and evaluate which ones are worth studying and which ones can be ignored. One of our graduate students modified this technique by adding possible test questions or paper topics and text page numbers to help her relate the discussion to her reading. Here is an example from her notes from a psychology of creativity class. Notice how she formatted the notes to follow the flow of conversation.

Discussion Notes

Question Posed	Professor's comments	Student comments
Must creativity result in a product?		Depends on how you look @ it-whose perspective? Artist-process
TQ? Process is more important than product. Defend or refute this statement	So which is more important process or product?	Public-product
p. 283 creativity outcomes	Does an idea count as a product?	Product. Have to have tangible evidence of creativity

- **Myth 4: If My Professor Provides Notes by Putting them on the Web or Handing them out in Class, I Don't Have to Take Notes.** We have noticed that students tend to earn lower grades in classes where the notes are provided. This is probably because most students don't interact with their notes and therefore don't learn the material until test time. We suggest that you print out the notes and take them to class each day. As you listen to the lecture, fill in gaps by adding detail and providing examples. You can also make special note of topics emphasized by the professor. Then, to be sure you understand the concepts in your notes, after each class use the T-Method.

The T-Method

1. Draw a T at the bottom 1/4 of your last page of notes (you can use the back of the page if you need more room).
2. On the left side of the page, summarize the key points of the lecture.
3. On the right side of the page, predict some test questions about the material.

Example of the T-Method

Summary	Questions
Memory consists of 3 systems 1. encoding, 2. storage, 3. retrieval.	1. What are the three memory systems? Define and describe characteristics?

(continued)

Summary	Questions
Information first goes into short-term memory through rehearsal (maintenance or elaborative) where it is either encoded or forgotten quickly (less than 30 sec) Information that is encoded goes into long-term memory	2. Compare and contrast maintenance and elaborative rehearsal. 3. How does information move from STM to LTM?

☐ Real College
Chad's Challenge

DIRECTIONS: Read the following *Real College* scenario and respond to the questions based on what you learned in this chapter.

"Why did I ever sign up for this 8 o'clock class?" Chad wondered as he dragged himself out of bed at around 7:30. Everyday it was a real challenge . . . and he even liked Professor Wilson's anthropology class. He was, however, experiencing some trouble.

Chad never had problems taking notes in high school. His teachers spoke slowly and would repeat information when students asked. Plus, most of his high school teachers gave study guides to prepare for the tests, so all he had to do was to look up the answers that came mostly from the teacher's lectures. But Professor Wilson talked so fast and tried to get so much in one lecture that Chad usually only got a small portion of the key ideas that were presented. Then, because he was often late to class, he would walk in during the middle of an extended comment and would be unable to figure out what Professor Wilson was talking about. His notes were disorganized and full of doodles and more than once he almost fell out of his seat when he nodded off. Chad tried two different solutions prior to the first exam. First, he gave up taking notes altogether and brought a tape recorder to class. Second, he borrowed a classmate's notes and copied them. He made a very low D.

After this poor performance, he decided that he really didn't know how to take notes from Professor Wilson. He wanted to put in a concerted effort to take notes once again, but he was unsure of what to do.

What advice would you give to Chad so that he can improve? (You are not allowed to advise him to drop the class and take it later in the day during the next term.)

☐ Thinking Critically
Something to Think About and Discuss

We have offered some reasons why self-questioning works in practice here and in other chapters in this book. From what you have learned so far:

- What are the benefits of testing yourself on your notes?

- How important do you think it is to share and discuss your notes with a classmate?

- What are the benefits and drawbacks to reviewing your notes each day?

☐ Follow-Up Activities

1. Try taking notes in all of your classes using the split-page method, discussion, or T-method for one week. Be sure to write questions or annotations. Then evaluate what you like and don't like about these methods. How might you modify these methods to suit your own note-taking preferences?

2. For each of your current classes, try to determine how much overlap there is between the text and the lecture. Do your professors' test questions come primarily from the lectures or the text? How will this information affect your note-taking?

CHAPTER 11

USING TECHNOLOGY TO LEARN

Read this chapter to answer the following questions:

- How is technology being used in college classes?
- What are the benefits and drawbacks to distance learning?
- How can technology be used in studying?
- How should students evaluate Internet information?

SELF-ASSESSMENT

DIRECTIONS: On a scale of 1 to 5 with 1 being "not at all true of me," 3 being "somewhat true of me," and 5 being "very true of me," respond to each of the statements below.

1. I can use a computer to check and send e-mail.   1   2   3   4   5
2. I can use a word processing system well to type   1   2   3   4   5
   my papers.
3. I know how to send file attachments.   1   2   3   4   5
4. I can find information easily on the Internet.   1   2   3   4   5
5. I seek out my professors' Web pages when   1   2   3   4   5
   available.

6. I have taken or am considering taking a   1   2   3   4   5
distance-learning course.

7. I feel comfortable using a computer.   1   2   3   4   5

8. I use my computer when I study.   1   2   3   4   5

The more number 5's you have marked, the more at ease you are with the technology that will play a major role in your life for the next few years. Read on for some tips about the use of technology in college learning.

Computers are becoming a necessity on most college campuses today. In fact, a good number of colleges are now requiring freshmen to purchase or lease a computer before they begin their first semester. Chances are you have had some opportunity to interact with computers in your high school, but most students have not considered how technology can be used to make learning more efficient in college. This chapter will discuss ways that technology is currently being used in college classes and how you can use technology to aid your learning.

Technology in College Classes

Most of your college professors will incorporate technology (specifically computers and the Internet) into their classes. But expect to find a wide range in the level of integration. Some professors will be from the old school—low-tech holdouts who won't even have an e-mail account. Other professors will use high-tech presentations during class with special effect extravaganzas. Most professors fall somewhere in the middle and use technology where they find it to be most beneficial for explaining course content and supporting classroom instruction. You can expect to see some or all of the following uses of technology as part of your college courses:

- **Computerized Class Presentations (such as PowerPoint).** Many professors use computer slides to outline their lectures. They may use overheads of diagrams or show video clips to emphasize points. They may also display Web pages or other Internet sources of information during class.

- **Computerized Notes.** It is becoming more common for professors to put their notes up on the Web. As discussed in Chapter 10, Web notes are best used as a supplement or guide for taking your own notes in class. You may also find yourself in a classroom equipped with computers or computer hookups that allow you to take notes on a laptop. Such classrooms are called "smart classrooms" and are equipped with the latest technology. This is a wonderful service that we suggest you take advantage of if it is available on your campus.

- **Computer Modules or CD-ROM Supplements.** Some professors place sample questions or problems on the Web so that students can evaluate their understanding of the course material as they prepare for exams. Other professors (especially in the sciences) provide supplementary material on CD-ROMs. These CDs generally contain information that cannot be depicted in a text format, such as a video of a chemical reaction, but enhances the information discussed in a lecture or in the text.

- **Computerized Course Management Systems (such as Web CT).** Professors using these course management systems find many creative uses for them. They may place their syllabi, quizzes, assignments, and other course information on there. They may also post student grades or have virtual chats with the class. We even know a professor who conducts exam reviews online. If your professor uses these systems, plan to visit the site often to keep up on new assignments or important information.

- **Course Exams.** Some courses will require you to take exams on a computer. Many mathematics courses are moving toward computerized exams and many English courses require students to write in-class essays on computers. Taking an exam on a computer is a bit different than the old paper and pencil type. But, basically you should not abandon your old-test taking strategies. Continue to read each question carefully and answer the items you know first. However, you should find out whether you can return to a question or if you must answer each item before moving on to the next one. Some students say that having exams on computers takes some getting used to, but once you have some experience, it is just like taking any other test.

- **Readings.** Your professors may assign readings that can only be found online. They may be from Web-based journals, supplied by the campus library's online service, or from any number of other sources. If you find you have trouble reading online, as many people do, we suggest you print it out in advance.

- **E-mail Assignments.** Professors may require you to turn in assignments over e-mail. If it is a short assignment, typing your response straight into the e-mail message is generally acceptable. If, however, you are required to turn in a longer assignment (more than one page), it is best to type it in a word processing program and send it as a file attachment. Be sure to use the file type requested by your professor. If you do not know how to do this, go to the nearest computer lab to get some help.

- **Group Presentations.** At some point in your college career, you will probably find yourself in a course that requires a group presentation that has a technology component. Some professors require a Web-based presentation or a presentation that utilizes several types of media. We suggest that you meet with your group early and often and try out the technology several times before presenting it in class to work out any problems.

- **Discussion Groups and Listservs.** These supports are used to generate discussion outside the class. Some professors even require each student to post a certain number of messages each week to ensure that the listserv is used. You can ask questions or see what other people are thinking to gain multiple perspectives on the course information.

You will probably find several other ways that professors incorporate technology into their courses as new tools become available.

NETWORKING

Building Background Knowledge

You can use the Internet to help you build your background knowledge of the content for your college courses. For one of your classes this semester, choose a topic that interests you and then visit several sites on the Web to find out more about it. Often getting some additional information will help you understand difficult material (and can even help you become more motivated to learn in the class).

Distance Learning

Most college campuses offer some form of distance learning. Distance learning was started because colleges wanted to find a way to serve a greater population of people who, for a variety of reasons, could not attend courses on campus. Currently, many full-time students are taking distance-learning courses as well because they find them a convenient way to round out their schedule.

There are two main types of distance-learning courses:

1. **Asynchronous courses.** These are the most common type. In an asynchronous course, classes do not meet at any particular time and you can learn at your own pace. If you have any questions, you usually ask them via e-mail. These courses are especially good for students who need the flexibility to do the course work at any time of day.

2. **Synchronous courses.** In this type of course, students and the professor meet on computers at the same time of day. Such courses more closely follow the traditional classroom format. In fact, your professor may even use a computer interface that shows a row of desks and a teacher in the front of the room. Synchronous courses allow for more interaction between professors and students and questions can be asked as needed.

SUCCESS AT A GLANCE

Benefits and Drawbacks to Distance Learning

Benefits	Drawbacks
• Can complete course work anywhere and at any time	• Less (or no) face-to-face contact with professor and other students

(continued)

Benefits	Drawbacks
• Fosters independent work	• Students need to be self-motivated, good time managers, and have the ability to learn on their own
• Provides greater access to college courses	• Can run into technology problems that interfere with the ability to get course information
• Good for students with work and family obligations	• The technology can distract from the content
• Allows students to set their own learning pace	• Often, there is no one available to respond to questions quickly

To figure out if a distance-learning course might be right for you, think about the benefits and drawbacks listed above. Do you need the flexibility that a distance-learning course can provide? Will you be able to manage your self and your time so that you complete course requirements with very little guidance?

Using Technology to Study

Some students have found that using a computer can greatly aid in learning and studying for courses. Here are some of the ways that students are using technology in learning:

- **Organizing Lecture Notes.** Some students like to retype their lecture notes because typing them on the computer helps them reorganize the information. We know of one student in an art history course who cut and pasted slides of paintings from her professor's Web site (and some from museum Web sites) right into her own notes. That way she could see the painting as she studied her notes about it. Some students like to take notes on their personal digital assistant (PDA—such as a Palm Pilot) in class as another way to help organize all of the course information.

- **Creating Maps and Charts.** There are several software programs that can help you create wonderful concept maps and charts in a snap. These maps and charts help you organize and synthesize ideas (as discussed in Chapter 13).

- **Meeting with Virtual Study Groups.** Students can set up online study groups to meet at designated times before exams. This is a great way to study with others because the group tends to stay more on task than in a face-to-face study group.

- **Researching Information for Papers and Presentations.** The Internet can be a wonderful source of information when researching information for class presentations or papers. Of course, you need to be careful about the quality of the information you get (see the next section for strategies for evaluation Internet information). You also need to be careful that you do not plagiarize information from the Web.

This list is certainly not exhaustive. And with new technologies coming out every day we are sure you will find other ways to incorporate technology into your learning and studying.

COLLEGE CAMPUS TODAY

Plagiarism Taboos

With more and more students gaining access to Internet information, many campuses have seen an increase in student plagiarism. We believe that this is partially due to the fact that many students do not understand what plagiarism is. So let's lay it out for you. Plagiarism is taking someone else's ideas

(continued)

and representing them as your own. This includes a theory or idea, a direct quote, a paraphrase of an idea, or pieces of information that are not common knowledge. To avoid plagiarism, be sure to give credit to the author whenever you use someone else's ideas in your own work.

Of course, plagiarism also includes direct cheating such as buying a paper online, turning in another person's work as your own, or copying directly out of another text without quoting the author. It is easy to avoid this type of plagiarism—just don't do it. When you find information on the Internet (or from any other source) be sure to report where that information came from.

Evaluating Internet Information

You can find it all on the Internet: world-class thinking to pure garbage to blatant lies. Anyone can put up a Web page that looks good. But just because it is well designed, it doesn't mean that the content is good. How can you decide what to believe? There are several ways to evaluate the credibility and quality of the information you find online. Consider the following criteria each time you surf the Web:

- **Sourcing.** Who is the author of this information? Is it a noted expert in the field, a high school student doing a report for school, a fan, a business, or an organization? Your answer to this question will tell you a lot about the quality of the information. In general, it is best to trust the information from the authority in the field over a fan or hobbyist.

- **Purpose.** What is the reason for this site to exist? Is it trying to educate, inform, or is it trying to market a product? Although commercial Web sites can sound very persuasive, if they are trying to sell you something, you need to take that into consideration when evaluating the information you find.

- **Corroboration.** How does this information compare with other Web sites? Usually there is a good deal of overlap, but if you find a site that is claiming ideas that no one else is discussing, that should send up a red flag for credibility. Try to check out a few sources to help you determine corroboration.

- **Accuracy.** Is the information you find correct? Several of the criteria on this list should help you determine the truthfulness of the information you are finding. One idea that applies in this case is that if the information sounds too good to be true then it probably is false.

- **Timeliness.** How current is the information? Because the Web is an ever-changing source of information, in general, the more current the source, the better. Most Web pages tell you the last time the site was updated. If no one has updated it in a long time, you might want to visit a more current site.

- **Bias.** Does the information seem to represent a particular point of view or is it trying to present an unbiased view? Most sites will contain some sort of bias. Your job is to use these other criteria on this list to figure out what it is.

QUICK TAKES

Internet Intelligence

The ability to evaluate the credibility and quality of information is a skill that will serve you for a lifetime. We are continually exposed to new information—on the computer, from television, radio, newspapers, friends, and so on. In fact, as access to technology increases, so does the amount of information with which we must cope each day. Of course, not all of this information will be of high quality, so the evaluation criteria discussed in this chapter will help you determine what to believe and what to question. Knowing how to evaluate information will help you when you watch the news, read a movie review, hear about the latest medical statistics, or just about any time you are presented with new ideas.

□ Real College
Leah's Laptop

DIRECTIONS: Read the following *Real College* scenario and respond to the questions based on what you learned in this chapter.

Leah's parents bought her a state-of-the-art laptop computer as a high school graduation gift. She has had a great time using it to chat with her old high school friends and surf the Internet. Her father asked her how the computer was helping her in her studies and she just stared at him speechless. It hadn't even occurred to her to use her computer to study.

Leah decided that she would like to use her computer to study (she says that she'll take all the help she can get). This semester she is taking a history course that requires her to read a textbook, a daily newspaper, and to watch two movies about the Vietnam conflict. She will have to take several essay exams and write a paper connecting current events to the movies she chose to view.

She is also enrolled in an accounting course, which has turned out to be tougher than she expected. She is starting to get to know some of her classmates and hopes to form a study group before the next exam so that they can review problems together.

Leah is enjoying her biology class, but realized after speaking with her father that she had not even opened the CD-ROM that came with the book, which provides examples, diagrams, and sample problems. She is not sure how to approach using it to help her study.

Leah is not sure where to begin. She knows that she can use her laptop in all of these courses, but does not know what to do. Based on what you have learned in this chapter, give advice to Leah. How can technology help her in each of these different situations?

☐ Thinking Critically
Something to Think About and Discuss

- Think about the courses you are taking this term. How is technology being utilized? Are some courses more technology-based than others? To what do you attribute the differences you find?

- How can you use technology to help you learn and study in each of your courses? Are there some courses that lend themselves better to the use of technology? If so, why?

☐ Follow-Up Activities

Use the criteria for evaluating credibility and quality on your favorite Internet Web site.

1. What component of credibility do you find? What components are lacking?

2. What is your overall impression of the believability of information on this site and why?

PART FOUR

IDENTIFYING YOUR LEARNING STRATEGIES

Part IV introduces you to a wide variety of strategies for active learning. We have included three brief selections from college level texts. The first piece, from a history text, discusses the Cuban missile crisis. The second piece, from a psychology text, presents research on the effects of prototypes. The third piece, from a biology text, discusses covalent bonds. The information from these text excerpts is used throughout the remainder of *College Success Strategies* as we present the learning and study strategies.

In Chapter 12, you learn about strategies for gearing up and for concentrating as you read. You learn about the importance of creating a good environment for learning. You also learn strategies for staying active and concentrating during reading.

In Chapter 13, you learn about the importance of rehearsal and review strategies. We discuss strategies for both verbal and written rehearsal to help you remember and retrieve what you have studied. You also learn strategies to help you organize information to review as you prepare for exams.

from **Penguin Academics**

The American Story

Robert A. Divine
University of Texas

T. H. Breen
Northwestern University

George M. Fredrickson
Stanford University

R. Hal Williams
Southern Methodist University

Containing Fidel Castro: The Bay of Pigs Fiasco

1   Kennedy's determination to check global communist expansion reached a peak of intensity in Cuba. In the 1960 campaign, pointing to the growing ties between the Soviet Union and Fidel Castro's regime, he had accused the Republicans of permitting a "communist satellite" to arise on "our very doorstep." Kennedy had even issued a statement backing "anti-Castro forces in exile," calling them "fighters for freedom" who held out hope for "overthrowing Castro."

2   In reality, the Eisenhower administration had been training a group of Cuban exiles in Guatemala since March 1960 as part of a CIA plan to topple the Castro regime. Many of the new president's advisers had doubts about the proposed invasion. The president, however, committed by his own campaign rhetoric and assured of success by the military, decided to proceed.

3   On April 17, 1961, fourteen hundred Cuban exiles moved ashore at the Bay of Pigs on the southern coast of Cuba. Even though the United States had masterminded the entire operation, Kennedy insisted on covert action, even canceling at the last minute a planned American air strike on the beachhead. With air superiority, Castro's well-trained forces had no difficulty in quashing the invasion. They

killed nearly five hundred exiles and forced the rest to surrender within forty-eight hours.

4   Aghast at the swiftness of the defeat, President Kennedy took personal responsibility for the failure. In his address to the American people, however, he showed no remorse for arranging the violation of a neighboring country's sovereignty, only regret at the outcome. Above all, he expressed renewed defiance, warning the Soviets that "our restraint is not inexhaustible." For the remainder of his presidency, Kennedy continued to harass the Castro regime, imposing an economic blockade on Cuba, supporting a continuing series of raids by exile groups operating out of Florida, and failing to stop the CIA from experimenting with bizarre plots to assassinate Fidel Castro.

Containing Castro: The Cuban Missile Crisis

5   The climax of Kennedy's crusade came in October 1962 with the Cuban missile crisis. Throughout the summer and early fall, the Soviets engaged in a massive arms buildup in Cuba, ostensibly to protect Castro from an American invasion. In the United States, Republican candidates in the 1962 congressional elections called for a firm American response; Kennedy contented himself with a stern warning against the introduction of any offensive weapons, believing their presence would directly threaten American security. Khrushchev publicly denied any such intent, but secretly he took a daring gamble, building sites for twenty-four medium-range (1000-mile) and eighteen intermediate-range (2000-mile) missiles in Cuba. Later he claimed his purpose was purely defensive, but most likely he was responding to the pressures from his own military to close the enormous strategic gap in nuclear striking power that Kennedy had opened.

6   On October 14, 1962, American U-2 planes finally discovered the missile sites that were nearing completion. As soon as he learned of the Russian action, Kennedy decided to seek a showdown with Khrushchev. Insisting on absolute secrecy, he convened a special group of advisers to consider the way to respond.

7   An initial preference for an immediate air strike gradually gave way to discussion of either a full-scale invasion or a naval blockade. The president and his advisers ruled out diplomacy, rejecting a proposal to offer the withdrawal of obsolete American Jupiter missiles

from Turkey in return for a similar Russian pullout in Cuba. Kennedy finally agreed to a two-step procedure. He would proclaim a quarantine of Cuba to prevent the arrival of new missiles and threaten a nuclear confrontation to force the removal of those already there. If the Russians did not cooperate, then the United States would invade Cuba and dismantle the missiles by force.

8   On the evening of October 22, the president informed the nation of the existence of the Soviet missiles and his plans to remove them. He spared no words in blaming Khrushchev for "this clandestine, reckless, and provocative threat to world peace," and he made it clear that any missile attack from Cuba would lead to "a full retaliatory response upon the Soviet Union."

9   For the next six days, the world hovered on the brink of nuclear catastrophe. Khrushchev replied defiantly, accusing Kennedy of pushing mankind "to the abyss of a world nuclear-missile war." In the Atlantic, some sixteen Soviet ships continued on course toward Cuba, while the American navy was deployed to intercept them five hundred miles from the island.

10   The first break came at midweek when the Soviet ships suddenly halted to avert a confrontation at sea. "We're eyeball to eyeball," commented Secretary of State Dean Rusk, "and I think the other fellow just blinked." On Friday, Khrushchev sent Kennedy a long, rambling letter offering a face-saving way out—Russia would remove the missiles in return for an American promise never to invade Cuba. The president was ready to accept when a second Russian message raised the stakes by insisting that American Jupiter missiles be withdrawn from Turkey. Kennedy refused to bargain. Nevertheless, while the military went ahead with plans for the invasion of Cuba, the president, heeding his brother's advice, decided to make one last appeal for peace. Ignoring the second Russian message, he sent a cable to Khrushchev accepting his original offer.

11   On Saturday night, October 27, Robert Kennedy—the president's brother and most trusted adviser—met with Soviet ambassador Anatoly Dobrynin to make it clear this was the last chance to avert nuclear confrontation. "We had to have a commitment by tomorrow that those bases would be removed," Robert Kennedy recalled telling him. Then the president's brother calmly remarked

that if Khrushchev did not back down, "there would be not only dead Americans but dead Russians as well."

12   In reality, John F. Kennedy was not quite so ready to risk nuclear war. He instructed his brother to assure Dobrynin that the Jupiter missiles would soon be removed from Turkey. The president preferred that the missile swap be done privately, but twenty-five years later, Secretary of State Dean Rusk revealed that JFK had instructed him to arrange a deal through the United Nations involving "the removal of both the Jupiters and the missiles in Cuba." In recently released transcripts of his meetings with his advisers, the president reaffirmed his intention of making a missile trade with Khrushchev publicly as a last resort to avoid nuclear war. "We can't very well invade Cuba with all its toil," he commented, "when we could have gotten them out by making a deal on the same missiles in Turkey."

13   President Kennedy never had to make this final concession. At nine the next morning, Khrushchev agreed to remove the missiles in return only for Kennedy's promise not to invade Cuba. The crisis was over.

14   The world, however, had come perilously close to a nuclear conflict. We now know the Soviets had nuclear warheads in Cuba, not only for twenty of the medium-range missiles, but also for short-range tactical launchers designed to be used against an American invading force. If Kennedy had approved the military's recommendations for an invasion of Cuba, the consequences might have been disastrous.

15   The peaceful resolution of the Cuban missile crisis became a personal and political triumph for John F. Kennedy. His party successfully overcame the Republican challenge in the November elections, and his own popularity reached new heights. The American people, on the defensive since *Sputnik*, suddenly felt that they had proved their superiority over the Russians.

16   The Cuban missile crisis had more substantial results as well. Shaken by their close call, Kennedy and Khrushchev agreed to install a "hot line" to speed direct communication between Washington and Moscow in an emergency. Long-stalled negotiations over the reduction of nuclear testing suddenly resumed, leading to the limited test ban treaty of 1963, which outlawed tests in the atmosphere while still permitting them underground. Above all, Kennedy displayed a new

maturity as a result of the crisis. In a speech at American University in June 1963, he shifted from the rhetoric of confrontation to that of conciliation. Speaking of the Russians, he said, "Our most basic common link is the fact that we all inhabit this planet. We all breathe the same air. We all cherish our children's future. And we are all mortal."

17   Despite those hopeful words, the missile crisis also had an unfortunate consequence. Those who believed that the Russians understood only the language of force were confirmed in their penchant for a hard line. The Russian leaders drew similar conclusions. Aware the United States had a four-to-one advantage in nuclear striking power during the Cuban crisis, one Soviet official told his American counterpart, "Never will we be caught like this again." After 1962, the Soviets embarked on a crash program to build up their navy and to overtake the American lead in nuclear missiles. Within five years, they had the nucleus of a modern fleet and had surpassed the United States in ICBMs. Kennedy's fleeting moment of triumph thus ensured the escalation of the arms race. His legacy was a bittersweet one of short-term success and long-term anxiety.

---

from **Psychology: The Brain, the Person, the World**

Prototypes That Lead to Heavy Drinking

Stephen M. Kosslyn
Harvard University

Robin S. Rosenberg
Adjunct Faculty
Lesley College

1   Prototypes not only play a key role in thinking, they also affect how we behave. Gibbons and Gerrard (1995) theorized that whether someone will engage in a health-risk behavior, such as excessive

drinking of alcohol, depends on how similar they think they are to a prototype of the typical person who engages in that behavior. Blanton and colleagues (1997) tested this theory by studying 463 adolescents (roughly half male, half female) who lived in rural Iowa. To assess prototypes for drinking, the participants were told, "We would like you to think for a minute about the *type of person your age who drinks (alcohol)* frequently." They stressed that they were not interested in anyone in particular, just "the typical teenage drinker." Following this introduction, the participants were given a set of adjectives and rated the degree to which those adjectives described their prototype. On the basis of these ratings, Blanton and colleagues inferred the degree to which the typical teenage drinker was generally viewed by the participant as "self-assured–together (such as self-confident and independent), unattractive (unattractive and dull), or immature (immature and careless)." To the extent that an individual participant rated people who drink high on the first factor and low on the other two, he or she was said to have a "positive prototype" of drinkers.

2   Three results are of particular interest. First, participants who had more positive prototypes of drinkers reported drinking more. This was exactly as predicted, if feeling that you are similar to the prototype shapes your behavior. Second, the positive prototype itself was apparently a consequence of the participant's peer group; the more their peers tended to drink, the more the participants tended to drink. Third, adolescents who had poor relationships with their parents were more likely to associate with a drinking peer group. Thus, the parents had an indirect influence on drinking by affecting the choice of peer group, which in turn affected the prototype.

3   Consider these findings from the levels perspective: The brain is set up to store representations of prototypes. In this case the prototypes arose from social experience, particularly with the peer group. In addition, social interactions with the parents led teens to favor particular peer groups, which in turn helped mold a positive prototype for drinking. And the prototype in turn affects behavior. The events interact: By becoming a heavier drinker, a person will tend to spend more time with a peer group of drinkers, which in turn will further mold his or her prototypes.

from **Biology: Concepts & Connections,**
Third Edition

Covalent Bonds, the Sharing of Electrons, Join Atoms into Molecules

Neil A. Campbell

Lawrence G. Mitchell

Jane B. Reece

1   The second kind of strong chemical bond is the **covalent bond,** in which two atoms share one or more pairs of outer-shell electrons. Two or more atoms held together by covalent bonds form a **molecule.** For example, a covalent bond connects the two hydrogen atoms in the molecule H_2, a common gas in the atmosphere. The figure at the right shows three ways to represent this molecule. The symbol, H_2, called the molecular formula, merely tells you that the molecule consists of two atoms of hydrogen. The middle diagram shows that the atoms share 2 electrons, and in doing so, both fill their outer (only) shells. At the right, you see a structural formula. The line between the hydrogen atoms stands for the single covalent bond formed by the sharing of one pair of electrons.

2   The number of single covalent bonds an atom can form is equal to the number of additional electrons needed to fill its outer shell. H can form one covalent bond; O can form two; N, three; and C, four. However, as you can see in the figure here, in an O_2 molecule, each O atom does not form two single bonds. Instead, the two O atoms share two pairs of electrons, forming a **double bond.** In the structural formula, the double bond is indicated by a pair of lines between the O atoms.

3   H_2 and O_2 are molecules, but because they are composed of only one element, they are not compounds. An example of a molecule that is a compound is methane (CH_4), a common gas produced by certain

bacteria. As you can see in the figure, each of the four hydrogen atoms in this molecule shares one pair of electrons with the single carbon atom. The same type of bonding occurs in molecules of water, a compound so important to life that we devote the next six modules to it.

ALTERNATIVE WAYS TO REPRESENT MOLECULES

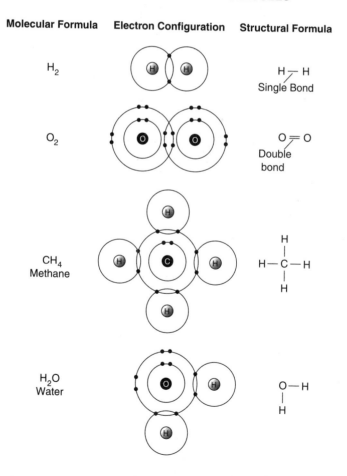

Molecular Formula	Electron Configuration	Structural Formula
H_2		H — H Single Bond
O_2		O = O Double bond
CH_4 Methane		H—C—H (with H above and H below)
H_2O Water		O—H (with H below)

CHAPTER 12

STRATEGIC READING

Read this chapter to answer the following questions:

- Why do you need to gear up before reading and studying?
- What are some strategies for gearing up?
- What is the difference between active and passive reading?
- What are some strategies for concentrating on textbook reading?

SELF-ASSESSMENT

DIRECTIONS: Answer each of the following questions by answering yes or no. This will give you an idea of how actively you read your textbooks.

	Yes	No
1. Do you have an idea of the concepts that are presented in the chapter before you start to read?	___	___
2. Do you set some goals prior to reading?	___	___
3. Do you reflect on what you are going to read?	___	___
4. Do you try to personalize your reading to help you understand it better?	___	___
5. Do you write in your textbooks when you read?	___	___

6. Do you try to put important text information in your own words? _____ _____

7. Do you think about the visual aids in the chapter? _____ _____

8. Do you try to summarize what you have read? _____ _____

9. Do you reflect on ideas during reading? _____ _____

10. Do you understand most of what you have read? _____ _____

11. Do you ask for clarification when you don't understand what you have read? _____ _____

12. Do you keep up with your reading? _____ _____

If you answered yes to most of these questions, you are off to a good start. If you answered no to most of these questions, this chapter should help you get on track.

Reading is something that every college student needs to do every day. But are you getting what you need out of your text reading, or are you just spinning your wheels? Do you find that your first half-hour is unproductive because you are not concentrating on what you are doing? Do you close your book after an hour or so and feel as though you have accomplished little? Maybe the reason is that you have not geared up for reading actively.

Gearing Up For Reading

Picture a track meet at a local college. The athletes pile out of a van just as the first race begins. They throw off their sweats and start running. Would that ever happen? Of course not. Just as an athlete would never run a race or even practice "cold" you should not expect to start reading or studying without warming up in some way. Athletes warm up to get their muscles ready to perform. Students, on the other hand, need to warm up their brains so that they will be more efficient and productive when they read.

There are several activities you can engage in order to gear up for reading. You should:

1. **Create a good learning environment.** Think about the place where you currently read and study by asking yourself the following

questions: Do you study in a setting that allows you to concentrate and study effectively? Are you constantly distracted by people, noise, or other diversions? Your learning environment can help you in a positive way when reading or studying or, if you do not have a good setting, it can actually hinder your efforts. You need to create a place that is free from distractions and allows you to maximize your studying time, so consider these factors:

- **Noise level.** Some students say that they need complete quiet to study. Even hearing a clock ticking in the background is enough to distract them. Other students say that they study best in a crowded, noisy room because the noise actually helps them concentrate. Some study most successfully when they are in familiar surroundings such as their bedroom; for others familiar surroundings do not make a difference. Some students like quiet music playing; others do not. The point is, you should know the level of noise that is optimal for your own studying. However, one general rule for all students is that the television seems to be more of a distraction than music or other background noise, so we suggest you leave the TV off when you are reading or studying. Also, don't let yourself become distracted by computer games or Internet surfing when you are trying to study.

- **Your special "learning" place.** You can also concentrate better when you read or study in a straight-backed chair, such as a desk or kitchen chair, than you can on your bed. In addition, your ideal learning place is one where the only thing you do there is study. If you have a desk, set it up so that you have everything handy—pens and pencils, a tablet of paper, calculator, your books and notes or anything else you need to study. If you find that you cannot create an effective learning environment in your home because there are too many distractions, try to find a quiet place on campus to study, such as the library or the student union.

2. **Survey your textbooks.** After setting up your learning environment at the beginning of the term, the next step in gearing up is examining your textbooks for each course. Some textbooks are written and formatted in a way that is very reader friendly. Such textbooks have some or all of the following features:

- Preview questions or an organizer at the beginning of each chapter to help readers focus on what they are about to learn.

- Diagrams, pictures, and figures to give readers a better picture of the topic.

- **Bold-faced** or *italicized* words to emphasize key terms. summary or review questions at the end of each chapter.

- Large margins so that readers have room to write notes as they read.

In order to determine if your textbooks are reader friendly, examine the way they are arranged. Surveying your texts will help you by:

- Familiarizing you with the topics to be covered so that you can activate what you already know.

- Increasing your interest in reading the chapters.

- Giving yourself the time you need to gear up for reading effectively.

3. **Preview your reading assignments.** You have found a quiet place to study and you have all of your studying tools at your fingertips. Now you're ready to gear up for the day's reading by previewing. Previewing the chapter doesn't take very long, but just as surveying your entire textbook helped you gear up for each course, previewing what you will read today will help to activate your prior knowledge and it will build your interest in the topic. Previewing consists of the following steps:

- **Read the chapter title.** The title tells you about the overall topic of the chapter and may clue you into the author's intent.

- **Read the headings and subheadings.** The headings and subheadings will tell you about the specific focus in the chapter and may suggest the author's approach to the topic. For example, a subheading in your history text called "The Horrors of War" would introduce very different material than a subheading called "War: Benefits and Advances."

- **Read the boldfaced or italicized terms.** These terms will clue you in to ideas that will be emphasized in the text and will point out new vocabulary or content-specific terms that will be discussed in the chapter.

- **Note the typographical aids.** Besides boldfaced or italicized words, many texts use graphs, charts, tables, or illustrations to emphasize key ideas. Read these sections to find out what is important in the chapter.

- **Read the introduction.** If your textbook offers chapter introductions, it is a good idea to read this section when you preview the chapter to get an idea of what the topic is about and the scope of information that will be covered in the chapter.

- **Read the summary.** If your textbook contains chapter summaries, it is a good idea to read this section **before** you actually read the chapter. The summary section outlines the key information you should have learned when reading the chapter.

- **Read the end of the chapter material.** This may include study questions, vocabulary lists, or application exercises. The end material will also tell you what is important in the chapter.

Although this might sound like a lot to do before reading, previewing actually takes a only few minutes to accomplish because you are not getting bogged down in the details of the chapter. Your purpose in previewing is to get a general idea of the concepts that will be covered in the chapter.

4. **Determine your reading purpose.** As you preview a chapter you should begin to think of some questions about the key topics. For example, in previewing the "Turbulent Sixties," which includes the excerpt on the Cuban missile crisis, you might ask yourself how the Soviet Union was involved, Kennedy's response to the crisis, and how it was resolved. By asking questions, you are starting to think about the key ideas contained in the text, which will make your reading more effective. Jot down your questions and try to answer them as you read.

It is always a good idea to read with a purpose in mind. When you are reading your textbooks for a class, your primary purpose is to learn the information contained in each chapter. However, this is a tall order. If you tried to learn every idea contained in every chapter, you probably would have a difficult time. What you need to do is figure out and focus on learning the key ideas contained in each chapter. A good way to help you determine what's important is to use your class syllabus and lecture notes as a guide.

Reading Done "Write": Staying Active During Reading

Have you ever finished reading a text chapter only to realize that you don't remember anything you just read? If so, chances are you were not reading actively. Because reading textbooks rarely tops any student's list of favorite activities, and also because reading textbooks is one of the most common college tasks, it is important to learn strategies that enable you to understand and remember what you read. If you finish "reading" 10 pages of text and can't summarize what you have read, you have just wasted valuable time. So where do you begin?

Put Away Your Highlighters

When we ask students how they go about reading their textbooks, many students tell us that they try to pull out key ideas from their texts by highlighting or underlining during reading. Although this is a popular strategy, highlighting is actually a very passive activity because students do not really understand the ideas they are highlighting. Many students actually put off reading for understanding until after they have highlighted the text. In other words, they skim the text looking for important information, highlight entire sections that seem important, and plan to return to those sections later when they study for the exam.

College Campus Today

Breaking the Highlighting Habit

Some students just gasp when we tell them to get rid of their highlighters. They believe that highlighting is the strategy of choice for most college students. As we try to change their minds and talk more about text annotation, we have them make the transition from highlighting to annotating by purchasing a pen with a highlighter on one end. Such pens are commonly found in college bookstores and office supply stores. We get them into the annotating mode, but when they feel this absolute need to highlight and annotate, they have everything they need right there.

When students mark their texts through highlighting, they are not being very selective; sometimes entire pages are highlighted in bright pink or yellow or blue. Students who highlight most everything have not been very discriminating about what to mark. They will have just as much information to cope with when they begin to study . . . and they will have to go fishing in a pink, yellow, or blue sea in order to find the key points.

On the other hand, some students highlight too little. If these students tried to rely on their highlighting for their test review, they would not have adequate information so they would probably end up rereading the chapters. Our advice to you is to put away your highlighters because you will want to use strategies that promote greater active involvement in reading and learning.

Make a Note of It

Active readers gear up to read by previewing and then they are ready to focus on their reading. One way to be sure that you are concentrating on and understanding what you read is to annotate your text, which requires you to write in your books. We realize this might take a bit of adjusting to because most of you were not allowed to write in your textbooks in high school. But in college, you buy your own books. Be sure you get your money's worth and "write on."

NETWORKING

Learning from Web Pages

Many colleges and universities offer advice for learning from text on their Web pages. First, try to locate these resources at your own institution by looking at an Academic Assistance or Learning Center page. Then, seek out advice from Learning Centers at other institutions using the following keywords: learning center, tutoring center, study strategies, study skills, textbook reading.

What Is Annotation?

In a nutshell, annotation is summing up the information in your text by briefly writing the key ideas in the margin. Unlike highlighting, which promotes passivity, annotation requires that you understand what you are reading. It requires you to actively make decisions about what is important because you are putting the ideas in your own words. As shown below, an annotated piece of text includes key ideas as well as examples, definitions, and other important details about the concepts.

Model Annotations of a History Text

Oct. 1962-Cuban missile crisis
- USSR built up arms in Cuba

- JFK warns Castro
            BUT
Soviets secretly built sites for med. and inter. range missiles

- Khrushchev claimed it was a defensive move; not really so.
- Soviets wanted to close strategic advantage b/t USSR and US

The climax of Kennedy's crusade came in October 1962 with the Cuban missile crisis. Throughout the summer and early fall, the Soviets engaged in a massive arms buildup in Cuba, ostensibly to protect Castro from an American invasion. In the United States, Republican candidates in the 1962 congressional elections called for a firm American response; Kennedy contented himself with a stern warning against the introduction of any offensive weapons, believing their presence would directly threaten American security. Khrushchev publicly denied any such intent, but secretly he took a daring gamble, building sites for twenty-four medium-range (1000-mile) and eighteen intermediate-range (2000-mile) missiles in Cuba. Later he claimed his purpose was purely defensive, but most likely he was responding to the pressures from his own military to close the enormous strategic gap in nuclear striking power that Kennedy had opened.

Excerpted from: Divine, R. A., Breen, T. H., Fredrickson, G. M., & Williams, R. H. (2002). *The American Story.* New York: Longman.

In order to annotate properly, you need to think about what you read before you write. If you find that your mind is wandering or that you are not concentrating, you have to get back on track. Because you stop reading after a few paragraphs to annotate what you have read, you will be able to reconnect with the reading.

Why Annotate Your Text?

Annotating your text is an effective strategy for several reasons. Annotation helps you:

- **Isolate Information.** By annotating your texts, you are selecting important information you want to remember.

- **Reduce Information.** You reduce the information you need to study into more manageable amounts.

- **Organize Information.** Sometimes your textbooks don't do a good job of organizing information. Through annotation you can reorganize the material in a way that is meaningful for you. And that will make it easier for you to remember what you have read and to prepare for exams.

- **Identify Key Concepts.** Annotation also helps you differentiate between major concepts and supporting ideas. Although for most courses you will have to know something about both major concepts and supporting details, by determining what is really important you will know how to focus your studying

- **Monitor Your Learning.** Because you annotate in you own words, you can monitor your understanding of what you are reading. If you are unable to put the information in your own words, you are alerted to the fact that your comprehension is breaking down.

How Do You Annotate?

There are some basic guidelines to follow regardless of what type of text you are annotating. Although you might have to modify these guidelines slightly for special kinds of texts, they will work in a majority of instances.

- **Read First, then Annotate.** To help you decide what to annotate, read a section and then think about what would be important if you were going to teach the material to someone else. When students try to read and annotate at the same time, they end up writing either too much or too little. We generally suggest that if your text does not have clearly defined sections, read at least three or four paragraphs before stopping to annotate. Another alternative is to keep reading until the text seems to move to a new topic.

- **Write Your Annotations in Your Own Words.** Don't copy directly from the book, unless you are annotating something that must be learned exactly as it is stated in the book, such as a chemistry or statistics formula, for example. When you are annotating definitions, you will want to simply paraphrase the author's words so that you don't change the meaning of the definition. Otherwise, put all information into your own words. (See the example below for the difference between paraphrasing and writing in your own words.) Keep in mind that stating things in your own words is a good way of monitoring what you understand. Information that is not understood should not simply be skipped over. Ask for help from another student or from your professor.

Difference Between Paraphrasing and Writing in Your Own Words

	Your text states . . .	Your annotations . . .
Paraphrasing	Two or more atoms held together by covalent bonds form a **molecule.**	Molecules–atoms connected by covalent bonds.
Writing in your own words	Prototypes emerge from our experience with the external world, and new items that might potentially fit within their category are then compared with them. The more attributes new items share with an existing prototype, the more likely they are to be included within the concept.	Prototypes–a system for organizing concepts into categories based on similar traits. Items with more traits in common are more likely to be included.

What Type of Information Should You Annotate?

In Chapter 10 when we discussed taking lecture notes, you were briefly introduced to the concept of annotation. Annotating your textbooks is similar because you are isolating the information you need to study and learn. Regardless of the content area, you should look for the following types of information whenever you annotate:

- **Definitions,** especially content-specific terms and concepts. Content-specific terms are words you find in that particular subject. For example, **prototype** (p. 174) is a content-specific term in the brief psychology passage. **Covalent bond** (p. 176) is a content-specific term from the biology excerpt. **Ostensibly** (p. 171) from the history excerpt is not a content-specific word. If you did not know the definition for ostensibly, you might look it up in the dictionary, but you would not include it in your annotations.

- **Examples** are also important to annotate because they depict specific instances, theories, experiments, cases, and so forth. Text examples often show up on your tests, so it is crucial to note them. You also should include personal examples when you can, because relating the information to what you already know will help you better remember the information. Or if the text does not provide an example, but you can think of one that helps you, add that information to your annotations.

- **Predicted test questions** are also an important consideration. When you read, try to predict some likely test questions about the material. Be sure to ask higher-level questions as well as questions that connect your reading to the class lecture. Higher-level questions are those that require more than just memorization of facts; they require application of the concept.

- **People, dates, places, and events** are important in certain types of courses like history, social science, and political science. A word of caution, however. This should not be the only type of information you annotate. The types of questions you will usually be asked in college require you to think at a higher level about the significance of the names, dates, and events. The only reason you annotate this type of information is to get a chronology of events. Be sure that you think about how the information fits into the larger context of the material.

- **Numbered lists or characteristics** contained in your text should also be annotated. If your text states that "there are 3 major causes of," or reasons for, or factors that contribute to a certain idea, annotate them by numbering them in the margin. In this way, you are connecting and learning those ideas together. Reader-friendly texts generally cue you to how many reasons or characteristics you should annotate, but less friendly texts do not. Even though the text may not point out how many there are, you should be aware and number the lists.

- **Relationships between concepts,** such as causes/effects or comparison/contrasts, are important to note. When you read your text, look for relationships between concepts, even if the text doesn't explicitly point them out. They will help you reorganize the information in a meaningful way.

- **Graphs, charts, diagrams** and other visuals are important to annotate because they often contain information that is not anywhere else in the text. In addition, graphs and diagrams can also provide good examples of the concepts discussed in the text.

Quick Takes

Annotation Beyond the Classroom

Although previewing and annotation may seem like strategies you'll never use after college, in many professions they come in handy. People in business preview long reports before reading them through, attorneys annotate cases, and teachers may even teach these valuable strategies to their students. The point is that these strategies are very useful in a variety of situations. Once you have learned them, they help you become a life-long learner.

Studying Your Annotations

If you have done a good job of annotating, studying from your annotations is actually a cinch. To use your annotations to help you study, cover up the text with your hand or a piece of notebook paper. Read over your annotations a few times to be sure that you understand the concepts. When you feel comfortable with your understanding of the material and that your annotations are complete, talk through the major points in your annotations without looking at the text. You should be able to talk about each topic that is annotated and you should be able to give examples and details as well. If you find that there is a section that you don't know, then you should reread your annotations. If you still don't understand, then reread that section in the text, ask a friend, look at your lecture notes, or ask your professor.

When you talk through your annotations, be sure that you are precise and complete in your explanations. Preciseness means that what you are saying is accurate information, that the conclusions you are drawing are logical, and that you can see relationships between ideas. Completeness means that you know all of the important information, not just the main point. It's also important to know examples, explanations, and, in many cases, details. For example, you should understand the why's and how's of the Cuban missile crisis, not just the chronology of events.

It's also a good idea to review your annotations a little bit each day so that when you are ready to study for an exam, you already know a lot of the material. These review sessions are a good time to link your lecture notes, secondary texts, and discussion group notes to your annotations. Pulling everything together as you go along makes studying from your annotations an active approach that is efficient and effective.

Annotation Pitfalls

There are three major problems students can experience when they are learning to annotate (Simpson & Nist, 1990). In order to help you avoid these pitfalls and to assess your own annotations, we will outline these pitfalls and offer some suggestions for overcoming them.

1. **"Medieval monk" syndrome.** This happens when a student annotates by copying the text almost word for word. Sometimes

students fall into this trap because they are trying to memorize information instead of really learning it. Students who write too much in the margins may be afraid that they will leave out something important if they try to paraphrase. However, with practice, you should be able to tell the difference between key ideas and details. If you find yourself experiencing the medieval monk syndrome and that your annotations are really just copying the author's words, be sure to do a thorough job of previewing the text before you read so that you are somewhat familiar with the chapter contents. Read one section at a time before marking. After reading each section think about what would be important information to tell someone about the material you just read and write it in your own words.

2. **"Nothin' here" syndrome.** Students who use this approach do not annotate very much at all. They may have random words annotated, or may just copy the heading or bold-faced words in the margin. This is a problem because if there is not enough information annotated in the margins there is little content to study. It leads students to believe that they have learned all the important material when, in fact, they have not. Sometimes students don't annotate enough because they feel that the strategy takes too much time. If this is a concern you have, try annotation with one course this term. You will probably find that it actually *saves* you time when you go to study because you have already thought about the information and organized it in some way. Occasionally, students do not annotate enough because the margins in the text are very small. If this is a problem, invest in some posting notes on which to annotate and stick them in the margins to give you more room to write.

3. **"Rest of the story" syndrome.** Students who demonstrate this pitfall may identify the key topics but do not annotate complete ideas. Sometimes students only partially mark ideas to save time, but because they do not pull out entire ideas, they will have trouble using their annotations to help them study. This is especially a problem in courses that give cumulative finals. If you did not annotate in enough detail, you may have to resort to rereading just to make sense of the information. Sometimes, students try to annotate only the information they don't know. In other words, when they come across a topic that they know a little bit about, they will only annotate the new

SUCCESS AT A GLANCE

Annotation Pitfalls and Models

Medieval Monk	Nothin' Here Syndrome	Rest of the Story
Climax of JFK's crusade came in October 1962	Arms buildup in Cuba	Cuban missile crisis
Summer and fall—Soviets build up massive amounts of arms in Cuba to protect Cuba		
		Why?
US Republicans call for a firm US response; JFK gives warning	US needs to respond	Result?
	Khrushchev says USSR not doing anything wrong	
Khrushchev ignores JFK and builds 24 medium range and 18 intermediate range missiles		
He claimed it was a defensive move but he was probably responding to pressures from his own military to close the strategic gap in nuclear striking power		

information. However, one of the benefits of annotation is that it helps you connect new ideas with prior knowledge, which helps you remember the new information. A student who doesn't link the information together will be less likely to remember it on an exam. To

Model Annotations	**Passage**
Oct. 1962-Cuban missile crisis	The climax of Kennedy's crusade came in October 1962 with the Cuban missile crisis. Throughout the summer and early fall, the Soviets engaged in a massive arms buildup in Cuba, ostensibly to protect Castro from an American invasion. In the United States, Republican candidates in the 1962 congressional elections called for a firm American response; Kennedy contented himself with a stern warning against the introduction of any offensive weapons, believing their presence would directly threaten American security. Khrushchev publicly denied any such intent, but secretly he took a daring gamble, building sites for twenty-four medium-range (1000-mile) and eighteen intermediate-range (2000-mile) missiles in Cuba. Later he claimed his purpose was purely defensive, but most likely he was responding to the pressures from his own military to close the enormous strategic gap in nuclear striking power that Kennedy had opened.
Resulted fr. USSR arms buildup in Cuba	
US Repubs. want JFK to respond b/c US security in danger	
Khrushchev denies intent while building missile sites in Cuba.	
• *claimed it was a defensive move; not really so.*	
• *Soviets wanted to close strategic advantage b/t USSR and US*	

overcome this pitfall, write everything you think you will need to remember, even if the information seems common sense now. Read over your annotations to be sure that they are complete and that they make sense. One way to know whether they are complete is to ask yourself, and be honest about this, if you were allowed to use only your annotations to prepare for an exam over the material, would you be able to pass based on what you have selected to annotate?

Practicing text annotation will help you become better at locating the key information and pulling out complete ideas. By taking the time to create good, quality annotations, you will save yourself time when you go to study the information. However, doing a halfway job will not be much help come exam time.

Source: Simpson, M. L., & Nist, S. L. (1990). "Textbook annotation: An effective and efficient study strategy for college students." *Journal of Reading, 34*, 122–129.

Some Common Concerns About Annotation

Annotation is a strategy that many students find is one of the best ways to help them focus on their reading. However, many students have concerns about their annotations.

How do you know what is important to mark? Deciding what is important to annotate is sometimes tricky. Obviously, you want to note what the text focuses on, but you also want to annotate lecture information. You can often tell what is important by looking at the headings and subheadings in your book. You will probably find that the more you annotate in a textbook, the more familiar you will be with how the text is written and what the professor stresses in class. Therefore, even if you are having trouble organizing the information right now, eventually you should feel more confident about it.

Doesn't this take a lot of time? Yes, in the beginning annotation does take more time than reading alone. Maybe even twice as long. However, if you have annotated properly, you have already taken a big step in preparing for exams. When you annotate, you have pulled out all of the information you will need to study, so you shouldn't have to reread the material unless you need some clarification about a specific concept. In addition, because you have actively interacted with the text material from the start, you will be able to remember more. This will cut your study time prior to an exam. Most students say that they find that the extra time spent annotating is worth it when they go back to study because they are sure they understand the material.

How can you be sure that you are annotating the information that will be on the exam? By listening to class lectures and discussion, you should be able to determine most of the important information. However, the goal of annotation is to your learn the concepts that are presented in the text, not to guess exactly what will be on the exam. If you understand all of the information in the text, you will be prepared for almost any exam question on that topic.

☐ Real College
Hillary's Highlighter

DIRECTIONS: Read the following *Real College* scenario and respond to the questions based on what you learned in this chapter.

Hillary is a returning student. After 20 years she has decided to quit her job and return to school full-time. Because she wants to get off to a good start, she bought herself all the supplies she thought she would need—pencils, notebooks, pens, and especially highlighters. Hillary doesn't see how she could study without her highlighter. Her approach is to open her textbook to the assigned chapter and immediately put her highlighter to work. Her daughter jokes that most of the pages in her books are now bright yellow.

For Hillary's sociology class this term she must read her textbook and the local newspaper. When she reads the text, she tries to highlight everything that seems important. One problem is that it *all* seems important so she sometimes ends up highlighting whole pages. There are so many details in the textbook that she is not sure what the professor will focus on for the exam. She is especially careful to note every name and date discussed in the book, but she doesn't spend a lot of time reading the newspaper because the professor barely mentions the newspaper in class. Basically, she just skims the articles for the facts. Hillary did not do well on the first essay exam even though she studied for hours because it seemed to focus on relating the sociology topics to the newspaper articles. She knows that she needs a new approach to learning because when she studies, she finds that she rereads almost every chapter because it was all highlighted. She hardly has time to read all of her text once, much less twice.

Using what you know about annotations, give Hillary advice on switching from highlighting to annotation and some insight into how Hillary should approach annotating her sociology readings.

☐ **Thinking Critically**
Something to Think About and Discuss

- Examine the textbooks you are reading this term. Which of the following features do they contain?

	Textbook 1 Subject:	Textbook 2 Subject:	Textbook 3 Subject:	Textbook 4 Subject:	Textbook 5 Subject:
Preview Questions					
Boldfaced Terms					
Summaries					
Diagrams					
Formulas					
Glossaries					
Application Activities					

	Textbook 1 Subject:	Textbook 2 Subject:	Textbook 3 Subject:	Textbook 4 Subject:	Textbook 5 Subject:
Large Margins					
Review Questions					
Text Boxes					

- Discuss three (3) benefits you see to using annotation.
- Discuss three (3) concerns you have about using annotation.

☐ Follow-Up Activities

1. Preview and then annotate the history text excerpt which begins on p. 170. How might you annotate this text differently than you would the biology excerpt on covalent bonds?

2. Preview and then annotate the text for one of your classes for one week. Remember to annotate in your own words and to mark all of the important information contained in the text.

3. Reflect on your learning of the material you previewed and annotated. Do you remember the concepts in the chapters you annotated better than the concepts in other chapters? How do you feel the strategy will benefit you when you begin to study for your exam?

Studying Smarter: Don't be a one-trick pony!
Use different rehearsal and review strategies for
different content areas.

CHAPTER 13

REHEARSING AND REVIEWING AFTER READING

Read this chapter to answer the following questions:

- What are rehearsal strategies?

- Why is it important to know how to use a variety of rehearsal strategies?

- What is the difference between rehearsal and review?

- Why is it important to have a specific study plan for each exam you take?

SELF-ASSESSMENT

DIRECTIONS: Think about the types of rehearsal and review strategies you currently engage in. Answer yes or no for each of the following questions. Do you:

	Yes	No
1. create CARDS, concept maps, or charts to rehearse information?	___	___
2. review when you have small pockets of time?	___	___

	Yes	No

3. change your studying techniques depending on the course?   ____ ____

4. create a study plan before each exam?   ____ ____

5. review at the beginning of each study session?   ____ ____

6. review several days before an exam?   ____ ____

7. study with classmates?   ____ ____

8. rehearse and review by asking yourself questions over the material?   ____ ____

If you answered yes to most of these questions, you are probably on the right track and doing what you need to in order to complete the studying process. Read the remainder of the chapter to see what additional rehearsal and review strategies you might use. However, if you answered no to several of these questions, you might want to rethink how you rehearse and review as you read the remainder of this chapter.

What Is Rehearsal?

Just as actors rehearse their lines to remember them, so students must rehearse what they want to learn. Rehearsal means engaging in activities, either written or spoken, that will help you learn information from a variety of courses. You might say the information out loud, write down the information in an organized fashion, or discuss it with a classmate. There are many ways that you can go about rehearing that we will present later in the chapter. What's important at this point is that you understand what rehearsal is and why it is important to your academic success.

Rehearsal strategies help you organize the concepts that your professor expects you to learn. In the previous chapter, we stressed the importance of engaging your mind even before you begin to read by prereading. This warmup activity, which gets the mind ready for mental exercise, enables you to actively read and annotate. You're putting the information in your own words and beginning to see how the concepts relate. If everything goes well, you understand what you have read. Well . . . sort of. You have comprehended it, but you just can't remember all of it. This is where the next step—rehearsal—enters the picture. Rehearsal helps you to actually learn and remember the material. You organize the information from your text and lectures, make it meaningful in some way, write it, and then say it to yourself. If you rehearse properly, you will be able to retrieve or have access to the information at exam time.

Why Is Rehearsal Important?

We already touched on why rehearsal is important, but let's think about this a little more by reviewing how memory works. In Chapter 3, we discussed two theories of memory—the parts theory and the levels of processing theory. It matters little which theory you believe more accurately reflects how memory actually works. What does matter, however, is that in order to get information into LTM or to process it deeply, you must rehearse in some meaningful way. Just reading over the material is not enough. At the rehearsal stage of learning, it's time to further organize by pulling out key ideas and supporting concepts and to personalize or *elaborate* the ideas to the point where you have not just memorized: You have conceptualized and truly understand.

Written and Verbal Rehearsal Strategies

Now that you have an idea of what rehearsal is and why it is important to use rehearsal strategies, let's think about two different types of rehearsal strategies: written strategies and verbal strategies.

1. **Written strategies.** When you use written strategies, you write down the important information in an organized fashion. The way you organize depends on the task your professor expects from you, the materials with which you are interacting, and the particular way that you learn best. In other words, because the tasks and materials vary from course to course, the written strategies that work well for you in biology will probably be very different from those that work for you in political science. Likewise, what works well for you may not work for the person sitting next to you. Specific written strategies, which we will present and discuss in detail, include: CARDS, concept maps, concept charts, questions and answers, and time lines.

2. **Verbal strategies.** Verbal strategies are those rehearsal strategies that require "talking" rather than writing. They work best for students who are more auditory learners, meaning those who learn better through hearing information rather than by reading it or writing it.

You say the information out loud and then check your accuracy. Like written strategies, the verbal strategies you select depend on all the other factors that impact learning—your characteristics, the task, and the text—although we believe that talk-throughs seem to benefit all students. The specific verbal rehearsal strategies that will be presented are: reciprocal questioning and talk-throughs.

It is important to understand that there is no single best strategy, either written or verbal. The "best" rehearsal strategies are those that work for you in a particular situation. And the best students know and appropriately use a variety of strategies, both written and verbal.

College Campus Today

Public Speaking

Many students have a profound fear of speaking in public. One of the best ways to overcome this fear is through practice. It sounds strange, but the more experience you gain speaking in front of a crowd, the more comfortable you will feel. Most campuses offer a variety of opportunities to practice public speaking. You could join a debate team, act in a play, run for office, or take a speech communications class. You will find that the better prepared you are—by using rehearsal and review—the better your public speaking will be.

Components of Good Rehearsal Strategies

When you were in high school you may have used rehearsal strategies without even knowing it. Perhaps you made outlines after you read your text or put vocabulary words or foreign language terms on index cards. You may have had a family member or friend ask you questions before a test. All of these are examples of rehearsal strategies, some of which are better than others.

Good rehearsal strategies have several features. They

- **allow for self-testing.** When you self-test, you rehearse without actually looking at the "answer." For example, if you needed to learn the characteristics of short-term and long-term memory for a psychology exam you would want to say those characteristics to yourself or out loud, and then immediately check your rehearsal strategy to see whether you were correct. This process differs greatly from "looking over" or "reading though" information and having no real idea of whether or not you know the material. Good rehearsal strategies allow you to monitor what you know and allow for the element of self-testing.

- **include complete and precise information.** Have you have ever taken a test, particularly a multiple-choice test, and the information has seemed "familiar" to you, yet you had a difficult time selecting the correct answer? This is probably an instance where you didn't rehearse completely and precisely. Like good text annotations, good rehearsal strategies require you to say or write *all* the information related to a concept and to see relationships between ideas.

- **are organized.** Good strategies have some structure to isolate the information in a way that makes sense and helps you remember it. Your brain files information very much like a computer. That is, concepts are stored in a logical way. Likewise, your rehearsal strategies need to have a logical flow as well.

- **state the ideas in your own words.** Few professors test you over verbatim information from text or lectures. Rather, they paraphrase and synthesize concepts—they put it in their own words. Thus, trying to memorize material straight from the text or lecture will cause problems at test time when the exam questions are written in another way. If after a test you find yourself thinking "The professor never talked about the information that way in class," you probably aren't trying to put the information in your own words as you're studying.

Written Rehearsal Strategies

CARDS: Cognitive Aids for Rehearsing Difficult Subjects

Of all the rehearsal strategies we will present in this chapter, you are probably most familiar with CARDS: Cognitive Aids for Rehearsing Difficult Subjects. You may have just called this strategy "flash cards" if you used it when you were in high school. CARDS is a strategy that uses 3 x 5 index cards. As shown in the example below, you write the key concept that you want to learn on the front of the card. Write another word or phrase, called an organizing term, in the top right-hand corner. The organizing term helps you group like concepts together. In the example CARDS for *double bond*, the organizing term is *covalent bonds*. This suggests that *double bond* is only one of the ideas related to *covalent bonds* and that it is linked to other ideas. Also write the source of the information—the text page, date of the lecture, documentary notes, and so forth—on the front of the card.

Front of CARD

Covalent Bonds

Double Bond

p. 23

Back of CARD

def. Two atoms share two pairs of electrons

ex. Oxygen—O^2, Carbon dioxide—CO^2
O=O

On the back of the CARDS you write all of the material you want to learn about this particular concept in an organized fashion *and* in your own words. Notice that the example has not only a definition of double bond, but also some examples. Because most college professors expect you to go beyond memorization, you should include examples, links to other concepts, and a general synthesis of the key points you need to remember about the concept.

CARDS has several major advantages.

- **They Can Be Carried Around Easily.** You can stick them in your backpack or pocket, and then easily pull them out when you have a few minutes to rehearse, such as while you are standing in line at the bookstore or waiting for class to begin. When you rehearse 10 minutes here or 15 minutes there, the additional study time quickly adds up.

- **They are Versatile.** CARDS works well in classes where you have to learn numerous terms, and if done correctly, can help you to see connections between ideas. For example, suppose you were in a biology course and you were reading a chapter on meiosis. Many terms go with this overriding concept. Rather than making just one card with a weak definition of meiosis, you would use meiosis as the organizing term and write it in the upper right hand corner of all the cards relating to meiosis. Then you would clip all of your meiosis cards together so that you could see how the different terms relating to meiosis connect. CARDS also works well for learning vocabulary, rules, conjugations, and so forth in foreign languages or in mathematics, statistics, or chemistry where you have to learn and then apply formulas.

How do you go about studying your CARDS?

1. **Organize the CARDS.** Use the organizing term in the upper right hand corner to group all like terms together.

2. **Start with one organizing term.** Read the key concept on the front of the first card, flip it over to the back, and read the information through a couple of times. Flip the card back over to the front and see how much of the information you can say to yourself without actually looking at it. Turn the card to the back again, and see how much you remembered. Repeat with each concept. Then return to the organizing term. Think about how all of the concepts you just learned are related not only to the organizing term, but also to each other.

3. **Separate out what you have learned.** Review your CARDS each day, using those small pockets of time. Separate the CARDS you have learned from those you need to spend more time on. Spend larger time slots interacting with the concepts that are giving you the most trouble.

4. **Review with a classmate.** Once you feel that you know most of the material on your CARDS, have your classmate ask you the term and then check to see how much of the material you are able to say accurately and precisely. Then exchange roles. (See the section on

Reciprocal Questioning later in the chapter.) Be sure that you can clearly discuss how the smaller concepts relate to larger ones and how the larger concepts relate to each other.

Concept Maps

As shown in the examples below, concept maps are visual representations of information, and thus these strategies are very useful for students who tend to learn visually. A concept map is organized in such a way that it is easy to see the major concept that is being mapped, related concepts, and how everything is related. This map depicts a map of water molecules that shows two main concepts with several subconcepts for each.

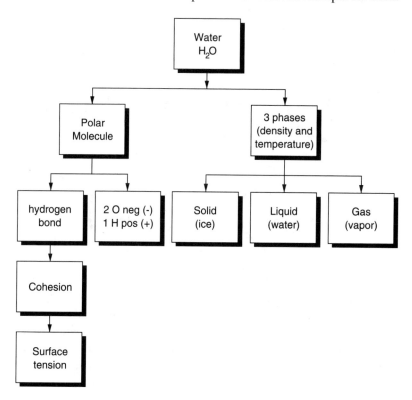

Concept mapping works well when it is important to see the relationship between complex concepts and it works particularly well in the sciences, where many ideas tend to be related and tend to interact. For example, mapping might work very well to see the relationship between hormones of the endocrine system or the different stages of meiosis and mitosis. Mapping is especially useful for students who like to personalize strategies, because there is no right or wrong way to map. The important thing is that the way ideas are linked together be clearly shown in your concept map. The next example depicts the fallout from the Cuban missile crisis. Note that the structure differs from the previous example yet it still presents the information in an organized fashion.

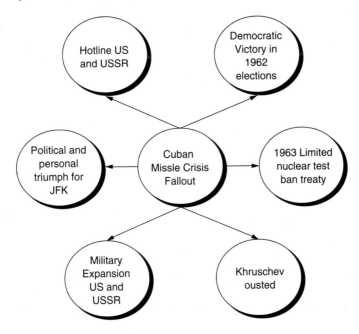

How Do You Go About Studying Maps? When you study your map, you can rehearse one concept at a time, then cover up everything except the main concept, and begin to talk the information through. Say the related material and then check your accuracy. Focus on how the concepts are related to each other because that is the major strength of mapping. Rather than viewing ideas one at a time, as is the case with CARDS, mapping enables you to understand how these ideas fit together.

Charting

Charting is similar to mapping but is useful in different kinds of situations. As shown in the next example, charting helps you synthesize information and is especially helpful when you are asked to compare and contrast ideas.

For example, suppose you were in a chemistry class where you learned about covalent and ionic molecules. Knowing that there was a strong possibility that this question would be asked on the exam, you would want to think about the similarities and differences between the two types of molecules. Start by making a jot list as seen in the example below. Then from your jot list, use those categories to create your chart as shown below.

Jot List for Molecular bonds

Covalent

- Molecules
- Shared electrons-covalent bonds
- Solids, liquids, or gases (water, ice, vapor)
- Small electronegativity differences
- Lower melting and boiling points

Ionic

- Positive and negative ions
- Ions held together by electrostatic attraction
- Crystalline solids (salt)
- High electronegativity differences
- High melting and boiling points

Chart for Molecular Bonds

	Covalent	Ionic
Composition	Discrete particles—molecules. Molecules made up of atoms held together by covalent bonds (shared electrons).	Pos (+) and neg (-) ions. Ions held together by electrostatic attraction—ionic bond (opposites attract)
Forms	Can exist as liquid, solid, or gas.	Exists as crystalline solids.
Example	H_2O, water (can be ice, water, or vapor).	NaCL, salt.

(continued)

	Covalent	Ionic
Properties	Lower melting and boiling points.	Higher melting and boiling points.
	Small electronegativity differences.	High electronegativity differences.

How Do You Go About Studying Charts?   You can study your chart by the categories either on the horizontal or vertical axis. In fact, it is best to study charts both ways. Using the above example, you would talk through the characteristics of covalent bonds thinking about composition, forms, examples, and properties. Then, you would talk though ionic bonds in the same fashion. Next, you would then study your chart horizontally by comparing and contrasting the properties of covalent and ionic bonds.

Question/Answer Strategy

Remember the study guides that your high school teachers gave you? These study guides were intended to help focus your thinking for a test, usually by posing a series of questions. The premise was that if you could answer the questions on the study guide, you would be able to do well on the test. The question/answer strategy uses a similar premise, only you are the active learner who is creating both the questions and the answers. You think about the important information in the text and lectures, pose questions that cover the material, and then answer each of the questions you posed.

In the next example, you'll see that the format probably looks different from what your previous teachers may have used. Using the question/answer strategy, you write your question on the left-hand side of the paper. The right-hand space is to answer the question and is wider and longer than the left side. This format should give you a clue that the questions you pose should require more than a one-word answer.

When you are posing your questions, think about Bloom's Taxonomy (discussed in Chapter 9). Try to create questions that focus on the higher levels, questions that typically begin with *why* or *how*. By higher level, we mean questions that encourage synthesis of the information to be learned. You will want to write memory level questions as well. Such questions typically begin with words such as *who, what,* and *when.* Most importantly, the questions you write should reflect the kinds of information that your professor expects you to learn.

The example below shows you the difference between writing primarily memory level questions and having a mixture of both. If you know that your professor is going to give you multiple-choice exams that have numerous application and synthesis questions, you would want to write questions such as those posed by the number. If, on the other hand, your professor simply expects you to memorize information, the questions posed in the parentheses may be sufficient for your rehearsal. Also note that the questions you pose using the question/answer strategy are more focused than those you predicted during the prereading stage when you were unfamiliar with the important information in the text chapter.

Example of the Question/Answer Strategy

1. Why would a "wet suit" not be considered as a prototype for the concept "clothing"?

1. A <u>prototype</u> is defined as the best or clearest example of a natural concept. Thus for the concept "clothing," a prototype might be "shirt" or "coat"— pieces of clothing that you might be more likely to mention. Because "wet suit" would not be mentioned very frequently when asked about the concept of clothing, it would not be considered a prototype.

(What is a prototype?)

2. How are prototypes related to behavior?

(What causes teen drinking?)

3. Discuss the three results of the study on prototypes and drinking?

(Which teens drank more?)

As with all of the strategies, your question/answer strategy will not be very effective if you leave out important information or include information that is wrong or incomplete. You should also be sure to put the material in your own words, whenever possible, because it will help you remember it better.

How Do You Go About Studying the Question/Answer Strategy?

When you study your question/answer strategy, fold your paper back so that just your questions are showing. Ask yourself the question, or get someone else to ask you. Then answer it by saying the information out loud. Check to see how much of the material you remembered correctly. If your answer matches what you wrote, repeat the process with the next question. If your answer was incomplete or wrong, read the correct answer several times and try to say it again before moving on to the next question. In addition, because the questions on the exam will most certainly be in random order, don't always begin with your first question and work your way through to the end. Instead, start with the last question, do every other question, or use some other pattern.

Time Lines

Unlike the other strategies we have discussed, time lines are only appropriate in specific situations. Basically, you can use time lines when it is important to know chronology—the order of something that happened over a period of time. For example, you might use time lines in a history course when it's important to know the chronology of the Vietnam Conflict, in an art class when you need to be able to compare and contrast major artistic movements, or in a geology course when you're expected to trace the evolution of the earth's crusts over millions of years. Hence, you can use time lines in many different disciplines but they do have a very specific function.

Time lines are flexible in that they can be constructed in a variety of ways. The following example shows the time line of events leading up to and during the Cuban missile crisis. Your textbooks may depict other types of time lines to show longer spans of time.

Time Line Example

Jan. 1, 1959	President Batista flees Cuba.
Feb. 2, 1959	Fidel Castro declared new president of Cuba.
May 27, 1960	US ends aid to Cuba.
April 17, 1961	Bay of Pigs incident.
Oct. 22, 1962	JFK announces that Soviet missiles are found off the coast of Cuba.
Oct. 27, 1962	Khruschev writes letter to JFK that he will remove missiles if US removes missiles from Turkey and promises not to attack Cuba. JFK agrees.
Aug. 30, 1963	Hot line established between US and USSR.

■   ■   ■

In the majority of studying situations, time lines should be supplemented with other strategies such as CARDS, concept maps, or charts. For example, if you were doing a time line portraying the major events of the Cuban missile crisis, it would indicate only the chronology—which events happened when. But that would be insufficient knowledge to have when preparing for an exam. For example, you would need to know *why* the Soviets placed missiles in Cuba, *what* the fallout from the resolution was, and *what* factors led up to the crisis. This information cannot be gleaned from the time line alone.

How Do You Go About Studying Time Lines?   When you are studying your time lines, use only your dates as the cue. Talk through the important events, laws, battles, etc. that occurred on that date. At the same time, use your other strategies to talk through the nature of each of the events, thinking about cause and effect, or how one event influenced another when appropriate. Use newspaper questions—who, what, where, when, why, and how—to be certain that you are fully describing each event. In addition, it's important to understand how events are related, so be sure that you see the big picture as well.

Verbal Rehearsal Strategies

Verbal rehearsal strategies are those that involve talk in some way — talking out loud, to yourself, or to a study partner. Although you might think it odd to talk to yourself as you study and learn, saying information out loud is a powerful tool because it is a form of active learning that keeps you connected with what you are learning. Talking and listening as you study helps you use other senses as well, and remember, the more senses you use when you study, the easier learning will be. We will discuss two different verbal strategies: reciprocal questioning and talk-throughs. Each of these strategies is a form of verbal summarization and each is generally used along with written strategies.

Reciprocal Questioning

Reciprocal questioning involves two learners, one who takes the role of the teacher, and the other who takes the role of the student. The "teacher" asks a question from one of the written strategies described earlier, from text annotations, or from lecture notes. Most should be questions that elicit higher-level or critical thinking rather than those that promote memorization or one-word answers. Then the "student" answers the question, checking his answer against the written strategy. If the student has answered the question correctly, the teacher asks the next question. If the question was not answered adequately, the teacher answers the question correctly and the two discuss the correct answer. Poorly answered questions should be asked again at the end of the study session.

After all of the questions have been asked and answered, and if necessary, reviewed, the two switch roles—the "student" becomes the teacher and asks the questions and the "teacher" becomes the student and answers them. The new teacher should be sure that she asks the questions in a different order and adds some new questions.

The example below gives you an idea of the difference between good and poor questions. These questions are about ionic and covalent bonds. Notice that most of the questions in the "Poor" column require only a one-word answer or simple memorization. The questions in the "Good" column are questions that require critical thinking, synthesis, and analysis.

Good Questions	Poor Questions
How does the composition of covalent and ionic bonds differ?	What is an ionic bond?
Explain and provide examples of the three forms of covalent bonds.	Name an ionic bond.
Describe why the electronegativity of covalent bonds is lower than that of ionic bonds.	Which has lower electronegativity, ionic or covalent bonds?

Reciprocal questioning can be a powerful strategy for several reasons.

- **It Brings More Senses Into Play.** You have read the information using the visual sense, you have written important concepts down in an organized fashion using the kinesthetic sense, and you are now hearing the information using the auditory sense. Using more than one sense helps you remember better because it makes you a more active learner.

- **It Encourages Multiple Perspectives.** The old adage "two heads are better than one" is true in this situation. One person may be very strong in understanding concept A and the other very knowledgeable about concept B. Pulling the ideas of two people together generally makes for clearer, more precise learning for both.

- **It Encourages You to use Your Own Words.** Because professors rarely write questions that come exactly from the text, it's important to put information in your own words so that you will recognize it in a slightly different form on the test. When you have two people putting it in their own words, you get another perspective of how the information might be phrased.

- **It Helps You to Monitor Your Learning.** When you are asked a question and then provide the answer, you get immediate feedback about your knowledge on that particular topic. This helps you monitor what concepts you know and on what concepts you need more work.

Talk-Throughs

As the name of this strategy suggests, talk-throughs involve saying the information (talking it through) to yourself, either silently, or out loud to monitor your learning. When you talk through the concepts you become both the student and the teacher, because rather than having someone ask you questions or ask you to explain concepts, you fill both roles. Start by making a talk-through list on an index card. As seen in the example below, a talk-through card simply lists, in an organized fashion, the concepts you need to learn and remember. Notice that the supporting ideas are indented so that it is easy to see which ideas are connected in some way. For example, in this talk-through card, it is easy to see that there are three main elements of thought covered in the subheading "Means of Thought: Words, Images, Concepts." In this case, the text's headings and subheadings were the basis for organizing the talk-through card and these headings are further supplemented with key terms. Although this is not always the case, headings and subheadings are a good place to start because they give you the overall "big picture" of the chapter.

Talk-Through Card Example

Means of Thought

1. Words

    Inner speech

    Language

2. Images

    Perception

    Mental space

    Visualization

3. Concepts

    Prototypes

    Organization

After you have made your talk-through card, begin rehearsal by saying what you know about the first major concept. Talk it through, looking back at your written strategies, if necessary, including text annotations and lecture notes. In fact, after you have said the information silently or out loud, it is a good idea to go back to your strategy and read over the information again to be sure that you are complete and precise. As you learn each piece of information, also be sure that you can make connections between the major concepts and the supporting details. Explain to yourself how the pieces fit together.

Strategy Selection

The strategies you select depend on a variety of factors: the task your professor asks you to do, the course for which you are studying, and how you learn best. This will be discussed further in Chapter 14, but the chart below summarizes the rehearsal strategies presented in this chapter and suggests when they might be most effective. But remember . . . active learners can modify strategies so that they can be used in situations other than those outlined here.

SUCCESS AT A GLANCE
Summary Table of Rehearsal Strategies

Rehearsal strategies	Use in	Types of questions
CARDS	Hard sciences, foreign languages, mathematics, statistics, any course where you have to learn many new terms	Best with objective questions; can be modified for use with either memory-level or higher-level questions

(continued)

Rehearsal strategies	Use in	Types of questions
Concept maps and charts	Hard sciences and social sciences, history; if you are a visual learner; when you need to see relationships	Can be used for both objective and essay questions; best for higher-level questions that require you to see the big picture
Question/ answers	All courses	Best for objective test questions unless you plan to modify it to predict essay questions
Time lines	History, art history, music history, anthropology, any course where you need to know chronology	Memory level questions; can supplement this strategy with other such as concepts maps, charts, or CARDS
Reciprocal questioning	All courses	All types of questions but works well when rehearsing answers to higher-level questions
Talk-throughs	All courses	All types of questions; helps you concentrate on key concepts rather than small details

Reviewing

Rehearsing and reviewing are different because they have different goals. Rehearsal enables you to learn the information. It not only helps you store the concepts you'll need to learn, but it also helps you to retrieve the material at test time. When you rehearse, you write, say, and listen to the information until you know it very well. You look for connections between ideas and understand how concepts are related. Reviewing, on the other hand, is a way of making sure that the important information has been learned in such a way that it is complete, organized, and precise. Reviewing ensures that the information will stay fixed in your memory. By reviewing daily, you remember about three times more than if you had not reviewed. Thus, there is a tremendous payoff in review.

You can use reviewing at various times during the studying process. For example, think back to Chapter 10 when we talked about lecture notes. We emphasized the importance of reviewing notes daily. Getting to class 10 minutes early and using those 10 minutes to read over your notes is a form of reviewing. In this case, reviewing refreshes your memory of what happened in the last class and prepares your mind to receive new information, making it easier to connect ideas. But the kind of reviewing that we will focus on in this chapter is generally done as a final phase of studying and test preparation. You review by self-testing to monitor your learning and gain a better understanding of what information you know very well and what information requires further study through additional rehearsal.

Using Your Talk-Through Card for Reviewing

We have already discussed how to make and use a talk-through card. Talk-through cards simply list the concepts you want to rehearse and learn as you study the material. You can also use your talk-through card to review. Start with the first concept and completely and accurately talk through the key points. If you know all the information related to that concept, check it off and go on to the next. If you have trouble remembering the material, return to your annotations or rehearsal strategies and say the information again. Keep in mind that if rehearsal has been done properly, reviewing should just be a matter of keeping the information retrievable in your memory and seeing which concepts are still giving you problems. Hopefully, you will remember most of the important information and see links between concepts when you are reviewing.

Making a Specific Study Plan

We have talked in other chapters about the importance of planning. Rather than having a unsystematic approach to test preparation, think about how much time you will spend studying and what you will do during those study sessions. It's particularly important to structure specific study and review sessions as the time for the exam draws closer. That's why we suggest that you develop a **Specific Study Plan** or SSP for each exam you take. Although some students get to the point where they know what they are going to do in each study session just by writing a few notes, it has been our experience that most students benefit from creating a more structured plan. Therefore, we suggest that you write out a study plan and clip it in your daily planner.

Construct your study plan about a week or so before the exam. Think about your goals by asking yourself a series of questions:

1. What grade do I want to earn on the exam?

2. How much time do I need to invest in order to make this grade?

3. Where will I find the extra time? Will I have to give up other activities in order to carve out time to study?

4. What kind of exam is it? Multiple-choice? Essay? What kinds of problems do I usually have when I take tests of this nature?

5. Do I know the balance of items? Is this a memorization task or will I be expected to answer higher-level questions? What proportion of questions will come from the text and the lectures?

6. What kinds of rehearsal strategies will I need to create because they will work best for this exam?

After you have answered these questions, you are then ready to construct your SSP. As shown in the following example, an SSP outlines what you will do in each particular study session. It shows what rehearsal or review strategies you will use, what concepts you will study, and approximately how long each study session will last. It's easy to see that the student in the example has three study sessions (1, 2, and 3) and two specific sessions set aside just to review with her classmates (4 and 6). One session (5) is set aside just for self-testing as a way of getting a handle on which concepts may still be problematic. Also note that each study session begins with a review of information that was rehearsed in the previous session. Each session should also end with a review of what was learned in the current session.

An Example SSP for an Exam Covering Both Text Chapters and Lecture Notes.

Session	What to do?	What to use?	Completed? Evaluation notes
#1 Sunday pm: 6:00-7:00	Study all concepts related to "covalent bonds"	CARDS, concept maps, lecture notes	took more than 1 hour (actual 6-7:45)
#2 Monday pm: 4:40-6:30	Review "covalent bonds"; Study all concepts related to "water molecules"	CARDS, concept maps, lecture notes	
#3 Tuesday pm: 7:00-9:30	Review "water molecules" and "covalent bonds"; Study all concepts related to "atoms and molecules"	CARDS, concept maps, lecture notes	

(continued)

Session	What to do?	What to use?	Completed? Evaluation notes
#4 Wednesday pm: 7:30-9:00	Review with study group	question/answer, reciprocal teaching	
#5 Thursday pm: 9:00-10:30	Self-test	question/answer, talk-through card	
#6 Thursday pm: 7:30-9:00	Review with study group	talk-through card, oral question/answer	

EXAM FRIDAY!

■   ■   ■

As you construct your SSP and think about the time you will need to rehearse and review the material, remember from the principles discussed in Chapter 4, you should always allow more time than you think you will need. If you block out two hours for a study session to learn a set of concepts, and it takes you only an hour and a half, you have gained a half-hour in which you can do something else. But if you set aside the same two hours and it actually ends up taking you three hours to feel comfortable with the concepts, you have lost an hour. Thus, it's important to have some flexibility in your schedule that allows for additional time should you need it.

When you complete each study session, check it off, evaluate how long it actually took you, and determine any specific problems you had that you might need to return to in your next session. Did you exceed the amount of time you allotted or did you need less time? This will help you as you develop an SSP for the next exam in this course.

Another thing to note about the SSP is that it sets aside time to do three different types of review.

1. You **begin** each session with a review of what you learned previously. Using your talk-through card as a guide, say what you remember

from the earlier study session. If there's material that is still giving you problems, begin the current study session with it.

2. At the **end** of each session, you review only those concepts you concentrated on in the current session. This type of review serves as a monitoring device to let you know what you actually remember from the session. If you start this review and find that you are having problems, you can return to those concepts immediately and rehearse some more. This is the monitoring part of your review when you discover whether you will need to devote more time to the study session than you originally planned.

3. **A day or two before the test,** you continue to monitor your understanding of all of the concepts you will be tested over. Concentrate the time you have left on the material that you understand least. Many students make the mistake of spending equal amounts of time on everything before an exam, even information that they know fairly well. Learn from their mistakes. The closer the exam, the more you want to concentrate on concepts you don't know well.

QUICK TAKES

Specific Plans Beyond College

Once you have mastered using SSPs in college, you will find them useful once you enter your career. Of course, you will not be planning for a test, but being able to set goals and then ask questions to figure out how to reach them is a skill that you will find extremely valuable.

Setting some goals for yourself and making an SSP for each exam helps you stay on track with both rehearsing and reviewing. Note that it is important to focus on learning specific concepts, not on the amount of time you actually have allotted for studying. For example, if you were studying for the test outlined in the example, you would want to learn all of the information related to the concept "covalent bonds" in your first study session. It is usually ineffective to go over all the information in every study session. Students who plan around time rather than around mastery of the information can easily go into a testing situation unprepared.

Forming Study Groups

One of the best ways to review is by forming study groups. Some students will form study groups that meet on a weekly basis to talk about and review what went on in class that week. Other students like to use study groups just before an exam as a way of reviewing and perhaps even getting a new or different perspective on what they have learned. Either way, study groups have big advantages if they are done right.

Perhaps the biggest advantage of being part of a study group is that it allows you to listen to information in another person's voice, which can provide insights that you may not have considered. In a traditional course, you listen to your professor's interpretation of the information during lectures, you read the text for another interpretation, and through these two sources, you come up with your own interpretation or meaning. You have listened, read, and written down material, so you have used several of your senses. All of this interaction should help you gain a greater degree of understanding of the material. It stands to reason, then, that by listening to and interacting with others who are also trying to understand the course information, you would gain a deeper understanding, be able to remember the concepts better, and subsequently do better on the exams.

Networking

Virtual Study Groups

Try to set up an online review session prior to an exam in one of your classes. You and a classmate can review by sending questions to one another via e-mail. Each of you can answer questions posed by the other and provide feedback as to the completeness and accuracy of your answers.

It's important to think about the characteristics of *good* study groups. Just meeting with people in the same course does not necessarily make a study group. Good study groups have the following characteristics:

- **Everyone Comes Prepared.** Study groups do not replace studying on your own. Everyone should come to the group prepared to review the information, pose and answer possible test questions, and voice questions about material they don't understand. If the study group members have to spend all of their time trying to teach a large portion of the course material to someone who didn't even attempt to learn it on her own, most members will not benefit.

- **Everyone Can Talk Through a Difficult Idea with the Group.** It helps everyone in the group if you choose something that is giving you a bit of trouble or something that you may have some questions about. As you are reviewing your understanding of the concept, others who may understand it better than you should be encouraged to offer additional explanation. Don't shy away from discussing information that you don't know very well; it defeats the purpose of the group.

- **Members of the Study Group Should Be Classmates, but not Necessarily Friends.** Everyone knows what can happen when friends get together to study: Everything goes fine for the first few minutes, but it's easy to get off track. It's much better to have serious students, who all have the goal of doing well, in your study group rather than just recruiting your friends. That's not to say that studying with friends will never work; it's simply harder to study with friends than it is with classmates working toward a common goal.

- **Meet at a Place That Is Conducive to Studying.** Campus libraries often have study rooms set aside for just this purpose. Such rooms are generally small and sound proof so that normal conversation and discussion can be carried out with ease. If your library doesn't have study rooms, dorms often have common areas equipped with study rooms. Empty classrooms can also work well. If your only alternative is to study in someone's room or at someone's home or apartment, remind yourself what the purpose of the session is—to review the course material for a test, not to socialize.

- **Have Clear Goals and Structure.** When you initially form a study group, you should have a more specific goal than to get together and study. Most groups meet at regular times. We know of a study group in a statistics course that meets weekly to review the important ideas presented that week, and then also meets a couple of times right before the exam to review what they know and to predict and solve possible test questions. Groups that have a game plan in mind before they come together are generally the most successful. Along those lines, if you're really serious about having a good study group, it doesn't hurt to set some ground rules right from the beginning to prevent difficulties later on. For example, what will happen if someone comes to the group without doing any preparation on his own?

Almost everyone can benefit from belonging to a study group at one time or another, but study groups work particularly well for students who learn better auditorily and through discussion and in courses they find problematic. We don't know of any student who is in a study group for *every* class, but if you are taking a particularly difficult course, it often helps to have the opinion and input of others.

☐ Real College
Conrad's Confusion

DIRECTIONS: Read the following *Real College* scenario and respond to the questions based on what you learned in this chapter.

Conrad is a first-year college student who is pretty nervous about doing well in his courses. He is particularly unhappy with his ability to see the big picture in some of his courses and is surprised that his classes seem to require him to study in different ways in order to do well. In high school, Conrad simply skimmed the parts of his texts to answer questions on the study guides that most of his teachers provided. He would memorize this information and do well on almost every exam. But in college, three of his professors expect him to conceptualize information. That is, he has to understand scientific processes in biology, his history professor expects the class "to put information in a historical perspective," and in his literature course, he has to think about how character development and use of language relate to the plot in the short stories they are studying. Conrad doesn't even know where to start studying for these courses. In high school he used to put lots of information on index cards and sometimes he would make complex outlines, but he doesn't even know any other study strategies to consider.

What would your advice to Conrad be? What rehearsal and review strategies would you recommend for each of his courses and why?

☐ Thinking Critically
Something to Think About and Discuss

- In the past, how have you rehearsed and reviewed information? Do the rehearsal strategies you currently use have the characteristics of good rehearsal strategies outlined in this chapter? What might you do to improve the quality of your rehearsal strategies?

- Try forming a study group for one of your classes, especially one that might be difficult for you. Remember that this group can meet throughout the term to review lecture notes or difficult topics from the text or lecture. Reviewing, like rehearsing, is an on-going process.

☐ Follow-Up Activities

1. Construct a set of questions/answers for a chapter in a course in which you are currently enrolled. Be sure to ask some higher-level questions that begin with the words "how" and "why."

2. Construct 20 CARDS, 1 concept map, or 1 chart for a course in which you are currently enrolled. Be sure to consider the task before you select your strategy.

3. For the next exam in one of your classes, set goals by answering the goal-related questions on page 218. Then construct an SSP. Remember to set aside time in your SSP for rehearsal and review. Plan to begin and end each study session with review.

PART FIVE

YOUR TEXT CHARACTERISTICS

In Part V, you learn about how the characteristics of the text influence active learning. Chapter 14 focuses on how to modify your learning strategies based on the discipline and the kind of text you are reading.

Chapter 15 discusses ways to become a flexible reader. It presents strategies for increasing your reading rate as well as discussing some common habits that may slow your reading.

*Studying Smarter: Choose your strategies for
learning based on the type of course and type of
tests you will experience.*

CHAPTER 14

STRATEGIES ACROSS THE DISCIPLINES

Read this chapter to find answers to the following
questions:

- How do my courses differ from each other?
- How do my textbooks differ from each other?
- How can I modify my strategies to suit different
  courses and texts?

SELF-ASSESSMENT

DIRECTIONS: Complete the following chart for each of your courses this
term. Think about how you prepare for each class.

	Course 1	Course 2	Course 3	Course 4	Course 5
(course name)	_____	_____	_____	_____	_____
I read the text before class.	Yes/No	Yes/No	Yes/No	Yes/No	Yes/No
I read the text after class.	Yes/No	Yes/No	Yes/No	Yes/No	Yes/No

(continued)

(course name)	Course 1	Course 2	Course 3	Course 4	Course 5
My class lecture follows the text.	Yes/No	Yes/No	Yes/No	Yes/No	Yes/No
I am responsible for reading multiple texts for this course.	Yes/No	Yes/No	Yes/No	Yes/No	Yes/No
I try to study in the same way for each course.	Yes/No	Yes/No	Yes/No	Yes/No	Yes/No

The way you have responded to these questions gives a good indication of how you approach reading and studying in your classes. Keep these answers in mind as you read the rest of the chapter.

As you have probably noticed by now, all of your courses are not the same. Obviously, the content is not the same in your history class and your chemistry class, but have you noticed that the ways in which your classes are organized and structured also differ? Some of your classes may involve taking lots of lecture notes, others may involve class discussion, you may have a lab class in addition to a lecture class, or you may have a lecture, lab, and discussion all in one course. In addition, the textbooks are often vastly different. In fact, you may have noticed that some of your textbooks are not even especially well written. Because class structure and text sources can be so wide-ranging, you will encounter different types of assessments depending on the course. You may have essay or multiple-choice tests, you may have to write journals or papers, or you may be required to complete any number of different tasks. When you begin to study for your courses, you will base your decision of which strategies to choose on the type of class, type of text, and type of assessment. In order to prepare you for the variety of tasks you need to do, we will examine discipline-specific differences in college courses.

SUCCESS AT A GLANCE

Questions to Think About

- How is the text arranged? Chronologically, topically, or otherwise?
- How much do the lecture and text overlap?
- Will I be able to read and understand the text before going to class?
- Will I be able to understand the lecture if I do not read before class?
- What kinds of strategies will work best for this discipline?

Textbook Characteristics

Saying that you can read each of your textbooks in the same way for each of your courses is like saying you can read *People* magazine in the same way as you read Shakespeare. Obviously, you have to adjust your reading to the type of course and textbook you are using. As you encounter different college textbooks you will notice some basic differences depending on the content area. Textbooks in the humanities are different from textbooks in the social sciences or physical sciences.

NETWORKING

Finding Resources on the Web

Many Web pages cover college learning in a variety of content areas. To find out more about approaching learning, find some

(continued)

resources using the following keywords: studying mathematics, science learning, studying humanities, etc. It may help to start out by looking up the learning center on your campus to find some of these resources. Find and report to the class on some additional strategies for learning in all of your courses.

Mathematics Textbooks

Reading a mathematics textbook is not like reading a novel or another textbook. Mathematics textbooks tend to use few words in order to keep ideas clearly outlined, so you must understand almost every sentence. You will be expected to comprehend abstract relationships and theories as you read about them. Mathematics texts tend to present new concepts, formulas, diagrams, and practice problems sequentially, which means that they build on one another. Learning mathematics is cumulative. The concepts you are learning this week are based on the concepts you have already mastered.

You will find that mathematics textbooks are not very repetitive, making every concept count. With little chance of picking up missed information by reading further in the text, you must be sure you have mastered each concept before moving on to a new one.

Study Strategies for Mathematics Courses   In general, college mathematics courses are based on problem solving. In addition to what we generally think of as mathematics courses, computer science, engineering, statistics, chemistry, and physics are also math-based courses. Whether you are in a class of 10 or 300, you will be asked to apply math principles and formulas in a variety of situations. Sometimes mathematics courses are discussion based, but often they are lecture based with the instructor explaining new concepts and the student taking copious notes. Many times mathematics instructors focus lectures on working out problems on the board.

To approach reading in mathematics, it is a good idea to preview the text before class. If you find that you can read and understand the chapter before the lecture that is even better, but many students find that they comprehend mathematics texts better after listening to the lecture and seeing some problems worked as examples in class. When you preview the text, note the concepts and formulas that are covered as well as any new terminology so that you will have some background information before listening in class. When you are in class, take good notes and ask questions. The more information and examples you have in your notes, the better it will be as you read the text.

COLLEGE CAMPUS TODAY

Computer Testing

It is becoming more common for college students to take tests on the computer rather than the more traditional pencil and paper method. On our campus, for example, students in all levels of math take computerized exams and receive immediate feedback on how well they performed. In chemistry, students also take exams on the computer and once they get their score, they can work on the items they missed and submit those items a second time for partial credit. Although many students don't feel comfortable taking computerized exams at the beginning of the term, most quickly adjust.

After class, read the text. It is best to read the chapter as soon after class as possible so that you will remember all of the key points and ideas discussed in class. Take your time as you read. Annotate key words, formulas, definitions, and symbols in the margins to help you remember them. Note the symbols used in your text, because they have very specific meanings and must be used correctly when working math problems. For example, to understand ab::cd, you must first understand that :: is the symbol for "is proportional to."

You cannot neglect math work. Plan to spend some time each night reading or working problems. As you read, work out the problems in your text. After reading examples, cover up the answer to the sample problem to work it out for yourself. It is also important to write down questions about concepts you need to have clarified so you can ask them during the next class period, before the class moves on to a new concept. Try to create your own problems and solve them for additional practice. If you find that you are experiencing difficulty understanding your textbook, you may find it helpful to use another math book (you can probably find one in the library) as a reference book to help clarify confusing points. In addition, try verbalizing the problems. Talking the information through by putting symbols into words, for example, can let you know where your understanding is breaking down.

Science Textbooks

Science courses can be divided into two categories—math-based science courses and text-based science courses. Each category will have vastly different texts. Texts for math-based science courses, such as chemistry or physics, will contain formulas like your mathematics texts, but they will also contain important diagrams explaining scientific processes.

Text-based science courses, such as biology, agriculture, forestry, botany, astronomy, and geology, are often more similar to social science courses than mathematics courses. There is little mathematics involved; instead, you will be required to read, understand, and apply scientific processes discussed in the text. These courses usually include a lab in which you experience hands-on application of scientific principles.

In science textbooks you will find many new terms and definitions. Often, those new terms will be used later in the text to define other terms, so if you don't understand the term when it is introduced, you will have trouble understanding future reading. Science textbooks also discuss proven principles and theories in terms of their relationship to each other. Therefore, it is important to be aware of and understand how the theories connect.

Strategies for Science Courses   Because of the amount of new terminology involved in learning science, it is important for you to read your science textbooks before class. In this way, you will be familiar with the terms and concepts discussed in the text and you will be able to build your understanding of the concept as you listen in class. It is also a good idea to connect the concepts discussed in class with the concepts described in your text by comparing your lecture notes to your text annotations each night.

As with your math courses, science concepts are usually presented sequentially, which means they build on each other so if you do not understand the concepts presented early on, you will have difficulty later. Your best defense is to test yourself as you read to make sure you fully understand each concept. Adopt a scientific approach and ask yourself questions, such as:

- Is this concept or phenomenon a theory or has it been proven?
- What other theories is this concept related to?
- How does this phenomenon work? What is the scientific process involved?
- Why does this phenomenon occur?
- What does it show us?

Making a concept map of key terms and concepts so that you can see how the ideas relate is another helpful strategy. When you preview each chapter, begin a concept map for the ideas contained in the chapter. As you read, fill in your concept map with the important scientific processes. Or you may want to make CARDS over the concepts and new terminology. However, in order to be effective, you must do more than just memorize the terms. Spread out your CARDS to show the hierarchy of terms or the order of the scientific process. This way you will be connecting the ideas together.

Science texts often contain diagrams or charts to explain concepts. Because science exams usually contain questions about the concepts described in diagrams or charts, you must be able to read and understand each one. As you read your text, annotate the diagrams and take the time to learn what they are depicting. A good self-testing strategy to make sure you fully understand the concept is to cover up the words in the diagram and try to talk through the information. If you can explain how the concept works, you've shown you understand it. In addition, although exams in your science classes may consist of multiple choice, essay, or short answer questions, many of your test questions will require you to apply science concepts to new situations. To answer these questions you must understand and be able to describe each concept. If you find that you cannot, reread your annotations and your lecture notes to be sure you understand the key points.

Humanities Textbooks

Humanities courses focus on all areas of human endeavor—invention, relationships, creation. Just about any area you can think of is represented in the humanities. Initially, many students think that humanities texts are easier to read than the texts in more fact-based courses like math or science, but humanities courses are challenging because they require students to interpret, analyze, and evaluate the text. In general, humanities textbooks do not introduce much new content vocabulary, but you may encounter unfamiliar use of words or dialects in your reading. Topics in humanities textbooks are often presented chronologically, as in a literature textbook that is arranged by the year each story, poem, and play was written. However, sometimes they are organized topically, as in a philosophy textbook organized by themes. Humanities textbooks are usually not sequential nor do the concepts build on one another, so you should be able to read any chapter in your humanities texts and understand it without reading the previous chapters. Unlike science courses where you look to find how concepts are related, in humanities courses you will look for similarities and differences between themes, metaphors, ideology, and philosophy. Therefore, you will need strategies to help you think critically about what you are reading.

Strategies for Humanities Courses Humanities courses include literature, philosophy, drama, music, art, and many more. In humanities courses, you are often asked to read from a variety of sources including novels, plays, and poetry, as well as from a traditional textbook. You also may be required to attend plays or musical events or other cultural activities in addition to class lectures.

Because many humanities courses are discussion-based, it is important to read the text before attending class. As you read, you should focus on analyzing and interpreting the information. Ask yourself questions such as:

- Why did the author choose to write this?
- What is the significance of what I am reading?
- What themes or metaphors are being used?

In class it is usually important to take notes about what your classmates are discussing, because professors often create exam questions based on the class discussion. In addition to reading before class and taking good notes during class, you should connect the reading to the class discussion during your review after class. This review may entail annotating your text about themes, metaphors, symbolism, or issues discussed in class, marking important passages or quotations, or connecting themes across readings. Because humanities courses often involve writing papers or taking essay exams, it is always a good idea to keep track of ideas for possible paper topics as you are reading and to try to predict essay questions after listening to the class discussion.

Social Science Textbooks

Social science textbooks are usually concerned with what happens in a society. The social sciences involve the study of people in terms of political, economic, social, interpersonal, and cultural aspects of society. These texts are often filled with terms that may seem familiar, but have a specialized meaning. For example, the word "class" would have very different meanings in a sociology course than it would in an education course. Social science texts usually present ideas in either chronological order or topical form. For example, a history textbook usually discusses events in the order they occur in time (chronologically) but sociology texts often discuss ideas by topic.

Sections of social science texts are often highlighted in a text box or by some other manner. In high school, you probably used the same tactic whenever you saw a text box—you skipped it. However, in college texts these boxes often contain important information that is not contained within the rest of the text. Sometimes they are supporting articles, or they are examples of a principle outlined in the text, or they are the original documents discussed in the chapter. But no matter what they contain, follow this general rule: **read the text boxes.** You may find that many of your exam questions come from this information. Professors are aware that students tend to skip text boxes and they want to make sure students pay attention to the important information contained in the boxes, so they base test items on them.

In your social science courses, you will be asked to read and understand many new concepts, so you will need strategies to help you organize large amounts of information.

Strategies for Social Science Courses   Social sciences courses include psychology, sociology, education, anthropology, history, political science, economics, and more. (We should note that history is viewed by some as a humanities course.) Students sometimes experience difficulty in social science courses because they try to memorize facts, forgetting that because the social sciences are based on theories, there are few "facts." Also, social science texts often deal with large time spans, making it hard to simply memorize facts. A history class could cover several thousand years all in one semester.

As with your humanities courses, you should read your social science textbooks before you attend class so that you are ready for class discussion or lecture. As you read, annotate both the text and any diagrams or other typographical aids. Identify comparisons or contrasts between ideas, because they often make their way into social science exams. In addition, note possible test questions.

QUICK TAKES

Being Prepared

Once you are out in the workplace, you wouldn't think about going to a meeting unprepared, but many students go to class each day without preparing. If you had to make a presentation to a new client you would want to be on top of things. If you get into the habit of being prepared for your classes when you are in college, you will likely carry these habits over into the world of work.

Because you will need to be able to identify trends, trace their influence on historical events, and draw parallels with current events, you will need to use strategies that help you identify relationships between ideas. Charting is a good way to keep track of these relationships. Often students lose track of the big picture in their social science courses and get bogged down in the details. By charting the information, you will be able to see how ideas fit together into a larger concept. You will also be able to track trends or discover principles about the information. Another good strategy is to create a time line to help you remember the sequence of important events. But remember that most social science courses will involve more than just memorizing names and dates, so use your time line to help you see the big picture as well.

☐ **Real College**
Caroline's Courses

DIRECTIONS: Read the following *Real College* scenario and respond to the questions based on what you learned in this chapter.

Caroline is taking five courses this term: biology, political science, American literature, statistics, and music appreciation. So far she has approached learning in each course in the same way. She goes to class, listens to the lecture, and then she reads the assigned chapters in the textbook. She tries to read the text the night before the lecture, but many times she does not get to the reading until right before the exam.

She is doing well in her music appreciation course, but is having trouble in all of the other classes. In American literature, the professor expects the class to discuss the novels and does not hold a lecture at all. Because she would rather listen to the professor before reading, Caroline usually doesn't have much to contribute to the discussion. Caroline does not take any notes in this class and feels that she doesn't really understand what she is supposed to be getting out of the reading. She has failed her first essay exam because the professor said that she was not reading critically enough.

In her biology class, the professor seems to lecture at 100 miles per hour. It seems as if he introduces twenty new concepts in every class. Caroline finds that she has trouble taking good notes because she never knows what the professor is talking about. She knows that something needs to change, but she isn't sure what she needs to do.

Statistics presents a whole other problem for her. She didn't understand what was going on from the first day of lecture. Now that they are about ten chapters into the textbook, she is completely lost and doesn't know what to do. They only have two exams in statistics, a midterm and a final. Caroline is nervous about taking the midterm, which is in two weeks.

In political science, Caroline has so many reading assignments that she has trouble keeping track of it all. The class has reading assignments from the textbook, the newspaper, two full-length biographies, and sometimes the professor brings additional readings to class. They are also required to watch the national news each night because they are supposed to be connecting everything they read to current political events. Caroline is not sure how to go about connecting all of the different readings to current events.

Using what you know about text and course characteristics, how would you suggest Caroline approach learning in the courses that are presenting difficulties for her this term?

☐ Thinking Critically
Something to Think About and Discuss

Think about the courses you are taking this semester and carefully examine each of the texts for these courses. Then discuss the following questions with your classmates:

- How do the textbooks differ from each other?
- For each different category of courses, which of the following components are contained in your textbooks?

  - New terminology (vocabulary words specific to the content)
  - New principles or theories described
  - Chronological format (concepts organized by date)
  - Sequential format (concepts built on one another)
  - Topical format (concepts organized by topic)

- What kind of background knowledge, if any, does each text assume you have?
- Which of the strategies presented in this book are the most effective for learning for each course type? Why?
- What type of tests do you have for each course type?

☐ Follow-Up Activities

Keep track of how you approach learning in each of your courses this term:

1. When are you reading the text, what strategies are you using to learn, how effective is your approach?
2. Make modifications to your strategy use based on the information presented in this chapter.

CHAPTER 15

BECOMING FLEXIBLE
Varying Your Reading Rate

Read this chapter to answer the following questions:

- What does it mean to be a flexible reader?
- How can I increase my reading speed?
- What are some habits that may slow my reading?

SELF-ASSESSMENT

DIRECTIONS: Read the following article to assess your current reading speed. Use a stopwatch or a watch with a second hand to keep track of your time. When you have completed the reading, record your time and answer the comprehension questions. Use the formula following the passage to determine your reading rate. Time yourself only for reading the passage but not for answering the comprehension questions.

It's Party Time
Amid a national epidemic of sometimes deadly binge drinking, many campuses are experimenting with ways to dry out.

By Claudia Kalb

Michael Tindle is a frat brother, a tennis player, and a music fan, the kind of guy who enjoys college as much for its social life as its academics. But

Tindle is also the kind of guy who has little love for rowdy drinking games and drunken roommates. So last year, when he entered the University of Michigan, he decided to live in a "substance-free" residence hall. The rules: no alcohol, no smoking. At first, Tindle, who is 19, worried that he would feel out of place. "I thought it would be all computer nerds who don't have any kind of social life," he says. But there were plenty of "regular people" just like him.

As social drinking turns toxic on campuses, students like Tindle are looking for ways to stay dry and many schools are reexamining their alcohol policies. A national survey conducted by the Harvard School of Public Health found that 44 percent of U.S. college students binge-drink, downing five or more drinks in one sitting. The effects range from dangerous—falling down a staircase or losing consciousness—to deadly. Experts estimate that 50 students die from alcohol poisoning or in alcohol-related accidents each year. "Regardless of selectivity or prestige, whether Ivy League, Pac-10, or small liberal-arts college down the road, it's a problem at all of them," says George Dowdall, a coauthor of the Harvard study and an associate dean at Saint Joseph's University in Philadelphia.

Students aren't just having beer or wine; they're mixing hard liquors together. And they're using tubes and funnels to pour it down. "In the past, drinking was more a means to an end—to feel comfortable in a social situation," says William DeJong, director of the Higher Education Center for Alcohol and Other Drug Prevention in Newton, Mass. "Now, it's drinking for the sake of drinking to oblivion."

Ninety-five percent of violent crime on college campuses is alcohol-related, according to the National Center on Addiction and Substance Abuse at Columbia University. And alcohol is implicated in everything from academic problems to sexually transmitted diseases and rape. Last year heavy drinking led to riots on campuses from the University of New Hampshire to Washington State University, as students clashed with police over their "right to party."

But the times may be changing. Last fall a string of alcohol-related deaths at MIT, the University of Virginia, and Louisiana State University jolted many students, parents, and college administrators into action. Schools that receive federal funds are required by law to have an Alcohol and Other Drug (AOD) policy—but in the past, many have been lax. Now administrators are stepping up and expanding their programs. MIT recently instituted a system of citations and fines for illegal drinking and is preparing to hire an administrator to oversee alcohol abuse. Many schools now provide substance-free housing. The University of Michigan, at the forefront of this trend, offered 500 substance-free slots in 1989. Today, thanks to their popularity, 2,600 places are available. "Students tell us that they view it as a way to opt out of the worst parts of a campus alcohol culture," says university spokesman Alan Levy. Other schools organize dry social events. At Holy Cross in Worcester, Mass., students congregate for "mocktails" and munchies or play midnight basketball. And at the five-college consortium of Amherst, Hampshire, Mount Holyoke, Smith, and the University of Massachusetts, a joint Web site dubbed Chilipeppers: Hot Without the Sauce lists community-wide activities where the drinks are everything but alcoholic.

Some schools choose more unorthodox approaches. At Salisbury State University in Maryland, the task force on alcohol abuse decided to create—not disband—a campus pub. Prohibiting alcohol "doesn't seem to us to be practical or philosophically make a lot of sense," says Prof. Jerry Miller, chair of the task force. "Students are going to drink. Our commitment is to encourage people to drink responsibly." Penalties for underage drinking in the pub are severe—a year's probation or loss of housing. Last year the University of Arizona ran a message on posters and in school newspapers: "64 percent of U of A students have four or fewer drinks when they party." The point: to acknowledge the drinking, but encourage moderation. Since the school adopted this direct approach in 1995, the school's binge-drinking rate has dropped from 43 percent to 31 percent.

Even fraternities, which have long played a major part in college drinking, are looking for solutions. The Harvard survey found that 86 percent of fraternity brothers and 80 percent of sorority sisters binge-drink. But those numbers could be shrinking. Three days after a Phi Gamma Delta pledge died of alcohol poisoning at MIT, the fraternity's national organization announced plans to ban alcohol from all of its college houses by the year 2000. Other national fraternities—including Phi Delta Theta and Sigma Nu—have made similar plans. And more are likely to follow; earlier this year the National Interfraternity Conference, which represents dozens of fraternities nationwide, adopted a unanimous resolution "strongly" encouraging its members to provide alcohol-free facilities and to rededicate themselves to core frat values like leadership and community service.

Experts say prospective students concerned about alcohol abuse should spend a night or two in a dorm and go to a couple of parties—both on and off campus. Talk to both school and town police and ask how often they're breaking up raucous parties or making underage drinking arrests. Visit the local hospital emergency room and find out how many intoxicated students are treated in a given week. Remember that when it comes down to it, you are a consumer. Think hard about attending a school that claims to have no drinking problem at all. The best colleges and universities acknowledge that alcohol abuse is a part of college life—and they're doing everything they can to combat it.

With Julie Weingarden in Detroit
Newsweek, Fall, 1998

Record your time: _____

Comprehension Check: Answer the following questions without looking back at the passage.

1. Which of the following is NOT an approach used by colleges to cope with binge-drinking?
   a. Issuing fines and citations for illegal drinking.
   b. Expelling binge-drinkers.
   c. Creating substance-free housing.
   d. Opening a campus pub.

2. The Harvard School of Public Health found that _____ percent of U.S. college students drink five or more drinks in one sitting.
   a. 64
   b. 54
   c. 44
   d. 34

3. Alcohol has been found to be related to which of the following problems on college campuses?
   a. Academic problems
   b. Violent crimes
   c. Riots
   d. All of the above

4. After a fraternity pledge died from binge-drinking, the fraternity planned to ___ by the year 2000.
   a. Ban alcohol
   b. Disband
   c. Ban fraternity parties
   d. Promote leadership

5. This article suggests that binge-drinking will:
   a. Decline significantly
   b. Remain the same
   d. Increase significantly
   e. Decline a little

   > Number of words: 971
   > Time: ___
   > (Use decimals for fractions of a minute. That is, if it took you 3 minutes and 45 seconds, record your time as 3.75 minutes.)
   > Rate of Speed (number of words ÷ time): ___
   > Comprehension score: ___%
   > (comprehension answers: 1. B, 2. C, 3. D, 4. A, 5. D)

What does the word flexible mean to you? You might think of a gymnast able to perform amazing physical feats. Or you might think about a choice (e.g., "What do you want to do?" "Whatever, I'm flexible"). No matter the context, being flexible means that you can adapt to the situation. You don't often hear the word flexible used in learning situations, but you should begin to think about being a flexible learner. Flexible learners adapt their approach to learning based on the four factors that impact learning discussed in this text: their characteristics as a learner, the task, the study strategies they select, and the materials with which they must interact. Flexible readers modify their approaches to text reading and adjust their reading speed to suit their purpose.

Flexible Reading

A flexible reader knows that it is unrealistic to attempt to read everything at the same speed. In other words, you cannot expect to read your chemistry textbook at the same speed at which you read the local news-paper. Your reading rate will vary depending on several factors:

- **The Difficulty of the Material to Be Read.** The easier the mater-ial, the faster you will be able to read.
- **Your Background Knowledge About the Topic.** The more you know about a topic, the faster you can read it.
- **Your Interest in the Topic.** The more interest you have in the material, the faster your rate.

The average adult reads about 200 words per minute; the average col-lege student reads about 250 words per minute. Given the amount of reading that is required in college, it is to your advantage to increase your reading rate without sacrificing comprehension.

When you were learning to read difficult material in elementary school, your teacher probably advised you to slow down. Many college students follow the same advice to this very day when they read some-thing difficult. However, if you are already reading at a slow rate and you slow yourself down even further, you actually might be making it harder to comprehend the text.

If a student is attempting to read the sentence, "The boy went to the store to get a loaf of bread and a gallon of milk." and is reading too slowly he would read the sentence as individual words instead of phrases:

The/ boy / went/ to/ the/ store/ to/ get/ a/ loaf/ of/ bread/ and/ a/ gallon/ of/ milk.

This student will have a more difficult time with comprehension because he must first recognize each of the individual words, then he must put the words together into meaningful phrases, and then he must put those phrases together into a sentence. By then, a good deal of time has passed (in reading terms) and a lot of the comprehension is lost. In this case, reading slower is **decreasing** the ability to comprehend the information.

Should you ever slow down when reading difficult material? Well, yes and no. You should slow down to the point of comprehension, but you should not read too slowly.

Habits That Slow Reading

Many students may have one of several habits that slow their rate of reading speed. They developed many of these habits when they were children and, therefore, may not even be aware of them. As you read the following sections, think about your own reading habits.

Backtracking

A person who reads the same words over and over is backtracking. Think about the example sentence used earlier about the boy going to the store. A person who backtracks would read the sentence as:

> *The boy went to the store/ went to the store/ store/ to get a loaf of bread/ loaf of bread/ and a gallon of milk.*

This habit can dramatically slow both reading and comprehension. Students backtrack when they are not confident that they have understood the reading or when they are not concentrating on what they are reading. If backtracking becomes a habit, students tend to do it no matter what they read, which is why it is one of the toughest habits to break.

To stop backtracking, you must convince yourself that you understand the information as you read. It is one thing to realize consciously that you do not understand a sentence and need to go back and reread it. However, most people who backtrack do not even realize they are doing it. One good way to stop this habit is to follow along with a pen or your finger as you read. You won't be able to backtrack unconsciously if you are following your finger, and it will help keep your eyes moving steadily forward. Another solution if you backtrack is to be sure to take time to preread. Having an idea about where the chapter is headed will help your concentration and, therefore, may also help your tendency to backtrack.

Subvocalization

If you say the words to yourself as you read, you are subvocalizing. Subvocalizers may move their lips, or they may say the words under their breath. When you were learning to read, you probably learned to sound out the words and the teacher asked you to read aloud. Later, when you began to read silently, you were still saying the words in your head. If you have never stopped "saying" the words you are probably subvocalizing. This habit slows reading rates because you can say only about 200 words per minute, but most everyone has the ability to read and comprehend at much faster rates.

Luckily, this is a fairly easy habit to break. If you find that you move your lips as you read, put your finger over your lips and when you feel that they are moving, will yourself to stop. If you are saying the words under your breath, put your hand on your throat as you read. You will feel a vibration if you are subvocalizing and again you can will yourself to stop. Some students have said that humming while reading helped them stop subvocalizing.

Fixations

Each time your eye focuses on a word or phrase it is called a fixation. Everyone fixates, but some people fixate too often or too long, which can slow reading down. Fixating on every word is also a habit left over from when you first learned to read. In elementary school you learned to recognize letters and then words one at a time, which made you fixate often. In fact, you probably stopped at every word. However, effective readers do not fixate on every word. Instead they read groups of words in a single fixation. A person who fixates too often would read the sentence as:

The/ boy /went/ to/ the/ store/ to/ get/ a/ loaf/ of/ bread/ and/ a/ gallon/ of/ milk.

This person is stopping on each word. To break the habit of fixating too often, a student needs to learn how to include more information in each fixation.

One way to break the habit of too many fixations is to use the **key word** method. In this strategy, you don't waste your time reading words like "the" or "and." Instead, you focus on the more meaningful words. As you fixate on the key words your eyes tend to include the words like "the" without having to fixate on them. A person using the key word strategy often would read the sentence as:

*The **boy went/** to the **store/** to get a loaf of **bread/** and a gallon of **milk.***

Experiment with this method to see how many times you must fixate in order to get the main idea of a sentence and to prove to yourself that you can comprehend without focusing on every word.

Another strategy to reduce fixation is **phrase word** reading. In this strategy, you go through the passage and stop in the middle of each phrase. When you stop, your eye takes in the entire phrase. It is different from the key word strategy because you are not looking for specific words; rather, you are taking in larger chunks of information at a time. A person using the phrase word strategy would read the sentence as:

*The **boy went/** to **the store/** to get a **loaf of bread/** and a **gallon of milk.***

Some students learn best using the key word strategy, but others say that they comprehend better using the phrase word strategy. Try out both strategies to see which one works best for you.

QUICK TAKES

Reading Fixations

How often do you fixate? Try this experiment with a partner to determine the number of fixations you make per line.

1. Punch a small hole in a sheet of paper with typed paragraphs on it.
2. Hold the blank side of the paper close to your eye so you can see through it.

(continued)

3. Have your partner read the paragraphs contained on the sheet of paper and watch her eyes.

4. Count the number of fixations (times she stops) per line.

5. Change places with your partner and repeat to have your partner count your fixations.

Discuss the habits that may be slowing you reading and your partner's reading.

Increasing Your Reading Speed

Many companies advertise speed reading programs that cost several hundred dollars. However, you can increase your reading speed, and sometimes even double it, without spending big bucks. All you need is something interesting to read and some time each day to push yourself to read faster.

The purpose of pushed reading is to increase your overall reading speed. When you practice reading faster you should not use your textbooks or even novels assigned for class. You cannot expect to be able to speed read a difficult textbook filled with new concepts and comprehend all of the information. Likewise, if you speed read a novel in your literature class, you will miss the language that makes the novel a great work. You may grasp the basic plot, but little else. When you are practicing reading faster, use a piece of text that you find enjoyable—the campus newspaper or a novel you are reading for pleasure—*but do not use material that you will be tested over.*

Networking

Increasing Your Rate

Many sites on the Internet publish short stories or magazine articles. Find some stories that interest you on the Web and use them for your reading rate practice. You might want to

(continued)

check out *Newsweek* or your favorite newspaper as a starting point. Then find some articles that will hold your attention for 10 to 15 minutes for your pushed reading. If you find that you read more slowly on the computer, as many people do, print out the stories you find before using them to increase your reading speed.

How to Read Faster

- **Choose High-Interest Material.** It is best to push yourself to read faster with material that you are familiar with and enjoy. For example, if you like to read mystery novels, choose one to use for pushed reading.

- **Practice Every Day.** To increase your reading rate, you will need to push yourself to read faster every day for 10 to 15 minutes. Use your local or school newspaper or anything that will sustain your interest for that amount of time. You might want to choose three or four brief articles and take a short break after each one.

- **Read at Slightly-Faster-than-Comfortable Speeds.** As you read, push yourself to read slightly faster than you usually do. You should feel a little uncomfortable reading at this speed and feel that you would prefer to slow down, but you should also sense that you understand what you are reading.

- **Check Your Comprehension.** Increasing your reading rate while losing comprehension provides no benefit. Therefore, you need to check your comprehension of the material you are reading. However, because you are changing a habit, it is okay to have comprehension of only 70 to 80 percent of what you read during pushed reading. In fact, if you are having 100 percent comprehension you can probably push yourself to read faster. To check your comprehension, try to summarize the information. Did you identify all of the key ideas? What about important details and examples? If you find that you are not comprehending the information, slow down a bit.

- **Try to Read at the Same Time Each Day.** Finding 15 minutes to read every day should not be much of a problem, but in order to keep an accurate record of your improvement you should try to find the time when you are most alert and try to read at that same time every day.

- **Don't Give Up.** Improving your reading rate is a slow but steady process. You may make some great improvements one week and then see little change the next. Don't worry about the fluctuations in your rate, as long as you are seeing an overall increase. However, if you find that you have gone several weeks without any improvement, make a conscious effort to push yourself even faster when you read.

SUCCESS AT A GLANCE

Keys to Reading Faster

- Choose high-interest material.
- Practice every day.
- Read at slightly-faster-than-comfortable speeds.
- Check your comprehension.
- Try to read at the same time each day.
- Don't give up.

How Fast Should You Read?

Students often ask how quickly they should read. This is not an easy question to answer because the rate at which you read depends on your purpose for reading and the type of material you are reading. Your goal is to be flexible in your reading and to choose a rate based on your purpose. In other words, you should be able to read a magazine or novel faster than a textbook.

In general, you should always strive to read faster than 200 words per minute because lower speeds can inhibit your comprehension. Otherwise, we are hesitant to give exact numbers because the rate at which you "should" read depends on several factors:

1. **How quickly do you currently read?** It would make no sense to tell a student to read at 400 words per minute if she is currently reading at 225 words per minute with 70 percent comprehension. Instead, we would tell her to use the pushed reading strategy described in this chapter to help increase overall reading rate without sacrificing comprehension.

2. **What is your purpose for reading?**

   - **Slowest speeds:** If you are reading to write a paper about a topic or to prepare for an exam you will read at fairly slow speeds. This includes reading difficult texts, poetry, technical manuals, textbooks, or literature with which you must take the time to notice and savor the language.

   - **Moderate speeds:** If your purpose is to read for pleasure or for general information, you will be able to read more quickly. This type of reading includes novels, newspapers, magazines, and other reading for enjoyment.

   - **Quickest speeds:** If you are scanning material for specific information, you will be able to read at very fast rates. This type of reading includes dictionaries, catalogs, phone books, and other reference books. Keep in mind, however, that this is not really reading in the true sense of the word.

3. **What is your task?** If you will be tested over the material, take more time to really understand it. It makes no sense to rush through your history text if you are not getting all of the information. If you are reading for pleasure there may be times when you want to read slowly to enjoy your book, and times when you want to use pushed reading to increase your rate. Be sure to leave yourself some time for both.

COLLEGE CAMPUS TODAY

Literacy Programs

Many campuses offer community literacy programs where college students team up with schools or community organiza-

(continued)

tions to tutor children who are having trouble with reading. Students who have participated in these programs find them rewarding, because they get to help a child learn to read. In addition, although students realize that reading sometimes feels like a chore, they can't imagine what life would be like if they could not read.

☐ Real College
Rudy's Reading Rate

DIRECTIONS: Read the following *Real College* scenario and respond to the questions based on what you learned in this chapter.

Rudy is first-year student at a small college. His goal is to finish his degree in computer science in 4 years, so he is taking 15 to 18 credit hours each term. However, he is overwhelmed by the amount of reading he has to do for each of his classes. He has to read technical reports and manuals for his computer science courses; novels, poetry, and plays in his English class; a very difficult textbook in his physics class; and a textbook and newspaper in his political science course. He knows that his problem is that he reads too slowly. Ever since grade school, he has always been the last one to finish his reading and the last one to turn in an exam. He is sure that if he could just learn to read faster, he would do better in school. He has signed up for a speed reading course where he spends a lot of time using computer eye-movement programs, but he does not feel comfortable reading with that equipment and does not think it is helping. He generally tries to read everything as fast as he can, but he finds that he gets tired quickly and can't keep it up. He also finds that he really doesn't understand what he is reading in some of his courses.

Using what you know about increasing reading rate and the habits that slow down reading, give Rudy some advice on how to go about increasing his reading speed.

☐ Thinking Critically
Something to Think About and Discuss

For the next week, practice pushing yourself to read faster each day using the strategies you have learned in this chapter. Remember to read at a slightly-faster-than-comfortable pace. Use a stopwatch or a watch with a second hand to keep track of your time. When you have completed the reading, record your time. Then, as a comprehension check, think about what you have read. How much can you recall?

☐ Follow-Up Activities

As you work on increasing your reading rate, keep track of your speeds and your comprehension in a journal. You should notice a steady increase in your rate over a period of time. Eventually you will find that your comprehension is reaching 100 percent at higher speeds. You can then decide whether to continue to increase your reading rate.

PART SIX

PREPARING FOR YOUR COLLEGE EXAMS

In Part VI we discuss strategies for exam preparation. In Chapter 16, you learn strategies in preparing for and taking objective exams. You are also introduced to some general test-taking strategies.

Chapter 17 presents strategies in preparing for and taking essay exams. You also learn about taking specialized exams such as open-book or take-home exams.

Studying Smarter: Don't run out of time before you run out of test. When you go into a testing situation, have a plan.

CHAPTER 16

PREPARING FOR OBJECTIVE EXAMS

Read this chapter to answer the following questions:

- What exam preparation strategies work in almost all situations?
- How should I prepare for objective exams?

SELF-ASSESSMENT

DIRECTIONS: Think about the following questions and answer them honestly. Once you have finished reading this chapter, think about how you can change your current objective exam preparation approach.

1. Taking a multiple-choice test is easy because all I have to do is recognize the correct answer. T F
2. To study for an objective test, I memorize all the key terms. T F
3. It is best to spread out studying time over several days. T F
4. When I study, I choose one strategy that works and stick with it. T F
5. Cramming works because I can only get motivated under pressure. T F

6. Multiple-choice tests can ask application and synthesis   T   F
   questions.

7. To study for exams, I read the text chapters.   T   F

8. When I study, I start with the first concept and work   T   F
   through all of the assigned reading in order.

Because we believe that preparing to take an exam begins on the day you begin to read about and listen to topics on which you will be tested, we almost feel as though having a special chapter on exam preparation goes against the philosophy of this book. That is, active learners are in a constant state of getting ready to take an exam. They have a difficult time distinguishing when prereading, reading, and taking lecture notes turns into the rehearsal and review that goes into test preparation. That said, we also know that many activities that occur as test time gets closer might be more appropriately labeled as test-preparation strategies.

General Test-Preparation Strategies

Although this chapter will focus on the specific strategies that you can use primarily in preparation for objective exams, there are some general test-preparation guidelines that apply to almost any type of exam. We will address these general strategies first because they are some "quick starters" that can get you moving in the right direction.

In general, you should:

- **Start Early.** Be sure that you have completed your assigned reading at least several days before the test. Remember that reading and studying are not the same thing. All of your reading should be completed *before* you begin studying.

- **Get Organized.** Organize all of your studying tools and strategies—notes, annotations, study strategies—so that you can dig right in.

- **Distribute Your Time.** Rather than trying to cram all of your studying into 1 or 2 days, distribute your time over several days. Spending a total of 6 hours studying spread over 5 days is much more effective than trying to spend 6 hours studying the day before, or even 3 hours a day for 2 days before the test.

- **Break Up the Work.** If you begin studying several days in advance, you will be able to break up the information you have to study into chunks of major concepts. In other words, don't sit down to study with the idea in mind that you will study every chapter and every page of notes. Study groups of information that seem to fit together, or at least identify which concepts you want to learn in a particular study session. This helps you stay more focused on the task at hand.

- **Stay Healthy.** Eat properly and get enough sleep. Try to remain in a studying routine rather than staying up all night cramming. Eat regular meals and exercise if that is part of your normal routine. As part of staying healthy, it's also important to monitor your emotional health by evaluating your stress level. When you get too stressed out, it influences other aspects of your performance and becomes a vicious cycle.

- **Self-Test.** It's important to have a firm understanding of what you know and what you don't know. Remember that self-testing involves asking yourself questions about the material, saying the information to yourself or to someone else, and then checking to see whether you are correct.

- **Study with a Classmate.** Studying with another serious-minded student has great benefits regardless of what kind of test you will have. One of the most successful models for studying with another is for both individuals to study on their own and then to get together to ask each other questions a day or two before the exam. Both parties can then find out which concepts they know very well and which ones they need to spend more time on.

Networking

Online Exams

Many professors now have sample exams online. Check out your professor's Web page or the department Web page to see what is available. In addition, visit the Web site of your textbook publisher. There are often quizzes, sample exams, links to additional information, and chat rooms where you can discuss the text with other students nationwide.

- **Look at Old Exams.** Talk to others who have previously taken the class. Finding out as much information about the test as possible, whether it's from looking at old exams or by talking to others, is simply a smart thing to do. It's not cheating; it's being an informed consumer, so to speak. If professors permit students to keep their exams, you can be fairly certain that they will not be giving that same test again. But it's probably also a safe bet that the kinds of questions asked will be similar. When talking with students who have already taken the class and the professor, it's a good rule of thumb to find out specifics about the level of questions and grading.

COLLEGE CAMPUS TODAY

Does Your Campus Have a Test Bank?

Many campuses have test banks: places on campus where professors can put copies of retired tests on file for students to examine. Sometimes test banks are located in the library and other times a student organization may be in charge of collecting and organizing them. Often Greek organizations keep test banks. If your campus has one, use it to find out the types of questions your professor asks. As long as the professor knows that his test is part of a legitimate test bank, it not academically dishonest to use these old tests.

Many of these general tips are common sense. But they are tips that students often overlook as they get caught up in exam preparation. In the next section, we will focus more specifically on preparation for and taking objective exams.

Preparing for and Taking Objective Exams

Preparing for Objective Exams

Objective exams can consist of several different kinds of questions. The most common types are multiple-choice and true/false questions, but matching and fill-in-the-blanks are also objective questions. Another name for this type of question is **recognition items** because all of the information is there; your task is to recognize it. For example, for multiple-choice questions, you have to recognize which answer out of the four or five choices is correct. For a true/false question, you have to recognize whether the statement is true or false. These items are considered objective because there is (or should be) only one correct answer, if the test is well written. In other words, in a multiple-choice question, only one of the answers should be correct. Moreover, if you studied and really know the information, the correct answer should be obvious to you.

SUCCESS AT A GLANCE
Studying for Objective Tests

- Make s jot list of key points
- Organize this information around broad concepts
- Begin each study session with a review
- Rehearse and self-test
- Concentrate on areas of weakness

Because of the precise knowledge required to answer objective items, it is extremely important that two key factors guide your preparation: (1) organization of information; and (2) thinking about the information the way in which your professor expects.

Organization. Let's start with an example. Suppose you are in an introductory level psychology course and every two to three weeks, you have a 50-item objective test—always all multiple-choice items. In any given testing period, you have about 30 pages of lecture notes and three or four chapters of information to study. Where do you begin? We have found that the best place to start when you know you will have an objective test is to make a jot list of all of the key concepts from text and lecture. The example below shows what this jot list might look like for two history chapters, one of which includes the excerpt on the Bay of Pigs incident and the Cuban missile crisis that you will find at the beginning of Part Four. Notice that the jot list is not particularly formal. Rather, it simply serves to force you to think about the concepts before you begin to study. Unless you make a conscious effort to jot down these concepts, you may leave out important information or simply gloss over concepts that you should spend a significant amount of time on.

QUICK TAKES

Learning Organizational Skills

Learning organizational skills—whether it's making jot lists, monitoring what you need to accomplish, or keeping a schedule book—will serve you long after you graduate from college. For most careers, organization is a must if you want to move forward, impress your boss, and have a social life at the same time. Sometimes, students think that these types of skills are just for college students, but they're not. Everyone needs to be organized. Once you learn and practice these skills in college, you will take them into the workplace with you.

Example of a Jot List

1950s and 1960s

Chapter 29 Affluence and Anxiety (1950s)	Chapter 30 The Turbulent Sixties
Levittown	JFK & cold war
Post-WWII boom	Flexible response
Upward surge in economy	Crisis in Berlin
cold war	SE Asia (containment)
Suburban life	Castro/Bay of Pigs
Role of consumerism	Cuban missile crisis
Critics of consumerism	New Frontier
Sputnik and reactions	Economy
Truman and the Fair Deal	Civil Rights
Eisenhower's modern republicanism	Court reform

(continued)

Chapter 29 Affluence and Anxiety (1950s)	Chapter 30 The Turbulent Sixties
Civil Rights and desegregation Black activism Areas of growth	LBJ era 1964 election Reform War in Vietnam Student protests Civil Rights and Black power Women's lib Nixon's return

■   ■   ■

Once you have made your jot list, then you can organize the information to study. You will need to:

1. Group together all of your rehearsal strategies related to the overriding concept. (Let's use the history topic of "the JFK presidency" as an example.) You should also know which sections of lecture notes go with this concept.

2. Look for overlap between the text and lecture and focus your studying on the big picture of the Kennedy years rather than just concentrating on text information one time and the lecture notes at another.

3. Focus each study session around a couple of broad concepts, such as "the cold war" or "or the presidency of JFK" rather than simply trying to "read through" everything you have to learn for the entire test. In other words, one night you might study all the material related to the Eisenhower presidency, the next night concentrate on JFK, and the third night learn issues such as civil rights or the cold war, concepts that spanned both of these presidencies. Following this procedure encourages you to think actively and critically. Use your jot list as a guide. Then rehearse and self-test the material from the next broad concept. Your study schedule might look something like the plan below. Note that each study session begins with a review and that after you have covered all the material, you end with a self-testing session where you identify specific areas of weakness.

4. Concentrate on any areas of weakness as you and your study partner question each other in one final study session before the exam.

5. On the morning of the exam, talk though the couple of ideas that were still giving you difficulty.

Example of a Study Schedule

Session 1—Monday
Focus: 1950s presidencies of Truman and Eisenhower

4:30-5:00	Organize all information
5:00-6:00	Study: Post-WWII boom, Truman, Eisenhower
6:00-6:45	Eat dinner
7:00-8:00	Review: Post-WWII Boom, Truman, Eisenhower
	Study: Civil Rights, desegregation, and Black activism

Session 2—Tuesday
Focus: 1960s presidencies of JFK and LBJ; major historical events

10:00-10:30	Review 1950s
10:30-11:30	Study: JFK and key events; e.g., Cuban missile crisis
11:30-12:00	Lunch
12:30-1:50	Class

Thinking. Organizing, both in terms of how you will group the concepts to be learned and how you will structure your study sessions, is crucial to performing well on objective tests. However, organizing won't help you much if you aren't sure about the level of thinking required. On essay tests (which we'll talk about in the next chapter), you can pretty much count on having to think critically and to analyze and synthesize information. But on objective exams, many students make the mistake of believing that the test questions are designed solely to see if they have memorized. That is, they think the questions don't go beyond asking for facts. Students who fall into this trap can experience grave difficulty and often don't do well. That's why it's important to know the kind of thinking that your professor expects. If she expects you to memorize the facts and most of the questions are factual in nature, you would study in one way. If, however, she asks application, synthesis, examples, and other types of higher-level questions, you would study another way.

To clarify this point, let's look at several example questions. Each of these questions is based on one of the excerpts in this book. The first example in each pair of questions is a memory-level task. The second is a higher-level question.(The * indicates the correct answer.)

Set A (based on the history excerpt)
1. The Bay of Pigs invasion was actually planned by
   a. Truman.
   b. Eisenhower.*
   c. Kennedy.
   d. Johnson.

2. As a result of the Bay of Pigs invasion,
   a. Cuban exiles had more intense training.
   b. the United States backed off of any further attempts to bother Cuba.
   c. Eisenhower lost his run for the presidency.
   d. JFK threatened the Soviet Union.*

Set B (based on the psychology excerpt)
1. One of the key results of the study that examined the relationship between prototypes and heavy drinking was
   a. an adolescent's parents have an indirect affect on her drinking habits.*
   b. those with negative drinking prototypes drank more.
   c. one's peer group has little influence on their drinking habits.
   d. All of the above are results of this study.

2. Which of the following statements about prototypes and heavy drinking is the most accurate?
   a. If you view the typical teenage drinker as unattractive and immature you tend to drink more yourself.
   b. Both your peer group and your parental relationship influence your drinking habits.*
   c. The prototype you have about other teenagers who drink has little or no effect on your own drinking habits.
   d. All of the above statements are accurate reflections of the study.

It is fairly easy to see the differences in these questions. The first question is very straightforward and requires little interpretation or thinking beyond the memory level. Studying for an objective test that asked this type of question would be a relatively easy task: Identify the key terms and ideas and memorize a definition, component parts, or the like. But think about the problem you might have if you simply memorized information and then had an exam that asked questions like the second one in each pair. You would have a much more difficult time because you had thought about the information in an incorrect way. Even if you studied quite a bit, if you only memorized when the task is to somehow go beyond memorization, taking the test would be a struggle.

The point is that you need to be clear about the professor's expectations and the way he tests. As we mentioned earlier, look at old exams, talk to students who have taken a class with the professor, or ask the professor. Whatever you do, have an accurate picture of the kind of test you will have. Then, as you are doing your rehearsal, review, and self-testing, you can frame your studying accordingly.

Taking Objective Exams

You have studied, you feel good about what you know, and you are absolutely ready to take your exam. Well, you're almost ready. The next (or final) thing you need to think about is a game plan. A sports analogy fits well here. The basketball team has studied the playbook, looked at films of themselves and the opponent, and is mentally ready to play this game. They are pumped and psyched. But if they don't have a game plan or fail to follow the game plan provided by the coaches, all their work may not result in a win. Any athletic team going into a game needs a game plan to follow—some sort of strategy for winning the game.

A testing situation for you is just like game day for the basketball team. You have prepared, you are mentally ready to take the test, and you want to do well. Now you have to follow through with your game plan for taking the test. To plan your strategy, it helps to ask yourself some questions before you get into the testing situation:

- How will I work through the test? Will I simply start with the first item and answer the questions in consecutive order?

- What will I do when I come across an item I'm not sure of? Will I skip it and come back to it later, or will I mark something before going on to the next item?

- How will I choose an answer when I absolutely can't even make an educated guess?

- How will I approach answering true/false questions?

- What will I do if I am running out of time and still have several questions to answer?

It's important to think about how you approach an exam before you are actually in a testing situation. We suggest the following guidelines.

- **Get to Class on Time.** Leave home early enough so that you don't have to rush. When you rush, you tend to get anxious, especially on an exam day. Once you get to class, get out your pen and anything else you might need. Relax and take a couple of deep breaths. Give yourself some positive reinforcement by saying such things as "I studied." "I know this stuff." "I know I should do well on this exam."

- **When You Get Your Exam, Take a Minute or so to Look Through it.** See how many items there are so that you know how to divide up your time. Very important and often overlooked: *Read the directions* so you know what you are required to do.

- **Read the First Item.** If you don't know the answer, leave it blank and go to the next item. Do this with each item until you find one of which you are certain. We believe it is good advice to do the items you know first and then come back and spend more time on those of which you are unsure. The only problem this seems to create is that students sometimes make mistakes by putting an answer in the wrong place on their answer sheet. Therefore, if you are going to skip around on the test, you need to make sure that your answer goes in the corresponding place on your answer sheet.

- **Eliminate Answers Whenever Possible.** On a multiple-choice question, you might be able to eliminate two answer choices immediately, but the other two alternatives might both be plausible. If this occurs, you at least have a 50/50 chance of choosing correctly.

- **Use Information from Other Items on the Exam to Help You with Items You Don't Know.** Once you have gone through the entire test, you can often pick up information from one question that will help you answer another. That's why it's a good idea to go through and answer the items you know first.

- **Use All of the Allotted Time.** Many students fail to use all of the class period to take their exam and then end up making careless mistakes such as leaving items blank when they could have guessed. Even when you have answered every question, it's best to go through the test one more time just to be sure. Remember, it's easy to mark a wrong answer when you actually know the correct answer.

- **When Faced with a Situation in Which You Have to Guess, Make a Selection and Move on.** Go with your gut selection and don't change your mind unless you have found information later in the test that helps you remember an idea related to the question. On a multiple-choice exam, for example, some students will select the same answer choice for every question they don't know. For true/false questions you might answer all true or all false for items on which you guess. Whatever you do, however, never leave objective test items blank unless you are penalized for guessing.

Taking exams does not have to be extremely stressful. If you have studied well and have a game plan for taking exams, you'll find that you are usually more relaxed going in and will tend to do better.

☐ Real College
Teddy's Tactics

DIRECTIONS: Read the following *Real College* scenario and respond to the questions based on what you learned in this chapter.

In high school, Teddy was always a model student. He wasn't one of those kids who waited until the morning of a test to try to cram as much information as possible into his brain. Teddy usually started a day or two before his scheduled exams and reviewed the study guides that most of his teachers gave him. An hour or so of reading over this information typically resulted in a good test grade for him.

Now, early in his first semester of college, Teddy finds that these tactics aren't working so well for him. He earned a D on his first anthropology exam and things don't look all that promising for the multiple-choice test that he has in a few days in psychology. It's not that he doesn't have the time; he just doesn't know what to do.

His professors don't seem to be of much help at all. Gone are the study guides that once made studying easy. Gone are the kind of tests he had in high school that simply asked him to memorize facts from class lectures. And gone are the frequent tests that were so common in high school. In anthropology he only has two more tests and a short paper. Teddy knows that he has to do something to get back on track.

For the impending psychology test, at least he has kept up with his reading . . . well almost. And he does know what the task is: He is responsible for five text chapters, all of his lecture notes, and two outside readings that focus on psychological research. The test will contain 50 multiple-choice questions, most of which the professor said would be example and application questions. There are another 10 matching items where he will have to match researchers with important research they carried out.

What advice would you give Teddy about how he should get back on track?

What general advice would you give Teddy for studying for objective exams? How might he have to change his studying from anthropology to psychology?

☐ Thinking Critically
Something to Think About and Discuss

One way to get a feel for the difference between thinking about the information in a factual way and in a more conceptual, higher-level way is to rewrite questions. Using the example questions that appear earlier in the chapter as a guide, use one of the text excerpts to write a factual question. Then write another question that draws from the same information yet taps higher-level thinking. Discuss these questions with a classmate.

☐ Follow-Up Activities

1. One of the most important things you can do to improve your readiness for objective exams is to monitor your learning through self-testing. Remember that when you self-test you try to answer questions without looking at the information. You put the information to be learned in your own words and say it to yourself or a study partner. When studying for your next objective exam, make an effort to self-test. Evaluate your confidence level on test day once you have self-tested.

2. Create a study plan for your next objective test. What concepts will you concentrate on for each study session? How will you know when you understand and can remember all the information? How will you review? What will your game plan be once you enter class to take the exam?

CHAPTER 17

PREPARING FOR AND TAKING ESSAY AND SPECIALITY EXAMS

Read this chapter to answer the following questions:

- How should you prepare for essay exams?
- What kind of a study plan should you have for preparing for essay exams?
- How should you study for special types of exams such as take-home or open-book exams?

SELF-ASSESSMENT

DIRECTIONS: The following questions are predictions for a history course. For each of the questions, decide whether the question is too broad (B), too narrow (N), or would make a good (G) essay question.

1. _____ From 1914 to the 1990s there have been obvious demographic shifts. Discuss the factors contributing to these shifts and the effects they have had technologically.

2. _____ How has life changed as a result of twentieth-century technology?

3. _____ Compare and contrast the weapons used in World War I with those used in World War II.

4. _____ What effect did the depression during the 1930s have on politics?

5. _____ What influences did technological advances have on the progression and expansion of World War II?

Of course, your ability to respond to these essay questions will depend on the content covered in class. Nonetheless, numbers one and five would be considered good essay questions, numbers two and four would be too broad, and number three would be two narrow. Keep this in mind when predicting essay questions for your own classes.

Preparing for essay exams involves different strategies than preparing for objective exams. This often comes as a shock, especially to first-year college students who may have had little experience with essay exams in high school or, if they have had essay exams, they prepared for them the same way in which they prepared for objective exams. As a general rule, essay preparation requires a different type of approach, a different way of thinking, and a different way of organizing.

When we use the term essay exam, we are referring to any type of question that requires you write an extended response. In this instance, essay tests would include:

- traditional multi-paragraph responses to questions
- short-answer questions that may require you to write a paragraph or two in response to a more narrowly focused question
- identification items, which require you to define a term, explain the significance of something, or write several sentences describing a person, place, event, etc.

Sometimes these types of exams are referred to as **recall** tests, because you are asked to recall all of the pertinent information from your memory. Unlike recognition questions (e.g., multiple-choice, true/false) that ask you to recognize the correct information, recall questions require you to remember the information on your own.

PORPE

PORPE (Simpson, 1986), which is an acronym for **P**redict, **O**rganize, **R**ehearse, **P**ractice, and **E**valuate, is a structured, organized strategy specifically designed to help you prepare for essay or short-answer exams. You begin the PORPE studying process after you have completed your reading, constructed useful study strategies, and have organized your lecture notes. As we explain each step of PORPE, we have included an example based on a predicted essay question from a psychology passage about the components of thinking.

Step 1: Predict. (Predict several days before the test.) The first thing you need to do is to predict some broad questions that your professor might ask you. Simply put, the better predictor you are, the better you will do on the exam. But predicting questions can be a tricky business. It has been our experience that when students begin to use this strategy, they either predict questions that are far too broad or way too narrow. For example, predicting a question such as "Discuss the presidency of Theodore Roosevelt" would be too broad; a question such as "What was the Fair Deal?" would be too specific for an essay question. Generally, the fewer the number of questions you are required to answer on an exam, the broader your prediction questions should be.

Keep in mind when predicting that rarely will your specific question be precisely what the professor asks. But once you become a good predictor, there will be considerable overlap between what you predict and the actual questions on the test. This is an example of a good essay prediction for a psychology course in which you were studying *Cognition*.

Step 1: Predict: Predict a question that you think might be asked on the exam.

Q: Thinking involves three basic components. First, explain each component. Then, explain how the three components are related and interact to produce thoughts.

Step 2: Organize. (Organize three or four days before the test.) After you have predicted several questions, you need to organize the information. Most students like to use an outline as a way of organizing so that they can see the key points they want to make and the support they want to provide for each key point. Other organizing strategies such as concept maps or charts also work well (see Chapter 13.) When you organize the material, think about both key generalizations and information to support those generalizations. Spend some time organizing your thoughts so that you will study worthwhile material.

As you become more focused and predict specific questions, your outline should be more comprehensive and detailed. To fill in your outline, use information that you included in your text annotations (Chapter 12), rehearsal strategies (Chapter 13), and what you have annotated in your lecture notes (Chapter 10). Be sure that you draw from both text and lecture as well as any other sources for which you are responsible. And be sure to do a detailed outline for each of the questions you predicted. The example below shows what an outline would look like for the essay question we predicted in Step 1 of PORPE.

Step 2: Organize. In an organized fashion, write down the ideas you want to include in your essay.

3 components of thinking—words, images, concepts

1. Words—inner speech and spoken thoughts.

- Thinking is not just talking to yourself—3 reasons
  - If true, one would not have trouble "putting thoughts into words."

- Words can be ambiguous, but thoughts are not.
- Some living things can think, but don't use language (e.g., cats).
- Linguistic relativity hypothesis (Whorf, 1956).
  - Suggests that thoughts are shaped by the language we speak
    - Ex.: Inuit tribe has different words for snow and can think about subtle differences in snow better than English speakers because they have more words to describe it.
    - Reverse ex.: Dani tribe only has 2 words for color (light and dark) but can perceive and learn shades of color despite the lack of words.
  - Language shapes some aspects of thought and memory. In fact, language can enhance memory.

2. Mental Imagery—when we form images, we think about it by scanning the image in our memory; images not like the real object; serve important purposes since people use images to understand and to increase their own motivation.

   - Mental Space—Kosslyn. 3 properties—spacial extent, limited size, and grain.

3. Concepts—mental categories that are similar; ex.: fruit is a concept.

   - Based on prototypes—best or clearest examples of a concept; ex.: a prototype of "art" would be paintings or sculptures rather than a neon light show.
   - Organized in several ways . . . by—features, visual images, or schemas (cognitive frameworks about our own representation of the world).

4. How concepts, words, and images interact—all 3 contribute to enabling us to think; language shapes how we view the world; concepts allow us to group things so that we can access information more quickly; images enable us to think about information from a perspective other than verbally.

■   ■   ■

Step 3: Rehearse. (Rehearse several times for each question, beginning three or four days before the test.) Now it's time to commit the information in your outline to memory. Read the question you predicted. Then read through your outline slowly and deliberately. "Listen" to what you are saying. Does it make sense? Do you have enough support? Do the ideas flow? After you have read through the outline several times, ask yourself the question again. This time, try answering it without looking at the outline. Be sure that you are rehearsing the concepts accurately. If you are not sure of something, immediately return to your outline and read that part through again, or if you are really experiencing problems, you might need to check your text or lecture notes to clarify or add support. Then try to restate the answer to that portion of the question. Always keep in mind that when you rehearse, it's important to also engage in self-testing.

Step 4: Practice. (Practice two days before the test.) Now it's time to practice writing out an answer to one of your questions. Write under the same conditions that you will have in class. For example, if you will be required to answer two essay questions in a 50 minute class period, take only 20 minutes to practice on one of your questions. That would leave 20 minutes to practice on the second question and 10 minutes to go back and proof your work.

You should also construct your answer so that it is organized the same way that you will organize it in class. Write in complete sentences, include appropriate examples, and be sure to have an introduction and a conclusion. The example below shows an answer for the question we predicted in Step 1.

Example of a Practice Essay

Thinking involves three basic components: words, images, and concepts. These components are strongly related to one another and interact to form thoughts. Without this interaction, we would not be able to think.

The use of words in both inner speech and spoken thought is an important component of thought. In the past, some have believed that thinking is the same as talking to yourself. However, this is not true because if thinking were the same as inner speech, we would never have trouble putting our thoughts into words. In addition, words are often ambiguous, but thoughts are not. For example, if you were thinking about "light" you don't wonder whether you are thinking about the light of the sun or the weight of an object. Third, there are many living things that think, but do not use words (e.g., cats and dogs).

Others have suggested that thoughts are shaped by particular words and language. This theory, the linguistic relativity hypothesis, is not entirely true. It is true that language can help describe small nuances such as the Inuit tribe's ability to think about subtle differences in snow because the language contains many words for snow. However, Rosch found that the Dani tribe, which only has words for light and dark but no words for colors, was able to perceive and think about variations in colors despite their lack of words to describe them. Thus, words do not entirely determine how we think, but they do influence some aspects and can even enhance our memory.

Mental imagery, or the "mind's eye," also plays a role in thought. Kosslyn discussed three properties of mental space. The first is spatial intent, or when we form images, we think about it by scanning the image in our memory. The second is limited size. This means that when we think about a small object we can "see" the whole thing at once, but when we think about visualizing a large object (such as an elephant) we either see only a small piece or it needs to be seen from further away to see the entire object. Third, mental images have a grain, which is similar to the resolution on a TV set. If you look at an item that is too small, there is not enough grain to view it and it will appear blurred. But images are limited because they cannot represent abstract concepts (such as "truth") and they are often ambiguous. Like words, images can contribute to our thoughts but cannot be the only means.

The final component of thought is concepts. A concept is a grouping of ideas, objects, or events in a meaningful way. Concepts tend to be based on prototypes, or the best and clearest examples of a particular concept. For example, most people would think of painting when they think of art, but not many would think about a laser light show. Concepts are organized both according to their levels of specificity and according to our schemas about the concept.

Thought is an interaction between words, images, and concepts. A concept may be described by words or images, but they differ from these components. Words and images are not concepts, but they can be used to express concepts. In addition, because concepts allow us to organize ideas together it aids our ability to represent the concept through words and images. Without these three components, thinking would be virtually impossible.

■   ■   ■

Step 5: Evaluate. (Immediately after practicing.) Now comes the most difficult part—evaluating your own writing. After you have finished practicing, read what you have written. After you have finished reading your practice essay, get out your outline and any other strategies you have been using to study from, and check for accuracy and completeness. Ask yourself the following questions:

- Is my introduction clear and focused?

- Are my generalizations complete and precise?

- Are my examples and supporting information accurate and complete?

- Do I have a conclusion that relates back to my introduction and overall thesis?

NETWORKING

Critiquing Essays over E-mail

If you have been working with a classmate this term in a course that requires you to write essay exams, you might try sending your study partner a copy of a practice essay over e-mail. Have your study partner critique your essay by evaluating its strengths and weaknesses. You can do the same for your study partner.

Once you have honestly answered these questions you can go back and do some rethinking and reorganizing, if necessary. You may even want to show your essay to your professor so that he can provide you with feedback. Or if your campus has a writing center, you may be able to get help with organizing your response.

QUICK TAKES

Writing Done Right

We believe that one of the most useful skills you can learn in college is the ability to write. Using components of the PORPE strategy can help you prepare for essays, but can also help you to organize a paper, group project or just about any other writing task you may encounter in college or beyond. Most careers require you to be able to express yourself clearly in writing and you just may find yourself using some of the elements of PORPE every time you write.

Taking Essay Exams

When you are in the actual test-taking situation, remember these three important factors: (1) How much time you are allotted to write each answer; (2) How you will structure each answer; and (3) The guidelines your professor provided about how she will evaluate or grade your essay. Each of these factors has a bearing on how you will spend your in-class, essay-writing time.

Time Allotted for Writing

Time is usually your biggest enemy when answering essay or short-answer questions. When you are deciding on your approach for taking the exam, think carefully about how you will divide up your time. For example, if you have one essay question and five fairly comprehensive

---

*Source for PORPE: Simpson, M. L. (1986). PORPE: A writing strategy for studying and learning in the content areas. *Journal of Reading*, 29, 407–414.

identification items to answer, would it be best to spend half of your time on the essay and the other half on the identification? Or would it be better to spend more time on the essay and less time on the identification items? It's all a give and take, but it's a good rule of thumb to begin with what you know best and feel the most comfortable with. If you know the answers to all the identification and feel a bit shaky on how best to approach the essay, start with the IDs and then use the remaining time to do the best job you can on the essay. In addition, consider the point value of each question. If the essay is worth 40 points and each ID is worth 3 points, you might want to spend more time on the essay.

Structuring Your Essay

Few professors provide students with guidance on how they want essay or short-answer questions structured. As a result, many students will write a paragraph to answer an essay question and a sentence or two to answer a short-answer item. Usually when professors ask you to write an essay, they want extended comment. That is, they want you to write considerably more than a paragraph. When you think of an essay, you should plan on writing at least an introductory paragraph, several paragraphs that discuss specific points you think are important to answering the question, and then end with a concluding paragraph. Short-answer questions, as a general rule, are a paragraph or two long and tend to be somewhat less structured than an essay.

If your professor tells you exactly how she wants you to structure your essay, *follow exactly what she says.* However, if your professor does not provide you with any guidance, the following structure is generally accepted in most disciplines.

- Write an introductory paragraph that outlines your thesis and indicates that you understand what the question is asking. By thesis, we mean the overall focus of your essay or the argument you will be making. If the question has multiple parts, be sure that your introduction pulls in *all* of the parts. The first paragraph should not be long and involved. But, it should be clear and concise and give the reader a picture of your overall points.

- Each of your next several paragraphs should begin with a generalization about one of the key points you want to make. Don't worry about following the five-paragraph essay format you learned in high school. Instead, use as many paragraphs as necessary to answer the question fully. For example, if the question asks you to discuss political, economic, international policy, and social issues, you would write four paragraphs, one dealing with each of the four issues. For each generalization, you should provide support in the form of events, names, dates, people, examples, and so forth—specific information that supports your point. Each paragraph should deal with only one key idea. Be careful about including several broad generalizations in the same paragraph. However, also be careful about writing a litany of facts without tying them together with generalizations. Whenever possible, have smooth transitions from one idea to the next by using words such as first, second, third; furthermore; in addition to; moreover; etc. In addition, unlike objective tests where we encourage you to guess if you have to, for essay exams, follow the "When in doubt, leave it out" suggestion. If you have included wrong information in your essay, your professor has no alternative but to take points off. But if your essay is sound and you have made numerous good points, you might get few or no points taken off if you leave out a bit of information.

- End your essay with a concluding paragraph that joins together the points you wanted to make. The conclusion doesn't have to be lengthy, but should return to your thesis and pull together the most important ideas related to that thesis.

Few professors would oppose this structure; so if your professor does not provide guidance about format, this one will rarely, if ever, get you into trouble. But, if your professor spends a lot of class time explaining the essay format he expects, be sure to get down as much information as you can about what he wants, and then when you practice your essay, use his model.

Evaluation Guidelines

It's a tall order to write essays within the allotted time frame, have an acceptable structure, and manage to keep the mechanics and grammar errors down to a minimum. That's why it becomes important to know your professors expectations before you go into the exam situation. For example, how strict will your professor be in taking off points for mechanics, grammar, and usage? If your professor doesn't say anything about his expectations in class, be sure to ask. Most professors do not expect perfection, but they will probably deduct points on a paper that has so many errors that it is difficult to read and understand the essay. The bottom line is to know what your professor expects and then do your best to balance time, structure/content, and grammar/spelling issues.

College Campus Today

Writing Intensive Courses

Most colleges have implemented some kind of writing across the curriculum program. In the past, writing courses had been largely confined to literature and English courses. But the current trend is to have "writing-intensive courses," or courses that require you to write papers or take essays, in almost every discipline. That means that you can take a science, engineering, or business course that requires lots of writing. You may even find a writing-intensive mathematics course on some campuses. Depending on your major, you will need to meet a writing requirement by enrolling in one or more of these types of courses. Use the strategies presented in this chapter (and the rest of the book) to help you prepare.

A Word About Identification Items

Identification items ask you to write what you know about specific events, people, laws, dates, and so forth. They differ from essay/short-answer questions in that they are more focused and usually require only a few sentences of explanation. Sometimes you can even write in phrases rather than in full sentences when answering identification questions. There are two ideas to keep in mind when preparing for identification items:

1. There are usually many options for the professor to choose from. In history, for example, where identification questions are common, every chapter and lecture is filled with material that could be included

on a test. So how do you decide which terms are the most important to study? A good place to begin is with your text. If your text provides a listing of key terms or if there is a chapter summary, making sure that you can identify what is in either of those sources usually is your best starting point. Match up those terms with what your professor has spent time on during lectures. Look for overlap, because identification items usually focus on material that has been addressed in a lecture or has been pointed out in the text.

2. You have to know the kind of information your professor expects you to include. Most of the time, professors will want you to include more than just definitional information. They may want you to discuss the significance, provide an example, or explain how it relates to some other issue or idea. Whatever the expectations, be sure that you know what they are.

Specialized Exams

We conclude this chapter by briefly discussing how to prepare for specialized exams. Specialized exams are those that may not happen as frequently in your college career, but you need to know how to prepare for them when they do come along. We will discuss three types of specialized exams: (1) problem-solving exams, the most common of the specialized exams; (2) open-book exams; and (3) take-home exams.

Problem-Solving Exams

Several types of courses require you to solve problems including mathematics, science, engineering, and business courses. Because many students fall into the trap of studying for exams of this nature by doing the same problems over and over again, we thought it was important to provide some additional strategies for studying for these types of exams.

Working the problems as a way of studying for this type of test is certainly a good idea and should be part of your studying routine. Note that we said "a part of," because if all you do is work the same set of problems over and over again, you will probably not do very well. The important thing to remember is that you have to think about and conceptualize what you are doing. You won't get those exact same problems on the exam, so you have to think about the concepts underlying the problems. That's why we suggest that you talk through your problems. As you do a problem, think about and verbalize what you are doing. If you can't talk through problems as you solve them, you probably don't understand the concept.

Let's look at an example and talk through some of the thinking that would make it easier to solve this problem. Thinking about math problems in this manner, especially word problems, also lets you know if you understand the reasoning behind your method of solving the problem.

The Problem: Susan begins a 20-mile race at 7:00 A.M., running at an average speed of 10 miles per hour. One hour later, her brother leaves the starting line on a motorbike and follows her route at the rate of 40 miles per hour. At what time does he catch up to her?

The Question: What is the problem asking for? You are supposed to solve this problem to find out what time he catches up with her, so you will need to make sure that the answer you come up with is reflected as time.

The Solution:

- **Visualize the problem.** This diagram shows that when Susan's brother overtakes her, they have both traveled the same distance.

  Susan >>>>>>>>>>>>>>>>>>>>
  Her brother >>>>>>>>>>>>>>>>>>>>>>

- **What is the basic idea behind the problem?** Both are traveling at a constant rate of speed so we would think about the basic equation as:

$$\textbf{Distance} = \textbf{(Rate)(Time)}$$
$$\textbf{d} = \textbf{rt}$$

- **Explain the variables.**

  Let t = # of hours Susan runs until her brother catches her
  Then $t - 1$ = # of hours Susan's brother rides until he catches up
  (He leaves 1 hour later so he travels 1 hour less.)

- **Write and solve the equation.**

  $10t = 40(t - 1)$
  $10t = 40t - 40$
  $-30t = -40$
  $t = \dfrac{-40}{-30} = \dfrac{4}{3} = 1\ 1/3$ hours = 1 hour and 20 minutes

The Solution: Remember that the question asked for time. Susan's brother caught her 1 hour and 20 minutes after she began the race. Therefore, he would catch up with her at 8:20 A.M. If you wrote 1 hour and 20 minutes as your answer, you would not receive credit because you did not answer the question that was asked.

- **Make Up a Test for Yourself with the Types of Problems You Will Be Tested on.** Put some problems on note cards and then use them as a way of seeing whether you understand the concepts. After you have worked through the problems, shuffle the note cards and work on them again in a different order, concentrating on those that gave you problems.

- **Get Help Early.** Courses such as mathematics, physics, and chemistry tend to be arranged sequentially. That is, the ideas build on one another. If you miss or don't understand something presented in week 2 of the term, chances are you are going to have trouble with what is presented after that. If you think you are "mathematically challenged," you should arrange to be part of a study group, get a tutor, or make regular appointments to speak with your professor right at the beginning of the term.

Open-Book Exams

Open-book exams allow you access to your text, and sometimes even your notes during the examination period. Open-book exams are generally given in the usual class period, which means you take them under timed conditions. This type of exam is often given in literature courses so that students can have access to specific pieces of text that they have been asked to read and interact with.

When students are told that they will have an open-book exam, they often breathe a sigh of relief. We have even heard students say that they didn't have to study because they were having an open-book test. But it takes just as much effort to adequately prepare for this type of test as it does to prepare for a more traditional objective or essay test.

Organization is the key in preparing for open-book exams. If you are getting ready for an open-book exam, first you have to go through the usual preparation steps of predicting, organizing, rehearsing, practicing, and evaluating. But you have to put extra time into organizing. You would want to mark information that you might use to support points you want to make or pull specific examples from the readings. You will need to have the information you deem important marked in some way so that it is easy to find. For example, you can tab important passages or pages in your text with adhesive notes. Because you are in a timed situation, you must know where things are and have the information organized so that you can find it quickly.

Take Home Exams

Take-home exams allow you to have access to your text and notes and put no time restrictions on the amount of time you can spend taking the test. The professor gives you the test questions, along with some basic instructions, usually to remind you that you can't get outside assistance to answer the questions. Some professors may even have you sign an academic honesty pledge. When professors give take-home exams, they generally expect a very high level of proficiency and thinking. For example, if they give you a take-home essay exam, they would expect your writing to display synthesis, analysis, and critical thought. They would expect a tremendous amount of support, and a paper virtually free of grammatical and spelling errors. Therefore, you usually have to spend a considerable amount of time working on take-home exams.

Even if you know you will have take-home exams in a course, it is extremely important for you to keep up. Do your reading, attend class, construct rehearsal strategies, and continue to review. Then, when you get your take-home exam from your instructor, you will be ready to organize all the information and spend less actual time on taking the test.

☐ Real College
Iris's Intentions (Gone Awry!)

DIRECTIONS: Read the following *Real College* scenario and respond to the questions based on what you learned in this chapter.

Iris had good intentions. And her semester was going quite well . . . up until this point, that is. Iris had some academic difficulties during her first semester in college, but she had learned from her mistakes, and so far so good. But now it was time for the real test. She knew that an exam was rapidly approaching in Dr. Jameson's history course and she was scared. Today was Thursday and this test was the following Tuesday. She had done a decent job of keeping up in her courses this semester, except for Dr. Jameson's, even though she had intended to stay on top of things in history. But somehow, she fell a little behind. Okay, a lot behind. Now it was time for the first of only two exams in the course and Dr. Jameson's exams had the reputation of being lethal. The most difficult thing was that half of the exam consisted of 30 multiple-choice questions and the other half was one essay question. That meant that she had to study in two different ways for the same test and she hadn't even completed the reading assignments yet. And to make things even worse she knew that most questions would come from the text and that she would have to pull in text-related information into her essay. Professor Jameson had already been very explicit about that in class.

Given the amount of time she has left to study and the kind of exam that she will have, what recommendations would you give to Iris? How should she prepare for and go about taking her history exam so that she can maximize her grade? If Iris had followed her intentions, what should she have done to prevent her problems?

☐ Thinking Critically
Something to Think About and Discuss

Think about the most difficult test you have had so far in your college career. What made this test difficult? How did you study for the test? Do you feel that you could have done better if you had studied differently? Looking back on the exam, how might you have prepared differently?

☐ Follow-Up Activities

For your next essay exam, try using the PORPE procedure and evaluate its effectiveness. Which parts of the strategy seemed most beneficial to you? What modifications will you make for the next exam?

Credits

Index

Additional Titles of Interest

Note to Instructors: Any of these Penguin-Putnam, Inc., titles can be packaged with this book at a special discount. Contact your local Allyn & Bacon/Longman sales representative for details on how to create a Penguin-Putnam, Inc., Value Package.

Albee, *Three Tall Women*
Alger, *Ragged Dick & Struggling Up*
Allison, *Bastard Out Of Carolina*
Austen, *Pride & Prejudice*
Austen, *Sense & Sensibility*
Behn, *Oroonoko, The Rover & Others*
Bellow, *Adventures of Augie March*
Bronte, *Jane Eyre*
Bronte, *Wuthering Heights*
Cather, *My Antonia*
Cather, *O Pioneers!*
Chesnutt, *The Marrow of Tradition*
Chopin, *The Awakening & Selected Stories*
Christe, *Death on the Nile*
Conrad, *Nostromo*
Delillo, *White Noise*
Dickens, *Great Expectations*
Dos Passos, *Three Soldiers*
Douglass, *Narrative of the Life of Frederick Douglass*
Golding, *Lord of the Flies*
Hansberry, *A Raisin in the Sun*
Hawthorne, *The Scarlet Letter*
Jen, *Typical American*
Karr, *The Liars Club*
Kerouac, *On the Road*
Kesey, *One Flew Over the Cuckoo's Nest*
King Jr., *Why We Can't Wait*
King, *Misery*
Lewis, *Babbitt*

McBride, *The Color of Water*
Morrison, *Beloved*
Naylor, *The Women of Brewster Place*
O'Brien, *The Things They Carried*
Orwell, *1984*
Paine, *Common Sense*
Postman, *Amusing Ourselves to Death*
Rose, *Lives on the Boundary*
Rose, *Possible Lives: The Promise of Public*
Shakespeare, *Four Great Comedies: The Taming of the Shrew, A Midsummer's Night Dream, Twelfth Night, The Tempest*
Shakespeare, *Four Great Tragedies: Hamlet, Macbeth, King Lear, Othello*
Shakespeare, *Hamlet*
Shakespeare, *King Lear*
Shelley, *Frankenstein*
Sinclair, *The Jungle*
Steinbeck, *Of Mice & Men*
Steinbeck, *The Pearl*
Stevenson, *The Strange Case of Dr. Jekyll & Mr. Hyde*
Stowe, *Uncle Tom's Cabin*
Truth, *The Narrative of Sojourner Truth*
Twain, *Adventures of Huckleberry Finn*
Wilson, *Fences*
Wilson, *Joe Turner's Come & Gone*